Same Sex

Our families are increasingly a matter of choice, and the choices are widening all the time. This is particularly true of the non-heterosexual world, where the last ten years

lesser ext

a variety

ONE WEEK LOAN

these de

changes i the meaning of fa

and that each can cast light on

of the different ways no

meaningful intimate relationships for themselves, and highlights the role of individual agency and collective endeavour in forging these 'life experiments': as friends, partners, parents and as members of communities. This topical book will provide compelling reading for students of the family, sexuality and lesbian and gay studies.

Jeffrey Weeks is Professor of Sociology and Dean of Humanities and Social Science at South Bank University, London. **Brian Heaphy** is Senior Lecturer in Sociology at Nottingham Trent University. **Catherine Donovan** is Principal Lecturer and Team Leader in Sociology and Social Policy at Sunderland University.

Same Sex Intimacies

Families of choice and other
life experiments

**Jeffrey Weeks, Brian Heaphy
and Catherine Donovan**

London and New York

First published 2001 by Routledge
11 New Fetter Lane, London EC4P 4EE

Simultaneously published in the USA and Canada
by Routledge
29 West 35th Street, New York, NY 10001

Routledge is an imprint of the Taylor & Francis Group

© 2001 Jeffrey Weeks, Brian Heaphy and Catherine Donovan

Typeset in Baskerville by Taylor & Francis Ltd
Printed and bound in Great Britain by St Edmundsbury Press,
Bury St Edmunds, Suffolk

British Library Cataloguing in Publication Data
A catalogue record for this book is available from the British Library

Library of Congress Cataloging in Publication Data
Weeks, Jeffrey.
   Same sex intimacies: families of choice and other life
experiments/Jeffrey Weeks, Brian Heaphy, and Catherine Donovan.
   Includes bibliographical references and index.
   1. Same sex marriage. 2. Gay male couples–Family relationships.
   3. Lesbian couples–Family relationships. 4. Gay adoption. 5. Gay
parents–Family relationships. I. Heaphy, Brian. II. Donovan, Catherine.
III. Title.

   HQ76.34 .W44   2001
   306.84'8–dc21   00-065293

ISBN 0–415–25476–0 (hbk)
ISBN 0–415–25477–9 (pbk)

Contents

Preface

This book is about same sex intimate relationships: what we call families of choice and other life experiments. Our aim is to show the different ways in which individuals whose lives have been lived at odds with the dominant sexual norms of our culture have been able, in the everyday circumstances in which they find themselves, to create meaningful, intimate relationships for themselves: as friends, partners, parents, members of communities. In this book, we document and analyse narratives of individual agency and collective endeavour, of creativity and choice, of personal autonomy and mutual responsibility, of care and love, of pleasure and commitment. They are stories of ordinary people and ordinary lives, made extraordinary by the circumstances in which they find themselves.

The book is based on interviews with self-identified 'non-heterosexuals', that is 'homosexuals', 'lesbians', 'gay men', 'bisexuals', 'queers', and the range of other possible labels which people adopt to represent their dissident sexual identities and sense of belonging. The interviews were carried out as part of a research project funded by the British Economic and Social Research Council (ESRC) in 1995 and 1996, entitled 'Families of Choice: The Structure and Meanings of Non-Heterosexual Relationships' (ref. L315253030). The project was based at South Bank University, and directed by Jeffrey Weeks, with Catherine Donovan and Brian Heaphy as research fellows, and in turn, was part of a wider ESRC research programme on 'Population and Household Change' (see McRae 1999).

The project was thus part of a wider study of changes in family and personal life, which provides the broad context for the research. In our own work, we sought to do two things. First, we wanted to analyse the emergence of the new relationship ethic in the non-heterosexual world, which has radically shifted the political and cultural focus of lesbian and gay communities across the liberal democracies and elsewhere. Campaigns for partnership recognition, same sex marriage and parenting rights are only the most public aspects of significant changes in everyday life. These are products of the growing maturity and complexity of the non-heterosexual world itself as a result of a long and vibrant history. But these shifts are also part of a wider transformation of intimate life, usually dramatised in terms of a 'crisis of the family'. The traditional family, we suggest, is indeed changing. But many of the values the family is supposed to represent are not in crisis. On the contrary, they are being reinvented in a variety of 'experiments in living' through which new patterns of commitment are being enacted in everyday life. The social changes we identify are affecting heterosexual and non-heterosexual lives alike, but they have a special resonance for those who are defined, and define themselves, as different. Underpinned by a widely accepted friendship ethic, women and men who have rejected what we call the heterosexual assumption are creating ways of being that point to a more diverse culture of relationships than law and tradition have sanctioned. 'Families of choice' are harbingers of new relational possibilities. In the wide-ranging chapters of this book, we seek to develop this argument.

We have regularly used the term 'non-heterosexual', which may sound rather clinical to many, and indeed it is not entirely satisfactory to us as authors. It is, however, difficult to find a better general label, since other terms are even more contested. The term 'homosexual' has too long been associated with the psychological textbooks to be in acceptable common use as a self-description. Moreover, it has historically obscured gender differences. As the novelist Gore Vidal once suggested, it is better used as an adjective than a noun. 'Lesbian' and 'gay' have been generally used since the 1970s, but again they have never had universal acceptance, and have often been rejected since the 'queer insurgency' of the early 1990s. The label 'queer' is even more contested. Long used as a term of abuse, or of self-mocking, it disappeared from polite speech in the 1970s, only to reappear as a sign of a radical rejection of 'assimilationism' in the era of AIDS and moral conservatism. However, it is not a term that many of the people we interviewed feel at ease with. Of all the options that we considered, the term 'non-heterosexual' seemed the most neutral, while at the same time keeping before our eyes the undoubted fact that, despite the dramatic liberalisation of attitudes in recent years, same sex relationships continue to be defined by, and against, the heterosexual assumption.

In *Same Sex Intimacies*, we attempt to be true to the relationship stories we were told. Throughout the text, we make frequent use of the voices of the people who we interviewed. The interviewees are identified by a code reference, a full listing of which is given in Appendix 2. They are vivid testimonies of the variety of ways in which non-heterosexual people 'do' family and intimate life. The stories they tell are part of the proliferation of stories of intimate life which are transforming not only the ways in which we talk about family life, but also the ways in which we live it.

Acknowledgements

Many colleagues, friends and 'families' helped us in researching and writing this book. We must first of all thank the ESRC for generously funding the research project on which it is based. Susan McRea was director of the Population and Household Change research programme, and gave us stalwart encouragement throughout. We would also like to thank the anonymous referees who supported the project initially, and who approved the final report. South Bank University housed the project, and we wish to thank all our colleagues for their interest, curiosity, stimulation and practical backing. Susan Howarth gave administrative underpinning throughout the life of the project, and we give her our thanks. Various papers arising from our research were given at a large number of seminars and conferences, and we are grateful for the ideas that flowed from these: sometimes we took them up, sometimes we did not, but the comments were always helpful and thoughtful. We must also thank the editors who published articles by us on various aspects of the research in journals and edited collections (for full references, see the Bibliography in this book), and their referees who made helpful suggestions. Together, they helped us polish those articles, and refine our thoughts for this book. We also greatly appreciate the comments of the anonymous readers of the draft of this book for their support for its publication. We want to thank all the participants in the Workshops on Sexuality, Identity and Values held monthly at South Bank University since 1995. They provided an intellectual community (and a lively Friday night social venue), and gave us lots of food for thought.

We owe special thanks to the following colleagues, co-thinkers and friends for practical and/or intellectual support: Peter Aggleton, Henning Beck, Terry Bogus, Bob Cant, Christopher Carrington, Peter Davies, John De Cecco, Onno de Zwart, Gillian Dunne, Jan Willem Duyvendak, Rosalind Edwards, Clare Farquhar, Tim Fisher, Jane Franklin, Linda Garnets, Philip Gatter, Gitte, Beverley Goring, Angie Hart, Ken Hassett, Gert Hekma, Henne, the late Benny Henriksson, Janet Holland, Stefan Jonke, Arlene Kochman, Ellen Lewin, Jane Lewis, Karin Lutzen, David MacFarlane, Astrid Mattijssen and the Clara Wichman Institut, Amsterdam, April Martin, Angela Mason, Pam Millar, Peter Nardi, Anya Palmer, Inglise Paulsen, Anne Peplau, Ken Plummer, Sheila Quaid, Jill Radford, Lisa Saffron, Theo Sandfort, Judith Schuyf, Carol Smart, Jenny

Spiegel, Judith Stacey, Fiona Tasker, Donna Thompson, Rachel Thomson, Randolph Trumbach, Jo Van Every, Kees Waalddijk, Matthew Waites, Kath Weston and Evan Wolfson.

Jeffrey Weeks gives his personal thanks to the following: Micky Burbidge, Chetan Bhatt, Kevin Porter, Philippe Rougier – for friendship. Mark McNestry – for love and partnership. Catherine Donovan gives her personal thanks to Richard Bliss, Ruth Charlton, Julie Ballands, Jacquie-Lee Jobson, Helen Stables, Gerald Donovan and Marie Louise Shalom; and special love and thanks to Melissa Jane Girling. Brian Heaphy gives his personal thanks to Steve Barrow, Michael Caine, Matthew Drennan, Grace Heaphy, Eileen Hourigan, William O'Connor, Clair O'Leary, Tom Schroeder and John Williamson.

Finally, we want to thank those people who freely told us their stories of friendship, chosen families, partnerships, and other life experiments. Without them this book would not have been possible. We dedicate the book to them.

Introduction

Happy families?

A comfortably well-off couple in their thirties begin to feel the clock ticking. They have been together for eleven years, and want to complete their partnership by starting a family. They have been unable to have a child of their own, and their efforts to adopt children have been hampered by the local social services officialdom. They therefore decide to use some of their now substantial savings to pay a woman to have their surrogate child (or in this case, twins).

An increasingly commonplace tale, perhaps: many couples today try to escape the failures of biology and bureaucracy by seeking a technological fix. The only difference is that in this instance the couple are two openly gay men. Suddenly, they find themselves in a media furore. Newspaper headlines range from the modestly factual, 'Gay men pay US woman to carry twins' (*Independent*, 1 September 1999), to the slightly frenzied, 'Fury over gay couple who are having surrogate twins' (*Evening Standard*, 1 September 1999). The usual suspects offer soundbites: 'They have no right to be parents', says Dr Adrian Rogers, adviser to the campaign group, Family Focus. A spokesman for Families Need Fathers warns that the children of gay parents could grow up confused. Valerie Riches, director of an 'independent think-tank', Family and Youth Concern, opines that: 'In all of this, we seem to forget the interests of the child. It will not know who to identify with …'. Against this background, one of the prospective fathers defends his stance: 'The kids will be loved as much as any other – and perhaps more than quite a few … we're all over the moon. I don't think the lack of a mother in the household matters very much.'

This story is one of hundreds that have appeared in the media since the 1980s concerning what we call in this book non-heterosexual 'families of choice' and 'life experiments': that is, the lives and life choices of self-identified lesbians, gay men, bisexuals, 'queers', and others historically consigned to the margins of our culture. These stories of same sex intimacies home in on touchstone issues about the ways in which we choose to live today, simultaneously evoking the weight of tradition and the shock of the new, the comforting envelopment of 'the family' and the threatening power of different ways of life. There is usually an immediate spark for the media flurry: surrogacy, a lesbian or gay fostering or adoption controversy, a child custody case, a dispute over employment law, a politician's 'unorthodox' private life revealed for all to gloat over, press coverage of developments of policy towards same sex partnerships in other countries, or an opportunist attempt to exploit an election campaign by playing on homophobic prejudices. The contingent circumstances vary. The wider context, however, is a profound, if uneven and certainly incomplete shift in concepts of identity, relationships, intimacy, parenting, and above all 'family', with homosexuality, as it has been for over a hundred years, a key, if always contested, marker of profound changes in social consciousness. Many of the old certainties about the 'right way to live' have been shaken. Traditional verities have been undermined. Old boundaries are being blurred. Non-heterosexual relationships sharply dramatise these upheavals: they signal the decline of the old, and the uncertain attitudes still prevalent about the new.

Times of uncertainty give rise to concerns about where the boundaries should be drawn between 'right' and 'wrong' forms of behaviour. The media tend to focus on such boundary conflicts, especially when they appear to challenge traditional roles and values. No wonder the very idea of same sex marriage intrigues, as a trail of headlines throughout the 1990s indicates: 'Bishop sparks gay wedding row by backing homosexual "unions" ' (*Independent*, 16 December 1996); 'Scots church to examine gay marriage' (*Independent*, 12 October 1998); 'Our vows show this love is so strong: Chris and Rick Farrah-Mills are gay, in love – and did something about it. They got married' (*Independent*, 28 September 1998). 'Doing something about it' seems to fascinate or horrify people in equal measure. What for many are the cornerstones of western civilisation – the institution of marriage, the biological imperatives of reproduction, the social conditions of parenting – are being radically challenged by the emergence of new patterns of intimacy and new claims to relational rights. This is occurring at a time when our social guidelines are in unprecedented flux, and where each society, in its own ways, has to find ways of living with difference. The media may massage the message, but there is a real story nevertheless.

The media frenzies reflect a new international agenda which has put the relationships of non-heterosexuals at the centre of moral and political debate. From the sober social democrat legislative changes in Scandinavia (see Bech 1997) and elsewhere, which pioneered the registration of lesbian and gay partnerships, and the more flamboyant legal action in Hawaii, which has sought the legalisation of non-heterosexual marriage (see Strasser 1997; Sullivan 1997), to the establishment in France of the 'Pacte civil de solidarité' (PACS) at the end of 1999 (Velu 1999), the question of same sex partnership rights, and issues relating to parenting, adoption, marriage, and family, are now clearly of major concern. Even in Britain – despite, or perhaps because, it is a country which has been slower than most other advanced democracies to recognise and enshrine any general concept of 'rights' – same sex partnership rights and the recognition of alternative families now form a major focus of concern for defenders of the traditional family, and not surprisingly a key part of the political agenda of many lesbian and gay activists. The British lesbian and gay rights lobbying group Stonewall, founded in the late 1980s to campaign for legal equality and justice, has put these claims at the centre of its work. Two of the 'five key challenges' of its equality agenda focus on:

- equal recognition and respect for same sex partners; and
- equal recognition and respect for lesbian and gay parents and their children.

Stonewall's manifesto states that:

> These are five challenges for equality which would alter every area of our lives – our right to grow up without fear and prejudice, our right to love, our right to work freely and openly, our right to form our own families, to live with our partners and our children. All these are basic human rights which for every other section of the population are protected in international and domestic law. These are rights which go to the heart of human existence.
>
> (Stonewall 1997)

In this new stress on non-heterosexual relationships and partnership rights, Stonewall is part of an international trend which has both refocused the strategic goals of campaigners for homosexual rights, and helped to identify important cultural shifts. The press, sometimes hysterically, sometimes with detached puzzlement, is picking up on an important – and for those most involved, a vital – social trend, and has simultaneously reflected and shaped popular reactions to these developments. At the centre of these controversies is the simple question, affecting heterosexuals and non-heterosexuals alike: what are the meanings of 'intimacy', 'relationships' and 'family' today?

In this book, we try to answer that question by examining the new stories that are emerging from many self-identified non-heterosexual people; stories about same sex intimacies, chosen families, personal life experiments, friendship and community, partnerships, sexuality and parenting, and new claims to full citizenship. These stories are important in their own right. But they also provide very important insights into the ways in which almost everyone in the modern world is faced by the fundamental question of 'how shall we live?' That question makes for anxiety and fear as much as hope and experimentation. It is hardly surprising, then, that two men deciding to father twins by controversial means causes waves. A lot is at stake.

'Pick and mix' relationships

'Knit your own life' was the headline of a special report on the changing nature of family life in the *Observer* (25 October 1998). Not everyone, unfortunately, agrees with such a pick and mix definition of the family. The defining moment in British engagement with the issue was the passing into law of the notorious

Section 28 of the Local Government Act of 1988, which outlawed support by local authorities for the 'promotion of homosexuality' and 'the acceptability of homosexuality as a pretended family relationship' (Weeks 1991: 137). A similar touchstone moment occurred in the United States in 1996 when Congress rushed into law 'The Defense of Marriage Act'. In response to the Hawaiian Supreme Court's judgement in favour of same sex marriages, the Act outlined the right of a state not to recognise same sex marriages conducted in another state and, for the first time in federal law, it defined marriage as exclusively an arrangement between a man and a woman (Sullivan 1997: Chapter 6). The key issues are why has this concern with changing patterns of intimate commitment emerged so powerfully in recent years, and why does the subject evoke such a rushed, even hysterical response? In both Britain and the United States, bills were rushed into law in response to perceived threats to 'traditional family values' offered by lesbian and gay campaigns. Attempts to repeal Section 28 in 2000 evoked bitter hostility in Britain. They were passed in Scotland only after a major political crisis, and were blocked for England and Wales in the House of Lords. But beyond such political explosions are more profound changes. We argue that this preoccupation with same sex partnerships and 'pretended families' can be seen as an aspect of a wider reshaping of both heterosexual and non-heterosexual patterns of relationships, the transformation of inherited family patterns, and the emergence of what in this book are described as new 'life experiments'. These everyday experiments range across a variety of patterns, from couple relationships to what we call 'families of choice': flexible, informal and varied, but strong and supportive networks of friends and lovers, often including members of families of origin. They provide the framework for the development of mutual care, responsibility and commitment for many non-heterosexual people – and indeed for many heterosexuals as well.

In many ways the development of non-heterosexual patterns of relating is paralleled by changes in the wider heterosexual world as traditional frameworks and constraints, especially those embodied in the idea and ideal of 'family life', radically change under the impact of long-term social, cultural and economic shifts. Many individuals in contemporary society have a strong sense that opportunities now exist on a greater scale than ever before for the construction of more open and democratic relationships than were allowed by the traditional family: this is what Giddens (1992) has described as 'the transformation of intimacy'. These relationships demonstrate some of the most important qualities attributed (in ideology at least; the reality is all too often different) to the traditional family: continuity over time, mutual support, a focus for identity and for loving and caring relationships, both for adults and for children (Pahl and Spencer 1997).

But while it is important to recognise these common features across the binary divide between heterosexuality and homosexuality, the public affirmation by non-heterosexuals of the importance of their chosen relationships represents a major shift in their life chances. Supportive networks of marginalised people, especially non-heterosexuals, female and male, have, of course, always existed (see Weeks and Porter 1998; Hall Carpenter Archives 1989a, 1989b). The developing patterns build on a long and often painful history. They are not fixed in concrete: on the contrary, they are fluid, flexible and adaptable. They are also marked by various dimensions of difference. Men and women often have a different take on the new possibilities, because of the related but often distinctive histories of lesbianism, male homosexuality and bisexuality, and their different positioning in the gendered world. There are differences arising from class, race and ethnicity, as well as age and geography. As Weston (1991: 3) argues in her pioneering study of 'families we choose' in the Bay Area of the United States, it is impossible to define simply the lesbian and gay family, because no single structure or model exists. It is a 'contested concept'. What we argue, however, is that emerging non-heterosexual ways of being can be seen as indices of something new: positive and creative responses to social and cultural change, which are genuine 'experiments in living' (Giddens 1992, 1994). The now regular, though not invariable, deployment by many non-heterosexuals of the language of family, which suggests continuity with traditional patterns, should not be allowed to obscure the emergence of an important change in the ecology of intimate life.

Stories we tell each other

Although references to non-heterosexual relationships and 'families' abound in the literature from the late 1970s (see Altman 1982), until recently the empirical study of these changes has been limited (for a review, see Weeks, Donovan and Heaphy 1996). This book is based on the findings of a research project designed to redress this absence. That project in turn was part of a major research programme, funded by the Economic and Social Research Council, on 'Population and Household Change' (see McRae 1999). The research was conducted in 1995 and 1996 in Britain, and involved in-depth interviews with 96 self-identified non-heterosexuals (lesbians, gays, bisexuals, queers – the self-descriptions varied), and was divided equally between women and men. In addition, a number of group discussions were held, and we participated in discussions with a number of agencies involved with lesbian and gay lives. We also conducted comparative work in the United States, Denmark and the Netherlands, where these developments are in some ways more advanced, and where certainly they have led to more engaged political and legislative debate (see Appendix 1, and Heaphy, Donovan and Weeks 1998 for a methodological overview).

We sought to make our interviews as representative as we could of different ways of non-heterosexual life. We interviewed men and women across a broad age range, from early twenties through to those in their seventies. We sought a geographical spread across the UK. People were drawn from different class and ethnic backgrounds, from different income groups, and from both urban and rural locations. A number of interviewees had previously been married, and more than we expected had experience of parenting. Thus, we can claim to reflect a range of experiences. We are not claiming, however, that these interviews are statistically representative of all non-heterosexuals – an elusive goal at the best of times. Quantitative studies based on surveys are, of course, notoriously difficult in relation to non-heterosexual people, not least because of the difficulty of establishing a representative sample for a 'hidden' population, and the problems of defining what is a 'homosexual lifestyle' (Plummer 1981; Weston 1991; see also Davies, Hickson, Weatherburn and Hunt 1993: 66–71). A questionnaire survey even of a self-defining sample would, moreover, fail to reveal the complexity of meanings around identity and relationships. A study based on semi-structured interviews, on the other hand, can provide a way of exploring shifting nuances of identity by providing brief life-histories of the interviewees, and allow for the development of narratives of 'intimate' and 'family' life.

We would emphasise some important effects of such a qualitative approach. First, we suggest that the personal stories we were told provide highly revealing examples of the type of life experiments that are both common, and perhaps inevitable, in the late modern world. Individuals' understanding of how, and why, they are living as they do, provide insights into new possibilities. Second, they are important evidence for the development of new narratives through which everyday experience is being reordered and new meanings emerge. Through narratives of the self and of their relationships and ways of being, as we argue below, people construct meanings which make things happen in everyday life. Third, the narratives provide insights into the processes through which non-institutionalised patterns of sexual and emotional interaction are being negotiated in a world of rapid cultural change.

One of the most important insights we gained, which illustrates all these issues, was that the non-heterosexuals we interviewed were not only very willing, but eager to tell their stories (see also Dunne 1997: 31). This is likely to have been influenced, in part, by the fact that we were open about our own gay (BH and JW) and lesbian (CD) identities to research participants. But there was something more significant at work. Our interviewees' eagerness to talk was often due to a desire to make lesbian, gay and bisexual lives visible as a strategy in validating their own domestic and emotional life choices (see Chapter 1). We see such responses as especially significant because they illustrate the power of the new narratives about intimate life in not only shaping individual choices but also in potentially changing the cultural circumstances in which these choices are made.

The notion of 'stories' or 'narratives' has been of crucial importance to our research (see Plummer 1995). Through narratives individuals give meaning to their lives, affirm their identities, and present their relationships as viable and valid. The stories about relationships and families of choice that are circulating within the contemporary non-heterosexual world tell us something very important about the new possibilities and new hopes for recognition that are re-shaping the lives of people historically consigned to the margins of society.

About the book

This book is concerned above all with agency, with the creativity and self activity of non-heterosexuals who are constructing ways of life valid to them in circumstances often not of their own making. Each chapter attempts to explore the various dimensions of this process of reinventing intimate life, highlighting what is particular to the non-heterosexual experience, but also drawing parallels with changes in society as a whole.

In Chapter 1, 'Families of choice', we analyse the context which has given rise to contemporary narratives of non-heterosexual relationships. We suggest this is a product of two interconnected changes: in the social world of homosexuality, and in the changing nature of the family and intimate life generally. Together these have provided the opportunity for new stories to emerge and circulate, which in turn expand the possibilities for everyday experiments in living.

Chapter 2, 'Life experiments', sets out to explore the meanings of non-heterosexual relationships. We begin by offering some stories of such relationships, as a way of revealing the diversity of patterns that exist, but also to underline the creative energy that goes into their making. Through these we begin to analyse the language of family, the meaning of 'family practices', the heterosexual assumption which continues to shape personal choices, and the discourse of resistance and self-invention which is a characteristic response of non-heterosexuals.

In Chapter 3, 'The friendship ethic', we explore the power of friendship for many non-heterosexuals in a world of institutionalised rejection. A particular emphasis is placed here on the different ways loyalties and mutual responsibilities are negotiated, and played out. This is linked to the emergence of new forms of commitment. Parenting raises key issues about care, commitment and responsibility. But so do other forms of relationship: between partners and friends, with families of origin. The AIDS crisis has posed dramatic challenges, particularly for gay men, which illustrate wider changes.

Chapter 4, 'In search of home', concentrates on notions of belonging, from memories of first home through to a sense of community, which often provide the social capital and specific knowledges which help individuals negotiate the hazards of everyday life. We explore the everyday practices of non-heterosexuality, among friends and partners, from home-building to caring, and the complex ways in which differences are negotiated in a world of conflicting loyalties and belongings.

The main aim of Chapter 5, 'Partnership rites', is to explore the working-through of an egalitarian ideal in relationships, and particularly partnerships. This chapter examines contemporary stories of intimacy to demonstrate the changing meanings of love and care, and the emergence of new ways of affirming attachment and commitment. It also explores the role of power in non-heterosexual relationships: examining various types of power relationship (age, physical, financial, emotional, sexual, racial), and how these are mediated and negotiated in everyday life.

Chapter 6, 'Sexual pleasures', is concerned with the erotic aspects of relationships. Non-heterosexual people have historically been defined by their sexuality and sexual preferences. This chapter explores the changing meanings of the erotic: the role of sexuality in relationships, similarities and differences between gay and lesbian erotic practices, how questions of fidelity and sexual need are negotiated, how sex is related to friendship and love. The chapter places particular emphasis on the relationship between sexual practice and the doing or undoing of gender.

Non-heterosexual parenting is probably the most controversial and contested aspect of families of choice. Even the European laws, which give recognition to lesbian and gay partnerships, generally stop short of sanctioning adoption. Yet many non-heterosexuals do parent, whether formally – as biological or adoptive parents – or informally, through fostering, and negotiated arrangements. Self-insemination, and more recently surrogacy, have opened up wider possibilities of parenting. In Chapter 7, 'Parenting', we analyse the stories of non-heterosexual men and women who tell of creating and caring for their children.

Despite dramatic changes in attitudes towards homosexuality in most western countries, many, if not most, non-heterosexuals have to live with risk and stigma. In conclusion, Chapter 8, 'Towards intimate citizenship', demonstrates how prejudice is confronted and lived with, and how networks, communities, and friendship circles not only face hostility, but also act as sources of social support and strength in combating it. The experience of oppression, and resistance to it, shapes what we call 'practices of freedom', and also gives rise to new claims to citizenship based on the recognition of relational rights.

Throughout these chapters we use the voices of self-identified non-heterosexuals themselves, to chart the everyday challenges that have to be confronted in shaping relationships. There are many different voices, based on different experiences, shaped by gender, age, ethnicity, class, and all the other factors that open up or foreclose life chances. Yet there is a unity provided by a common experience of the dominant heterosexual norms, and the need to create meaningful relationships in a world which remains hesitant in fully validating them.

This book has been a collective endeavour, both in the sense that we the authors have worked closely together on every stage of the research, and also because we have worked with the narrators whose stories and experiences we present here. We emphasise again that we do not claim to offer the comprehensive truth about non-heterosexual ways of life: they are too diverse for that. We offer instead what Plummer (1992) referred to in his book, *Modern Homosexualities*, as 'fragments' of experience. But these fragments are not randomly selected. They are part of a pattern of individual life choices and narratives that many people are adopting in a rapidly changing world. In this book we document and offer ways of understanding the development of same sex intimacies, families of choice and other life experiments.

1 Families of choice

The changing context of non-heterosexual relationships

The emergence of families of choice

In his book, entitled *Our Families, Our Values: Snapshots of Queer Kinship*, Robert Goss (1997: 19) argues that everyone 'has the right to create family forms that fits his or her needs to realize the human potential for love in non oppressive relationships'. It would be surprising indeed if everyone agreed that families could be 'created' so readily. But the fact that many non-heterosexual people are saying it, in ever proliferating stories of everyday life, signals a new development.

'Family' is a powerful and pervasive word in our culture, embracing a variety of social, cultural, economic and symbolic meanings; but traditionally it is seen as the very foundation of society. It is also a deeply ambiguous and contested term in the contemporary world, the subject of continual polemics, anxiety, and political concern about the 'crisis of the family'. It is surely of great significance, therefore, that the term is now in common use among many, though by no means all, self-identified non-heterosexuals. Increasingly, it is being deployed to denote something broader than the traditional relationships based on lineage, alliance and marriage, referring instead to kin-like networks of relationships, based on friendship, and commitments 'beyond blood' (Wakeling and Bradstock 1995). Such networks might also incorporate selected blood relatives. They may or may not involve children. But whatever the particular patterns, they have a cultural and symbolic meaning for the people who participate or feel a sense of belonging in and through them. 'Everyone has the right to define significant relationships and decide who matters and counts as family,' continues Goss (1997: 19). If this is the case, something is clearly afoot in the politics of the family, and in particular in the lives of those historically excluded from family life in most western cultures. We are witnessing the development and public affirmation of 'families of choice' (cf. Weston 1991).

New ways of thinking and talking about family are being absorbed into everyday life, as the following two quotations illustrate. The first is from Rachel, a black lesbian in her early thirties:

I think the friendships I have are family. I'm sure lots of people will say this, but, it's very important to me because my family is not [important] – apart from my mother, who is *kind* of important – on the whole, my [chosen] family is all I've got. And my family are my friends. And I think you make your family – because I've never felt like I belonged anywhere. And it's taken me a long time to realise that it comes from me. ... It doesn't matter where I go or who I am with, I'm not going to just suddenly be given a family, or a history, or an identity, or whatever. You don't just get it on a plate. You have to create your own. So far as I am concerned, that's how important friends are. (F02)

The second is from a white gay man, Luke, aged 36:

we [friends] call each other family – you know, they're family. I'm not sure whether that's family in the sense of being gay [family]. ... I have a blood family, but I have an extended family ... my friends. (M04)

Comments such as these raise a number of interesting issues. First, the use of the term 'family' suggests a strongly perceived need to appropriate the sort of values and comforts that the family unit is supposed to embody, even if it regularly fails to do so: continuity over time, emotional and material support, ongoing commitment, and intense engagement. Many non-heterosexuals, particularly lesbians, dislike using the term 'family' because of its historic baggage and oppressive heterosexual connotations. Yet, even in the process of rejecting the term, some of its meaning is preserved. Juliet, a 39-year-old lesbian, remarks that:

Because I have kind of, at the moment anyway, fairly negative feelings about my biological family, it maybe is not something I would actually immediately apply to my friends and the people who are important to me. Having said that, you know, I think the way I think about those people is the way that ... generally people would regard family. (F01)

For many others, friendship circles are spoken about as equivalent to the idealised family (and infinitely preferable to the real one). We can hear this in some characteristic comments on friends as family: 'a feeling of belonging to a group of people who like me' (Simon, a gay man, 32); 'affection, love if you like – you share the good things, and you share the bad things, too' (Dan, 71). These may not be everyone's definition of the ideal family, nor are they anywhere near the legal definition of kin, but the words carry intense conviction among those who have chosen to organise their relationships around new forms of commitment.

The second point is that this usage illustrates a very important ethos that now pervades the non-heterosexual world: a sense of the freedom and agency which the concept of 'created' relationships brings (cf. Henriksson 1995). For one gay man, Paul, friends are 'more important than family'. He goes on to say that:

I take my family [of origin] for granted, whereas my friendships are, to a degree, chosen, and therefore they are created. And I feel a greater responsibility to nourish them, whereas my family will always be there. (M21)

Paul's words are echoed by a black lesbian in her late twenties, Malika:

In the last few years since I've come out, I've learnt that family can be anything you want it to be. So I create my own family, basically, and that's been a difficult thing for me to get my head round, but I like it now. (F03)

This emphasis on creativity is crucial to understanding what is happening in terms of changing relationship patterns. It suggests a new self-confidence in the non-heterosexual world, and an awareness of new opportunities and spaces for choosing ways of being. However, running alongside this is a strong sense of the continuing hostility towards homosexuality in the wider world, despite the well-recognised changes which have opened up these new possibilities. Chosen families provide the 'life-line' that the biological family, it is believed, should provide, but often cannot or will not for its sexually different offspring. For a young lesbian, Jo, aged 22, her family of origin is 'homophobic'. Chosen relationships, based on friendship, on the other hand, are 'supportive, and understand in a way that your family should and often doesn't. And because of people's situations, they often end up spending more time with their [friends]. ... I think they become like family' (F43).

As these comments illustrate, people slide easily between viewing the family as a site of hostility, and as something they can invent. Friends are *like* family; or they *are* family. The family is something external to you, or something you do. This ambivalence in language is revealing. We are clearly in transition from one set of norms to another. The 'postmodern family', as Stacey (1996: 7) has described the current diversity of patterns, underlines the contested, ambivalent and undecided character of contemporary familial patterns, combining a mixture of experiment, pastiche and nostalgia. The language of 'family' used by many contemporary non-heterosexual people can be seen as both a challenge to conventional definitions, and an attempt to broaden these; as a hankering for legitimacy and an attempt to build something new; as an identification with existing patterns, and a more or less conscious effort to subvert them. The stories that many non-heterosexual women and men tell about families of choice are creating a new public space where old and new forms jostle for meaning, and where new patterns of relationships are being invented.

The concept of 'stories' or 'narratives' is an important element when considering the changes that are taking place. Through narratives, individuals give meaning to their lives, affirm their identities, and present their relationships as viable and valid. The new stories about families of choice that characterise the contemporary non-heterosexual world provide new truths, and these in turn circulate within communities, and give rise to claims for recognition and legitimisation as crucial elements of the claim to full citizenship (Plummer 1995).

As Lewin observes, 'same sex commitments are nothing new; only the demand for equity and recognition have changed the landscape' (Lewin 1998: 25).

The best way to conceptualise this changing landscape, we believe, is in relationship to the circulation of new stories that are significantly reshaping the ways in which we conceive of intimate life. In his book, *Telling Sexual Stories*, Plummer (1995) argues that:

> Society itself may be seen as a textured but seamless web of stories emerging everywhere through interaction: holding people together, pulling people apart, making societies work … [The] metaphor of the story … has become recognised as one of the central roots we have into the continuing quest for understanding human meaning. Indeed culture itself has been defined as 'an ensemble of stories we tell about ourselves'.
>
> (Plummer 1995: 5)

If this is the case, then the emergence of new ways of expressing basic needs and desires ('new stories') are very important. They signal both changing perceptions and changing possibilities. We can speak of intimate lives in new ways. New stories about sexual and intimate life emerge, it may be argued, when there is a new audience ready to hear them in communities of meaning and understanding, and when newly vocal groups can have their experiences validated in and through them.

In the case of the non-heterosexual world there is a growing audience, in the burgeoning sexual communities themselves, 'fattened up, rendered ripe and willing to hear such stories' (Plummer 1995: 121). And there are many individuals, like those we quote in this book, willing to vocalise new experiences, which has led to a conscious presentation of the viability of non-heterosexual ways of life. As Lewin observes, as narrators 'construct their stories they engage in a process of explaining their own worlds to themselves, thereby conceptualizing who they are' (Lewin 1998: 38), and, we would add, making sure that their stories are heard, not only among their immediate circles, but in the wider world.

This involves a high degree of reflexivity in the accounts we listened to. People offer stories to validate their lives, and simultaneously reveal their awareness of the similar stories circulating in the communities with which they identify. They provide examples of 'the reflexive project of the self', which the sociologist Anthony Giddens (1991) has argued is characteristic of the late modern world. Faced with the breakdown of traditional ways of life and older forms of legitimisation, people are forced to shape new values, norms and life patterns. In so doing, they draw on their own experiences and those of their significant others, and begin to define themselves anew. Pioneering books such as Kath Weston's *Families We Choose: Lesbians, Gays, Kinship* (1991), which was followed by a number of works, including *Valued Families: The Lesbian Mothers' Legal Handbook* (Harne and Rights of Women 1997), *We Are Family: Testimonies of Lesbian and Gay Parents* (Ali 1996), and *No Place Like Home: Relationships and Family Life among Lesbians and Gay Men* (Carrington 1999), simultaneously document these changes and circulate the new narratives, promote alternative ways of being, and offer models for 'doing family'. People are rethinking the meaning of their relationships, and the new meanings of family.

From this perspective, the emergence of the emphasis on 'family' and relationships in the life stories of many non-heterosexuals represents an important shift in the cultural politics of sexual nonconformity. Of course, many of the patterns that have recently come to public consciousness are not in any fundamental sense new. The burgeoning literature of lesbian and gay history offers plentiful accounts of same sex relationships in the past, from the passionate friendships of women (see Faderman 1981; Smith-Rosenberg 1985), and the emergent networks of homosexual men from at least the seventeenth century onwards (Bray 1982), to the intricacies of bisexual life (Garber 1995). Historians have documented patterns of religious same sex commitment ceremonies, which some have argued are prototypes of contemporary 'same sex marriages' (Boswell 1994; Hexter 1997). We are not, therefore, arguing that non-heterosexual relationships have emerged fully armed out of the flux of postmodernity. The myths of the promiscuous, hedonistic homosexual man, capable of no more than fleeting relationships, or of the sexless spinster, cosily ensconced in private life, have some passing contact with a difficult and complex history, but are belied by the realities of many non-heterosexual lives and the intense erotic, romantic and friendship commitments which have long existed. But at the same time as we acknowledge a rich history, we also need to recognise crucial contemporary changes in the life stories of those who have been forced to live outside what we describe in Chapter 2 as the 'heterosexual assumption'.

These changes are the result of two closely intertwined shifts in contemporary culture: a transformation over the past generation in the possibilities for living an openly non-heterosexual life; and wider changes in the organisation of sexuality and gender, which have given rise to both the so-called 'crisis of the family' and to complex transformations of intimate life. In the remainder of this chapter, we concentrate on these two transformations, and the new narratives which they offer.

From identity to relational rights

From being a subject 'hidden from history', homosexuality has in recent years come to dominate at least one form of writing about the past: sexual history (see Weeks 2000). This is due to a growing recognition that the history of heterosexuality is inextricably bound up with its 'other', same sex activity. We cannot understand one without the other. Different cultures, and diverse histories, have responded to same sex activities in a variety of different ways, so there can be no simple history of homosexuality as a transhistorical experience. There is always a dual movement in the history of sexual nonconformity, a story of difference, and a story of convergence. The sexually outlawed are regularly forced to live in at least two worlds: of outward conformity, and of secret transgression. Each defines the other. Sexual history has to be, inevitably, about both heterosexuality and homosexuality.

Since at least the eighteenth century, and increasingly codified from the nineteenth century (Trumbach 1998, 1999; Sedgwick 1985, 1990), the execrated category of 'the homosexual' has served to define the parameters of what it is to be 'normal', that is heterosexual. The fact that the boundaries between the two have always been permeable, as countless personal histories have revealed, and the for long ambiguous category of 'the bisexual' underlined (Garber 1995), made little difference to popular beliefs and prejudices or the legal realities. The divide between homosexuality and heterosexuality seemed rooted in nature, sanctioned by religion and science, and upheld by penal codes. It is not surprising, therefore, that distinctive social worlds emerged in which at first male and later female 'homosexuals' developed different ways of life (see Chapter 3 for a fuller discussion). These worlds were generally covert, and always vulnerable, but they provided the context for the solidification of distinctive sexual identities, and what Michel Foucault (1979) called a 'reverse discourse'. The hostile categorisation became the starting point for positive identification.

For recent generations of non-heterosexuals, however, the real turning point was the emergence of a radical lesbian and gay movement from the late 1960s, though this inevitably was rooted in longer-term developments (Weeks 1977/1990; D'Emilio 1983; Adam 1994). The new movement had a profound effect not only on the lives and relationships of people directly involved in it, but also in the wider community. One of the fundamental effects (if not the original inspiration) of the lesbian and gay movement was the assertion of identity and community: an affirmation of a positive sense of self and of the collective means of realising this (see Weeks 1995). Finding community, said one of the interviewees in Kath Weston's book, means discovering 'that your story isn't the only one in the world' (Weston 1991: 123). The new stories – embodied in a library of 'coming out' narratives – told of discovering the self, achieving a new identity, finding others like yourself, and gaining a new sense of belonging.

Although the radicalised movement of self-affirming lesbians, gay men, bisexuals, transgendered people and others proclaimed the desire to 'end the homosexual', and indeed the heterosexual (Altman 1971/1993) – that is to get rid of redundant and oppressive categorisations – the reality was different. Since the early 1970s, there has been considerable growth of distinctive sexual communities, and of what have been called quasi-ethnic lesbian and gay identities, and the proliferation of other distinctive sexual identities, from bisexual to sado-masochistic, and many sub-divisions (Epstein 1990). Difference has apparently triumphed over convergence, identity over similarity. The rise of a queer politics from the late 1980s can be seen as both a product of and a challenge to these developments, rejecting narrow identity politics in favour of a more transgressive erotic warfare (Warner 1993; Seidman 1997) – while at the same time, ironically, creating a new, post-identity identity of 'queer'.

Since the 1970s, the lesbian and gay movement has oscillated between two elements – a 'moment of transgression' and a 'moment of citizenship' (Weeks 1995: 108–23). The first marks a challenge to the existing sexual order, the subversion of existing norms and the questioning of conventional values in the name of something better. The second is about justice and equity, daring the existing order to recognise difference, and to redefine the grounds of full inclusion. In practice, sexual politics must always involve features of both, which implicitly, or increasingly explicitly, involves a challenge to heterosexual hegemony, and its most characteristic social form, the family.

The transgressive element of lesbian and gay politics offered a sharp critique of the family as the forcing house of hostility to homosexuality, and the subordination of women. As the Australian gay theorist Dennis Altman put it, 'straight is to gay as family is to no family' (1979: 47); while the French theorist Guy Hocquenghem (1978) encouraged gays to elaborate friendships as polar opposites to kin. Feminist sociologists Michele Barrett and Mary McIntosh made a similar point in their critique of (white, western) familialism in their significantly·entitled book, *The Anti Social Family*. They argued that: 'It is the belief that kinship, love and having nice things together are naturally and inevitably bound up together that makes it hard to imagine a world in which "family" plays little part. This mythological unity must be picked apart, strand by strand' (Barrett and McIntosh 1982: 159). A phrase in the manifesto of the London Gay Liberation Front (1971: 2) speaks for a host of radical challenges to the family in this moment of transgression: 'The very form of the family works against homosexuality.' In other words, it is a denial of identity.

However, since at least the early 1980s (see Altman 1982) a different emphasis has come to the fore, giving rise to the new narratives of intimate relationships that are at the heart of this book. They focus attention on the values of everyday life, and form the basis of new claims to full citizenship for those hitherto on the margins, especially where relationships are concerned (Weeks 1998). The achievements of the lesbian and gay movement have opened up possibilities for broader claims for validating a wide range of life experiences. The question of identity has not gone away, nor were issues about relationships absent from the early feminist and lesbian and gay movement. Barrett and McIntosh (1982: 149), after all, wrote of the need for 'experiments in new ways of living', thus voicing a widespread feeling that personal liberation necessitated radical changes to traditional domestic and family structures. It is therefore surprising, on the surface at least, that the growing emphasis on the recognition of relational rights for non-heterosexuals should be expressed in the language of the family. What significance can we read into this?

First, the usage is not in fact new, and can be traced through non-heterosexual narratives throughout the twentieth century, though often marked by the quotation marks of irony and self-mocking. Chauncey (1994) records its regular American use in his study of gay New York during the first half of the twentieth century, and it also recurs in British testimonies (for example, Weeks and Porter 1998). It achieved an anthemic apotheosis in the 1980s' pop song by Sister Sledge, 'We are family', which has graced many a lesbian and gay Pride celebration. The 'we' is the broad community, and the smaller platoons within it. Nor, it has to be said, is the usage uncontested. Many strongly resist the use of the term, even as they describe very complex relationships with family of origin, friends, lovers and offspring. People are uneasy with a term that is so clearly associated with an 'institution' which has often excluded them, and which continues to suggest the perpetuation of an exclusively heterosexual mode of being.

Even the most passionate theoretical advocates of the rights of non-heterosexual people to form their own 'families' are careful to emphasise the dimensions of difference. As Goss writes:

> The appropriation of the term *family* is not an assimilationist strategy of finding respectability in general society. *We are not degaying or delesbianizing ourselves by describing ourselves as family.* In fact, we are Queering the notion of family and creating families reflective of our life choices. Our expanded pluralist uses of family are politically destructive of the ethic of traditional family values.
>
> (Goss 1997: 12)

For others, however, the use of the term suggests a willingness to destroy the distinctive achievements of non-heterosexual history, a retreat into the fantasy of 'pastoralism' (Bersani 1995), and a restriction on the erotic possibilities of queer life. In the same volume of essays as Goss, Rofes writes that he and his lover:

> understand love as a wily social construct loaded with a range of question-able values, and romance as a social practice laden with obligation offered as love letters and power plays masquerading as roles. ... I argue that our attempts to equate childless gay male social formations with even a liberal definition of 'family' runs the risk of intermingling constructs with very different values and tainting the creative interpersonal processes used by gay men in constituting relationships.
>
> (Rofes 1997: 158–9)

Clearly, this is a continuing conversation, through which friendships, partner-ships and intimate life are being defined, lived and reshaped, and throughout this book we shall return to the value of the term itself.

However, the use of the term 'family' raises a second key issue: its circulation underlines the poverty of our language in describing alternative forms of intimate life (Weeks 1991). The language of familialism is all pervasive in our culture, and it is difficult to escape its entanglement. Even during its most militantly anti-family phase in the early 1970s, activists in the modern lesbian and gay movement used the familial terms 'sisters' and 'brothers' to affirm one another as signs of a political and emotional solidarity (Weeks 1977/1990), though in this case it was probably derived from the common usage of the American Civil Rights and British Labour movements. It is ironic that as this usage has disappeared, a more explicit use of the language of family has emerged as a key element in contemporary non-heterosexual politics. We can begin to explain this, however, by reflecting on a wider shift in family politics. The early polemics of gay liberation were concerned not only to critique but to outline *alternatives* to the family, which was seen as an imprisoning and outmoded institution. This reflected a wider challenge to the hegemony of the family, which was expressed both in theoretical critiques and in counter-cultural challenges to the existing order.

Since the 1970s, however, this rhetoric has almost completely disappeared. Increasingly, critics of the family have talked not of replacing the family but instead of recognising *alternative families* (Weeks 1991), an acknowledgement of the pluralisation of forms of family life. There are various types of family, they argue, differentiated by class, ethnicity, geography and simply lifestyle choices, but in the main, fulfilling the basic purposes of family. If there are indeed so many types of family, why should same sex families be ignored? As Stacey writes, lesbian and gay families are:

> Neither marginal nor exceptional, but rather represent a paradigmatic illustration of the 'queer' postmodern conditions of kinship that we all now inhabit. Gays and lesbians who self-consciously form families are forced to confront the challenges, opportunities and dilemmas of the postmodern condition with much lower levels of denial, resistance, displacement or bad faith than most others can indulge.
>
> (Stacey 1996:15)

The appropriation of the language of the family by many non-heterosexuals can, therefore, be seen as a battle over meaning, one important way in which the sexually marginal are struggling to assert the validity of their own way of life. It is striking, for example, that the usage became much more common in Britain after the condemnation of 'pretended family relationships' in Section 28 (Weeks 1991). It is a classic example of 'reversing the discourse': turning what was conceived of as derogatory into a resounding affirmation.

In so doing, non-heterosexuals are part of a wider struggle over meaning, both participating in and reflecting a broader crisis over family relationships. As Andrew Sullivan (1997) has argued, if the future of marriage is a critical ground of contestation in the wider world, it is hardly surprising that lesbians and gays should focus their demands on it. If parenting is perceived as in major need of rethinking, then why should non-heterosexuals be excluded from the debate? If families get ever more complex as a result of divorce, remarriage, recombination and step-parenting, why should the chosen families of lesbians and gays, composed of lovers, ex-lovers and friends, be denied a voice? As Browning (in Sullivan 1997: 134) makes clear, 'each of us, hetero or homo, has a stake in nurturing a diverse landscape of families' – and apparently of claiming as 'family' whatever our own arrangements are.

This has become even more important for many non-heterosexuals because of the unanticipated AIDS epidemic from the early 1980s. Weston has suggested that:

Situated historically in a period of discourse on lesbian and gay kinship, AIDS has served as an impetus to establish and expand gay families. In certain cases blood relations joined with gay friends and relatives to assist the chronically ill or dying. Sometimes a family of friends was trans- formed into a group of caregivers with ties to one another as well as the persons with AIDS. Community organisations began to offer counselling to persons with AIDS 'and their loved ones', while progressive hospitals and hospices modified residence and visitation policies to embrace 'family as the client defines family'. Implicit in a phrase like 'loved ones' is an open-ended notion of kinship that respects the principles of choice and self-determination in defining kin, with love spanning the ideologically contrasting domains of biological family and the families we create.

(Weston 1991: 183)

The HIV/AIDS epidemic dramatised the absence of relational rights for non-heterosexuals in a climate of growing prejudice and enhanced need. Same sex partners were often ignored or bypassed by medical authorities as their lovers lay sick or dying. Insurance companies refused cover for same sex couples. Mortgage companies insisted on HIV tests before agreeing (or more likely, not agreeing) housing loans. Individuals were cast out of joint homes when their lovers died, and were often denied inheritance rights (Heaphy, Weeks and Donovan 1999). The epidemic revealed how vulnerable non-heterosexuals were without full recognition of their significant commitments – without full citizenship (Watney 1994: 159–68).

Other developments – especially where children were involved – gave the same message. The first debates about the validity of non-heterosexual family type relations began in the 1970s in Britain and the US, with controversies over child custody battles of lesbian mothers (Hanscombe and Forster 1982; Rights of Women Lesbian Custody Group 1986; Lewin 1993). The so-called 'lesbian baby-boom' (see Chapter 7), and the claims by lesbians and gay men for equal rights in issues concerning fostering and adoption, further underlined the continuation of inequality, despite the gains that had been made over the previous decades. Not surprisingly, by the 1990s throughout western countries, but especially in Scandinavia and the United States, new demands for partnership rights, same sex marriage, and for recognition of new family forms were flourishing, often with regard to child care. As Nardi (1999) has observed, while the use of the term 'family' may be little more than metaphorical when applied to adult friendships, it has a strong affinity with conventional uses when applied to units with children. All these factors have created a new agenda for non-heterosexual politics, in which the language of the family has become a key battleground.

Leading social theorist Manuel Castells (1997: 71) has argued that contempo- rary social movements, like the lesbian and gay movement, have three characteristic elements: an assertion of identity; the identification of an adversary; and a societal goal. This can be translated into three key questions:

'Who are *we*?', 'Who or what are we *against*?', and 'What are we *for*?' The early years of lesbian and gay politics gave a resonant answer to the first question: 'we' were those who came out, affirmed our sexuality and identity, and developed a new sense of belonging in and through a concept of movement and 'community'. The result was the non-heterosexual world as we understand it today. The second question also provided emergent answers, though the language has shifted over time: discrimination, oppression, 'homophobia', 'heterosexism', 'compulsory heterosexuality'. In other words, the fundamental cause of hostility towards homosexuality was a culture which privileged heterosexuality, and denied the validity of other sexualities and ways of life. Lesbians, gay men, bisexuals and other sexual minorities have come a long way since the late 1960s, throughout the highly industrialised democratic nations, but the struggle for recognition, and against the denial of identity and different ways of being, is far from won. In many ways it is still at the heart of debates about what we mean by the rights of non-heterosexuals. But it also poses sharply the third question: 'What are we *for*?'

It is now clear that the assertion of identity is insufficient if basic forms of inequality persist. Cultures are perfectly able to accept the idea that some people are different without fundamentally shifting their values or power structures. Nor is 'sexual liberation' for many people the real issue. As Michel Foucault (1979) pointed out some years ago in *The History of Sexuality*, the meaning of liberation is fundamentally ambiguous. The loosening of old forms of restraint on sexual expression does not in itself change the dominant institutional patterns which place people in a hierarchy of acceptability (Rubin 1984). The broadening of non-heterosexual politics and culture into an exploration of relationships, with campaigns for relational rights to the fore, offers new possibilities for challenging entrenched forms of social and sexual exclusion, by defining the qualities of different ways of being. As Castells (1997: 219) argues: 'What started as a movement of sexual liberation came full circle to haunt the patriarchal family by attacking its heterosexual roots, and subverting its exclusive appropriation of family values.' In this sense, then, it is part of a much wider change in intimate life, in which questions of what constitute family values are central.

The politics of intimate life

Late modernity, Giddens (1992) has argued, is a post-traditional order in which the question 'how shall I live?' can only be answered in day-to-day decisions about who to be, how to behave, and whom we should love. In a world where old sources of authority are challenged, where new identities proliferate, and where individuals seem to be increasingly thrown back on their own resources for values and guidelines for their everyday actions, we have no choice but to choose (Weeks 1995, 1998). Giddens, among others, argues that this potentially opens the way to a radical democratisation of the interpersonal domain (see also Beck and Beck-Gernsheim 1995). For if individuals are the ultimate makers of their own lives, then the freedom to choose lifestyles and forms of partnerships on a democratic and egalitarian basis becomes crucial to the sort of lives we want to live. In practice, of course, there are strong cultural inhibitions and material constraints which limit individual opportunities, and the democratic relationship remains an ideal rather than a living reality (Jamieson 1998, 1999; Lewis 2001). Nevertheless, there is an increasing flexibility and 'moral fluency' (Mulgan 1997) in intimate life, which stretches across the heterosexual–homosexual divide. Many people are cast adrift from the old verities embodied in tradition: they have to invent new forms for themselves.

Non-heterosexual people have had to be the arch-inventors, because so few guidelines have existed for those living outside the conventional heterosexual patterns. But the emergence of a new discourse concerned with wider aspects of homosexual existence than simply sexuality and identity can be seen as part of a new set of preoccupations in contemporary cultures as a whole: a recognition of the opening up of all social identities, and of patterns of relationships. On a theoretical level, the poststructuralist and postmodernist challenges of recent decades have stressed the fluid, historical, negotiable, contingent nature of all social identities, including sexual identities (Weeks 1995). Abstract speculation about identity, however, is simply a marker for the growing awareness of multiple belongings and potential ways of being. Increasingly, we recognise that identities are not pregiven; they have to be articulated in increasingly complex social circumstances. The traditional ordered distinctions and balances between men and women have been radically challenged by both material and cultural changes, not least the impact of feminism. The binary divide between homosexuality and heterosexuality, which was codified in the nineteenth century and has come to be regarded as the very definition of natural in the twentieth century, has been significantly challenged by the public emergence of vocal lesbian and gay movements and collective identities. Boundaries dissolve, and new ones have to be hastily assembled. The relationship between adults and children has become particularly fraught, the subject of constant negotiation and renegotiation – as emphasised by a series of moral panics and public controversies, ranging from the outcry over violent videos to the perceived endemic threat of paedophilia. In this context, perhaps it is not so surprising that debate on same sex relationships often revolves around responsibility for child care. The lesbian, gay, bisexual, transgender, queer – the list is potentially long – assertion of identities is only one aspect of a wider pluralisation of identities in a culture of diversity. Diverse identities, and a variety of different ways of life, produce new and more complex patterns of relationships. Indeed, it can be argued, identity is shaped in and through intimate relationships.

'Families of choice' and other chosen relationships – creative adaptations to rapid change based on voluntary association – are characteristic responses to a shifting society, and sociologists have seen their emergence as a significant and developing feature of the heterosexual, as well as non-heterosexual, world. In modern society, most people, whether heterosexual or homosexual, live through very similar experiences of insecurity and emotional flux at various times of their lives, and relationships based on friendships and choice often become indispensable frameworks for negotiating the hazards of everyday life. As Litwak and Szelengi have argued, friendships provide 'alternative ways of doing things when the formal structure of society is clearly inadequate   ... when the normative rules of society have come to appear especially artificial and fragile' (quoted in Nardi 1992a: 109).

Even traditional organisations are noting a transformation in the ways in which people conceive of kin and supportive relationships through friendships. In 1998, a leading Church of England charity, The Children's Society, redefined the family as 'an emotionally supportive network of adults and children, some of whom live together or have lived together' (quoted in *Independent on Sunday*, 10 May 1998). This is precisely how many non-heterosexuals would describe their relationships, especially where there are dependent children. Sociologists Pahl and Spencer (1997; see also Pahl 2000) have gone further in seeing the growth of 'friend-like relationships' as characteristic of the late twentieth-century Zeitgeist. They argue that these forms are not necessarily supplanting kin relationships, but extending and enriching them. As old communities of fate and necessity decline, and family patterns change, the flexible patterns of friendship can provide more adaptable structures both for private life and for the labour market, offering effective 'bridging ties' to enable individuals to escape from communities of origin. The central aspect of these friendship networks, Pahl and Spencer maintain, is that they are voluntary, they are developed over time, not given, and they help to strengthen our individuality. They have to be worked at and they make us more reflexive about who we are and what we are doing.

But a culture based on choice also breeds uncertainty. The development of these new patterns has provided a happy hunting ground for those who hanker for the verities of the past. We need not succumb to the myth of a golden age to recognise many of the symptoms of breakdown in the traditional ordering of domestic life. The rising divorce rate, the incidence of single parenting, the delay of marriage, the rise of cohabitation, a rapid increase in single households, the emergence of new patterns of intimacy, of which families of choice are but one example: all these are indices of profound change. However we respond to these changes, there can be no doubt of the massive, and certainly irreversible, shifts in the inherited patterns of everyday life.

The rise of a new moral politics since the 1970s, concerned to defend (or resurrect) the traditional family, can be seen in part as a reaction to these changing patterns. Hostility to the claims for equal rights and justice from lesbians and gay men, and the idea of alternative families, have been central to their discourse, especially in the US (see Stacey 1996; Herman 1997). This in turn has reinforced the emergence of the new preoccupations in the non-heterosexual world itself, as 'anti-gay' propaganda mediated, in Weston's (1991: 135) phrase, a shift in the non-heterosexual community towards exploring new forms of commitment.

However, cultural pessimism seems totally unjustified when we look at the underlying trends. Despite cohabitation and divorce, most people still marry. Despite the growth of single member households and of single parents, most children still grow up in two parent families with siblings (see essays in McRae 1999, especially Scott 1999). Even the spectre of rampant homosexuality has been downplayed in recent sexual surveys. Despite the greater public presence of homosexuality, researchers suggest that self-identified non-heterosexuals form a tiny percentage of a given population (Wellings *et al.* 1994). There is still a surprisingly high degree of stability in family relationships, even if, as we argue, the form is changing (McRae 1999).

The inevitable question, therefore, is where is the problem? And why is there such anguish? Perhaps, as Silva and Smart (1999b: 3–4) suggest, what is in decline really is the normative force of marriage as the underpinning of family life, and this 'ideological slippage' is in fact what much of the political rhetoric is about. Certainly, it is the decline of marriage that appears to have had the greatest effect on cultural conservatives. But that, one would have thought, could as easily lead to the endorsement of same sex marriages, as it could to lament for the decline of heterosexual marriage, as the conservative gay commentator Andrew Sullivan (1995) observes.

A more fundamental issue, we would argue, for which the decline of the centrality of marriage is only one sign, is a transformation of the meanings of intimate life, which is leading to a new balance between the desire for individual freedom and the possibilities of commitment. The contemporary debate about the family regularly fails to recognise this, and instead we are presented with a stark polarity (Weeks, Donovan and Heaphy 1999). On the one hand, the media and conservative moralists (of all political cultures) offer an image of mutuality, interdependence and resilience, represented by an ideal type of the family. At its most evocative, this ideal type is seen as a haven of trust, mutual involvement and shared responsibilities, which many argue offers the best hope for a communitarian culture (Etzioni 1995). By its very nature, this traditional model is heterosexual, the norm against which all other intimate relationships must be judged.

On the other hand, set against this, many commentators present a vivid caricature of the perils of the search for autonomy, for an individual fulfilment that often avoids commitment, and is the product of an individualistic and hedonistic culture (see, for example, Davies 1992; Dench 1996; Dennis and Erdos 1993; Phillips 1999). Inevitably, the triumph of the latter ethos is seen as corroding and ultimately undermining the first. This is clearly put in an impassioned polemic by the British writer, Melanie Phillips, an exponent of tough-love liberalism (or moralism), in an article entitled 'The truth that dare not speak its name':

> To gain acceptance by the majority, the beleaguered minority claims it is not deviant, that gay sex is as natural as heterosexuality. Those who tell the truth, that this is a lie, then have to be suppressed by social or political ostracism. The very word normal has to be airbrushed out of existence. ... The result is not only that the oppressed and their defenders become oppressors. It also becomes impossible to conduct the urgently needed debate

about the damage being done to our gay *and* heterosexual young by a narcissistic culture that places at centre stage a crude and materialistic sexual individualism that denies proper concern for the common good.

(Phillips 1998: 25)

In this gloomy scenario, extra-marital lifestyles, especially non-heterosexual ones, are portrayed as the triumph of 'sexual individualism' over the obligations of family, precisely because of the undermining of the duties of traditional family life.

We believe that this radically misreads what is happening in society. The new narratives of intimate life that we have pinpointed do not represent a thinning of family commitments and responsibilities, but a reorganisation of them in new circumstances. Beck-Gernsheim (1998: 57 ff.) has observed that the 'obligation of solidarity' imposed on the family as a network of dependence and a 'community of need' in earlier times, is now being transformed by the new individualisation in western cultures, which also increasingly characterises relations among members of the same family:

> A shorthand way of saying this is that a community of need is becoming an elective relationship. The family is not breaking up as a result; it is acquiring a new historical form.
>
> (Beck-Gernsheim 1998: 54)

This is a result of less basic need in western societies as affluence grows, however unevenly it is distributed, and a recognition that family consists of different elements, of individuals with separate interests. As women become more autonomous, their interests explicitly diverge from those of men. Similarly, common interests between adults and children can tear apart. Thus, the coherence of the relationships among members of a family have to be worked out rather than taken for granted:

> people need to be able to rely upon well-functioning rules and models, but now an ever greater number of decisions are having to be taken. More and more things must be negotiated, planned, personally brought about.
>
> (Beck-Gernsheim 1998: 59)

This is both the effect of, and a major contributor to, a greater sense of risk and uncertainty in our everyday lives (Weeks 1995). Individualisation offers a greater sense of personal autonomy, of freedom from outmoded and often oppressive patterns of life. But it also threatens greater moral loneliness. Deprived of the fixed certainties, at least those which concern shared values, that earlier periods offered, individuals have to make choices about how they want to live in a time when the moral rules are often obscure. Trust and commitments are less assured, and yet individuals still need the security that these promise – perhaps, in fact, need them more in order to face a world of continuing insecurity in work and at home. This is the spur to the creation of chosen commitments, based on more democratic relationships.

Anthony Giddens (1992) has called this process 'the transformation of intimacy'. He suggests that there has been a long-term shift towards the ideal of the democratic egalitarian relationship between men and women, men and men, women and women. At the centre of this ideal is the fundamental belief that love relationships and partnerships should be a matter of personal choice and not of arrangement or tradition. And the reasons for choice are quite clear: personal attraction, sexual desire, mutual trust and compatibility. People stay together only so long as the relationship fulfils the needs of the partners. This is what Giddens (1992) terms the 'pure relationship': based less on romantic, and more on pragmatic notions of love, it implies an openness to the other which is dependent on equality and mutual trust, but also on a willingness to up and go when things go wrong:

> a situation where a social relation is entered into for its own sake, for what can be derived by each person from a sustained association with another; and which is continued only in so far as it is thought by both parties to deliver enough satisfaction for each individual to stay within it.
>
> (Giddens 1992: 58)

This argument has aroused a great deal of controversy, and we share many doubts about its overall validity (see Chapter 5). It suggests an attitude to relationships which sees them as both over-calculating and fragile, based on implied (and sometimes explicit) contract rather than the delights and vicissitudes of love and romance. The empirical evidence, moreover, underlines the distance from actuality for many people of this theoretical model. A number of critics have noted the embeddedness of inherited inequalities between men and women, as young people reproduce the sexual brutalities and struggles which optimists hoped had long disappeared, and older ones slip complacently into conventional gendered patterns (Jamieson 1998, 1999; Holland *et al.* 1998). These factors, which are above all about differential access to power, make the attainment of the ideal difficult and fraught. Yet the same evidence reveals an unprecedented acknowledgement of the merits of companionate and more equal relationships among the same people, even as we fail to achieve them. This is perhaps a more potent implied criticism of the advocates of a real transformation of intimate life. Their position often concentrates on individual processes of choice. The reality is that choice is shaped constantly, both negatively and positively, by complex relationships.

The main point, however, is that though the reality is often complex, the egalitarian relationship *has* become a measure by which people seek to judge their individual lives. This model of how we should live may be seen as an expression of a new norm, the quest for individual fulfilment in the context of freely chosen egalitarian relationships. From this point of view, it can be argued that heterosexual and non-heterosexual forms of life are to some degree converging, as Henning Bech (1992, 1997) has suggested in exploring the implications of the recognition of same sex partnerships. For on both sides of the sexual binary divide, there is a common interest in trying to find a balance between individual satisfaction and mutual involvement. This is not the collapse of the family, nor is it the triumph of unfettered hedonism. It is, we believe, the search for a new form of 'emotional democracy'. The new stories about 'doing family' (Chapter 2) can be seen as everyday efforts at achieving this ideal.

Living 'connected lives'

The stories that non-heterosexuals tell seek to validate the meaningfulness of chosen relationships, where the narrative of the self secures meaning through a narrative of 'connectedness'. The following quotation, from Peter, a 32-year-old gay man, vividly illustrates this point:

> I think that one of the things that socially always happens is that lesbians and gay men are made into individuals with sad lives who are lonely … and I'm really looking forward to there being something that says, 'there are all these lesbians and gay men and they are living completely connected lives, and they have got support, they have got community and they're doing things better than the heterosexual world, because they've created this thing for themselves'. … [having] people talk about their lives, is going to be really good and if it's only read by other lesbians and gay men, who maybe see something in somebody's interview that makes them think, 'Oh, God … that's like my life', it makes us into a real community, with real relationships and real lives, not sort of playing at it. So that's why I wanted to do it [be interviewed] because I thought, 'that's a good thing to do'. (M11)

We see this response as especially significant because it acknowledges the power of the new narratives about intimate life in not only shaping individual choices but also in potentially changing the cultural circumstances in which these choices are made. Through interactions in the social worlds they inhabit, non-heterosexuals shape new ways of understanding their relationships, and acquire the new skills necessary to affirm the validity of different ways of life. As Niamh underlines in the following quotation, the language of the social sciences, fully internalised, intersects with her experiences of non-heterosexual life, to produce a sharp comparison with what she sees as the inequalities of heterosexual life:

> Because they're embedded – you can tell that I'm a wild social construc- tionist – in a socially constructed framework which supports them and because there is an essential power imbalance [in heterosexual relationships] that you can't get round, and because there is an expectation that there are certain roles, which are backed up by economics and backed up by sanc- tions. And also people are … men and women are socialised differently in terms of what relationships are – what heterosexual relationships are. (F34)

The fact that the participants in the research that underpins this book want to highlight the positive realities of their relationships, in comparison to orthodox patterns, gives us important insights into the new narratives that are emerging about families of choice, and the ways in which these stories are becoming part of a collective identity.

Several key narrative strands emerge in these accounts which are central to our argument: people are telling new stories, or old stories in new ways, about identity, mutuality, choice, and the constant process of negotiation which make relationships possible. In many ways, these themes are particular to the non-heterosexual experience. But they are made possible, as we have argued, by broader changes in the everyday reality of intimate life, which is why we seek not only to understand the emerging patterns of the so-called 'sexual minorities', but also to relate these to wider disruptions of traditional family life.

Clearly, we cannot claim that our analysis reveals the comprehensive truth about all non-heterosexual life today. Our claim is both more modest and perhaps more theoretically and methodologically interesting: that the new stories about families of choice tell us something very important about ways in which social actors see the development of both the non-heterosexual and heterosexual world, and shape their lives accordingly.

Plummer (1995: 171) suggests that there are three valuable ways of testing the validity of people's accounts. The first method, the correspondence theory, assumes a matching of the story with details that can be documented. It assumes a transparency in what is said, so that the truth emerges fully from the narrative. Truths, we have suggested, do emerge from narratives. They provide evidence of changing lives and complex processes. But of course life stories always leave open the question of how representative they are. The second way, the aesthetic theory, is concerned with the grace and elegance, the literary effectiveness of a narrative, and with new ways of telling stories. It is as concerned with the way in which something is said, as it is with what is said. This, too, is valuable. Through the phrasing, the assertions and hesitations, we gain genuine insights into the ways in which perceived experience is expressed. But, Plummer argues, there is a third and more effective way of analysing the account, which partly builds on the last point, but goes further: to take the narratives seriously in their own right, not as historical truth (though historical truths do become apparent through them) but as narrative truth. Hence, it is possible to conceptualise the stories of non-heterosexual relationships in the following way: not so much as demonstrating final truths, but rather, as a way of understanding the consequences of telling a particular story, in a particular way, under specific circumstances. We thus concentrate on what can be said, why is it said now and not at other times, and the effects of telling a particular story in a particular way. This is what Plummer (1995) calls the 'pragmatic connection', by which stories can now be examined for the roles they play in lives, in contexts, and in social order.

In examining the stories of families of choice and non-heterosexual relation-ships offered to us, we hope to begin to separate out and clarify the forces at work, to throw new light on the motivations, hopes and desires of many non-heterosexual people. In so doing, we aim to convince the reader of the plausibility of our account, even if we decline to assert that it is the *only* plausible one (cf. Brewer 1994). At the same time, we hope to cast new light on wider changes in intimate and family life, to illuminate not only non-heterosexual patterns, but also the changing nature of heterosexuality. If the traditional family is indeed in crisis, then the experience of those who have often been forced to live outside its walls can tell us something important about new challenges and new possibilities.

2 Life experiments

The meanings of non-heterosexual relationships

Life stories

Contemporary social movements, the Italian theorist Alberto Melucci has argued, 'are prophets of the present. What they possess is not the force of the apparatus but the power of the word. They announce the commencement of change' (Melucci 1996: 1). The movement among self-identified non-heterosexual people in western societies to elaborate new narratives of love, commitment and 'family' – stories of 'completely connected lives', to quote Peter from Chapter 1 – is, we suggest, a sign of profound and sweeping change in the culture of everyday, intimate life. Beneath the rhetoric, in the intimate worlds where most personal lives are lived, many people are quietly reassessing and reconstructing bonds of trust, negotiating relationships, experimenting with ways of life which are meaningful for them, even if society has not yet given these grass-roots transformations meaning and recognition.

The stories recorded in this chapter are examples of the life experiments that non-heterosexual people have to undertake. They are ordinary stories of ordinary people in the sense that the individuals described do not see themselves as extraordinary or part of the cultural avant-garde. They are shaping their lives in the best way possible within their circumstances, and are preoccupied by ordinary virtues and vices. As Jill, a 42-year-old lesbian, says in comparing homosexual and heterosexual lives: 'I think, in terms of day-to-day living, the pressures are all the same. You know, the bills come in and you have to eat … and you have to get work' (F22). Or as Marilyn (aged 45) comments: 'There are similarities in that everyone can feel loyalties and love and affection, that side of things. … The basics of life, perhaps' (F33).

What makes the stories extraordinary is that they are often regarded as such by those whose lives are different, and who have the power to define difference as somehow deviant, inferior, less worthy of respect and recognition. As Stacey (1996: 109) observes, what unifies non-heterosexual lives is the experience of institutionalised hostility towards homosexuality, and the complex social, psychic, individual and cultural effects this then produces. Everyday life experiments are inevitably stories of diversity and difference. The experiences of homosexual or bisexual men and women are shaped by their gendered histories, and by the linked but significantly different histories of lesbianism and male homosexuality. Ethnic, racial, class, geographical and other social and cultural differences intersect and shape sexual identities and life patterns. However, regardless of the real and often searing differences and divisions, the climate in which non-heterosexual individuals are tested gives rise to commonalities, patterns and regularities. Stories of individual lives are shared with others in similar positions. What emerges is a collective experience, where new voices can be heard and new narratives can unfold – the 'power of the word'. We begin our analysis by offering some examples of these everyday stories.

Peter (M11)

Peter is a 32-year-old white gay man who describes himself as British and middle class. Originally from London, he moved to another large city approximately thirteen years ago to study at the local polytechnic. A self-defined gay man, he sees himself as someone who is firmly immersed in lesbian and gay culture:

> I have a completely gay identity – both in my social life, in my family and in my work … I see that as being the way I kind of primarily identify myself. Not just in terms of being out, but having a sort of gay perspective on everything I do, because I do very straight work, and I like to think that I have a different view of the way I do it because of having some sort of developed culture around being a gay man.

Peter grew up in a conventional family, with two parents, a brother and a sister, and he is close to all of them. He became aware of his sexuality in his early teens, and came out to friends and most of his family while at polytechnic. By the time he disclosed his sexuality to his father – when he was in his mid-twenties – he was 'out' to everyone. While he says that his father is still 'not as comfortable about it as my mother is', he feels that his homosexuality has been broadly accepted:

> I'm completely out and it's completely talked about. *My* sexuality is fine. You know, we can all chat away about it at family gatherings. … Coming out … was very easy and it was a very good experience for me. … I can't think of anybody who reacted in a way that upset me – that was important to me. So I've been one of the lucky ones, I think.

In Peter's narrative, being 'out' plays a crucial role in defining who he is to himself and to others: 'it's *completely* important to me … I can't ever imagine not being out'. In living openly as a gay man, Peter feels that he has been afforded important opportunities that are not as readily available to heterosexuals, for example the development of non-traditional ways of living. Thus, coming out has played a crucial role in opening up choices:

you have to think about [your lifestyle] all the time. So nothing that you do is ever just following the set pattern. ... I know it's all very restrained by the sort of oppressions out there, but within a group of lesbians and gay men, you get to choose the way you want to behave and you're not restrained by stupid bloody conventions.

Peter feels that over the years he has made key choices relating to community, family and friendship, and that these different factors are interconnected. He considers that he lives and operates within a strong local lesbian and gay community. This is not merely an imagined community, rather, as Peter emphasises, it exists in a particular geographical space:

it is a community. And whatever anybody tries to say about it, [such as] 'Oh, there is no lesbian and gay community ...', I always think, 'Well, you just don't live in [this city], so you can't know what it's like'. And it is [a community]. We all have these places that we go [to], and we live within walking distance of each other, and we can rely on each other completely. And it's brill. That's why I like living [here].

There is no doubt in Peter's mind that there exists a real gay and lesbian community, one in which like-minded people choose to live near one another. This allows for a sense of confidence and safety within the local neighbourhood: 'It's good from the point of view that I feel I can be completely out and feel completely safe at the same time.' However, not only is it about living in an area with a relatively high population of lesbians and gay men, but it is also about the fact that he and his closest friends have chosen to put down roots in the same location:

we all make choices about where we want to be – you know – like Marcia used to live on [name of] Road, and when she was buying a house she decided that she would hopefully live at the top end of [name of adjoining] Road – it had to be within three minutes walk of where I live and where Leonie is down the street ... we make these kind of huge life decisions on the basis of, 'Is it three minutes away from the people I already know?'

Here, Peter is referring to members of what he regards as his 'other' – chosen – family, built around friendships with lesbians and gay men that have been developed over time, and which are based on strong links:

love and trust are the two things that are most important about what I get from people [his friends] – that I know that I trust them, and they trust me; I love them, and they love me. ... it's not that love that you get with your family, it's that I know that they like me as well. So, they've chosen it, you know, in a way that you can't possibly choose it with your family. And that is probably why now, at 32, they're more important than my genetic family, in terms of the people that I want to spend time with and that I miss when I'm away. I go away and see my parents and I miss my friends ... [T]he longevity of it is what makes it so easy because, you know, when you've been through the mill and back and they've seen you at your worst ... and they know all the bad bits of your personality and all the good bits as well. ... And it's also about referring back to things and having a history together. That's what I like about it.

Friendship is very important for Peter: 'It's the thing that I am sustained by.' Although he has been in a (non-monogamous) relationship for a year, and is committed to having a future with his partner, they do not plan to live together. Critical of cultures that place a primary value on being a couple, Peter does not prioritise his relationship with his boyfriend as having more importance than his core friendship relationships:

> David is my partner, I suppose, but he is also my boyfriend, and I would describe him to the outside world as my boyfriend. Because 'partner' tends to make people think that you live with them, or ... that this is like 'the most important person in my life'. And he [David] is a very important person in my life, but ... there is no one person who's the most important person in my life.

In this narrative of intimate life, individuals who are part of the 'network' or 'family' are identified as being 'the most important' source of support, care and love. Plans for the future are framed in terms of mutual and collective care: 'we do talk about the future and how we would look after each other', comments Peter. In the end, the value attached by Peter to his various relationships is based on the extent they have developed unconditionally over the years. This is the case for both his 'traditional' and 'non-traditional' relationships:

> both my 'families' support me in everything that I do, which is really good ... it's quite a sustaining thing ... it's that unconditional love that you can't really find anywhere else. I mean, for all that they get on my wick, I know that my brother, sister, mum and dad love me unconditionally – however much they, as I say, might get on my nerves at times. It's 'over-arching' – and the same thing [applies] with the people that are important to me – that it [the friendship] is unconditional.

Rachel (F02)

Rachel is in her early thirties and lives on her own in a large city in England. She identifies as a black Jewish lesbian, who is middle class and British. Rachel was adopted by white parents when she was a baby. She has a sister and several nieces and nephews. At the age of 14, Rachel's family moved to her current house, and Rachel has continued to live there since her family left when she was

18. Rachel is quite close to her mother – who is living with her at the moment and is 'driving me mad' – and was also quite close to her father before he died.

The city in which Rachel lives has a predominantly white population. This has been reflected in the friendships she has made. Recently, Rachel has formed a black lesbian group, which has occurred in tandem with her beginning her first relationship with a black woman, Malika. Rachel's experiences have changed her perceptions of her friendships and her notions of community:

> there's a lot of people who used to be [my] friends and who aren't now. ... I think I've changed a lot over the past few years. ... And part of that is about how I feel about being a black lesbian in a *very* white town. ... The lesbian community has *never* given any kind of sign that it accepts or even allows black lesbians to exist.

When discussing the most important people in her life, Rachel talks about her lover Malika, friends, her ex-lover's child, Allie, and her mother. Friendships are very important to her: 'people you can rely on – one hundred per cent ... they would be there and they would basically do anything for me'. She also talks about getting from her friends 'that feeling of belonging. That feeling of being part of something'. For most of her life Rachel has lived with other people, including various lovers; she has only spent short periods of time living on her own. She has now made the decision to live only with other black women, preferably lesbians. She does not live with Malika (F03), with whom she has been in a relationship for three years. As Rachel says:

> we've made a decision – well, apart from the fact I've always said I would never live with another lover again – we'd like to keep it that way because it is very important to remain individuals and to keep our independence and our separate lives. We both do completely different things outside our working lives and we like that. We like to keep that.

Her relationship with Malika, who also identifies as a black lesbian, is a non-monogamous one, and the development of their relationship has been gradually negotiated:

> when we were first in a relationship we talked about non-monogamy and security, and insecurity and trust. And, basically, Malika's most important thing was to trust me ... basically I trusted her more than she did me be-cause she'd had really bad experiences around trust – or mistrust – and had no reason to trust anyone. And one of the things that she needed at the time was for me to reassure her that I wouldn't sleep with anyone else, or *how* I would [approach it] if I did. So ... it's kind of been a progression, in terms of what it is okay to do and what it's not okay to do. And we have to keep talking about that and to keep making sure that that's clear.

Rachel still keeps up contact with, Allie, the child of her previous lover, Tess. Rachel was in a relationship with Tess before she became pregnant, and she makes the comment that:

> I wasn't a co-parent. I just happened to be in a relationship with someone, [and] she wanted a child. And … it meant that I had to build a completely separate relationship with the child involved if I wanted to.

In general, Rachel doesn't much like spending time with children, 'but Allie I did like and I still do'. Rachel and Tess have been separated for over three years, but Rachel still sees Allie; she notes that, 'I don't know quite how constant it is to Allie, really, but it feels constant to me.' Since Tess has met a new woman, Lynn, there have been changes in the relationship between Rachel and Allie:

> it kind of feels like Lynn has finally taken my place in terms of Allie. Because … I know that's how she [Allie] used to talk about me all the time – and she doesn't do that any more. … I don't know why I feel a loss, really. Because, you know, what have I lost? I haven't actually lost anything. It's up to me to make sure that Allie sees me when she wants to, when I can. And that's all I've got really.

Rachel defines 'family' thus:

> [it] means people who care about you and that you care about. People who are there for you … people who you can rely on if you're in trouble, or just if you need help. The people who love you, I suppose.

Greg and Mark (M17 and M18)

Greg is 38, self-defined as middle class, and currently unemployed. Mark is 22, 'no class', and a care worker. Both men are white. Their daughter, Becky, is 12. They live in a medium-sized town and have been in a (monogamous) relationship for over three years, and have lived together for the majority of that time. Greg and Mark both describe themselves as English and as 'queer' or 'gay'. Mark is close to his mother, who lives not too far away with his stepfather. He is not very close to his brother. Greg was estranged from his parents from an early age: his mother and father were separated when he was 2, and his mother 'left me when I was 15'. His parents died when he was in his late teens, and he is close to his sister who is a lesbian. Neither Greg nor his sister have contact with their brother, since 'he doesn't talk [to us] because we are both queer and he doesn't approve'. When he was 19, Greg married Isabel, then 16, 'even though … I was out, and she knew what I was even though she wasn't entirely sure what she was'. They had Becky when Greg was 26, and separated shortly after Becky's birth. Isabel now identifies as a lesbian and lives with her partner Judy, with whom she has had a public commitment ceremony, attended by the entire family.

Becky lives with Greg and Mark for over half of the week, and with Isabel and Judy (who live one mile away), for the remainder of the week. Becky considers all four partners to be her parents:

Greg: I mean, do you think you've got four [parents], or two, or two plus two, or …
Becky: Four.
Greg: Given that you inadvertently call both of us 'dad', I think … and I know you do the same thing on your mum's side …
Becky: Yeah.
Greg: I mean, she has two blood parents and she has two other parents, which, if we were heterosexuals, they'd be called step-dad and step-mum …
Mark: That's sweet.
Greg: So, Becky has four parents, all of whom have to be taken into account.

Becky's care and living arrangements can require considerable organisation and negotiation among the five individuals involved, 'to the extent that we have family conferences where all five of us will sit down [to plan things]' (Mark). Since both female parents work full-time, Becky spends evenings after school with her fathers until she is collected by Isabel. During mid-term and summer breaks the time is divided more evenly between the households. Becky is given a key defining role in how 'the rota' operates:

Mark: We're fairly flexible, but there is always someone here to be there for her.
Greg: At the moment the rota is organised how Becky wants it. … And we've said to her if she wants to change it in any way, then she can, and the only exception to that would be if she wanted to live with one parent alone.

For Mark and Greg, their family provides 'the friendship, the security … and if we're lucky it stays there for always' (Greg). However, while the parents are generally 'out' as individuals, and Becky's family situation is known to certain schoolteachers, there are limits to the extent they are 'out' publicly – or recognised – as a family. This is seen as a protective measure and is influenced by Becky's needs and desires.

While Greg and Mark consider Becky and the four parents as key members of 'the family', it also includes others:

Greg: Personally, I have quite a strong definition of family because I lost both my parents when I was quite young. … I suppose if you put Becky at the centre, there are a core of people who rotate around it. The four parents, the two grandmas, my sister, the aunty, but family. … It does also extend to other friends. I mean, it's not tied by blood.

Mark: Because there's … Alex and Lucy and Frances [friends] and there's my mother. Yes, there's lots of external people. But because they've got emotions tied in to some person or for a long-term relationship-friendship-wise, that makes them a larger part and you always know that there are those people there.

In Greg's narrative, mutuality and trust are key elements of this family, which is 'something we've created, not as substitutes – that makes it sound inferior – but an alternative that we've created'.

Sam and Jackie (F04 and F05)

Jackie, aged 42, is a full-time teacher. She has a 9-year-old daughter from a previous heterosexual relationship. She defines herself as white, working-class British. With regard to her sexuality, Jackie does not want to identify as anything in particular, although she comments that, 'in terms of being right on, yes [laughing] okay, I'm a lesbian'. Sam is 31, and works full-time with children. Like Jackie, she sees herself as white, working-class British, but identifies as a lesbian. They live in a city in the midlands in England. Sam moved in with Jackie a few weeks after they got together, and they are each other's first lesbian relationship. They have been in a monogamous relationship for two years. Apart from a few of Jackie's friends who have been told, the couple have been completely in the closet about their relationship. Neither woman has told her family of origin. For Jackie, this means her mother: her father is dead and she is an only child. Until she moved in with Jackie, Sam lived with her parents. Sam has a very tight-knit blood family, and she feels particularly close to her only brother. Jackie has a very distant relationship with her mother, and before his death, her father.

About three months before the interview, the two had decided, as Jackie puts it, to 'widen our social circle', and they 'took the plunge' and went to a gay pub in their home town. They have since gone regularly, and have also started going to a lesbian/gay café. They have both decided to join different groups to make more, and separate, friends: Jackie wants to join an HIV/AIDS help-line and Sam intends to volunteer at the café.

The most important people for Jackie are: her daughter, Jodie, Sam, her mother and a (heterosexual) friend, Richard. The most important people for Sam are: Jackie, Jodie and her brother. Sam explains: 'I have lost contact with the majority of the friends that I had previously to my relationship with Jackie, because I couldn't deal with their reaction or their judgement, I saw them less and less and just let it go, really.'

Jackie has noticed that Jodie is starting to express hostility about homosexuality – which she has never done before. When Jodie asked Jackie if she was a lesbian, Jackie replied, 'Well, I suppose I am really – yes.' To which Jodie responded, 'Please don't be a lesbian. I don't want you to be.' Although Jackie and Sam have talked about moving away 'and starting again', they are prevented from doing so because of Jodie's education and the difficulty in getting work. They talk about negotiating living together: in the past, they have argued about money, domestic work, Jodie and sex. Sam was used to having her own money and never having to do domestic work, and the transition to living in a shared household has created problems:

Jackie: I know the adjustments Sam had to make because, you know, from being a single person and having your own income, it's like when I suddenly had Jodie. Your money's not yours any more. You don't view it like that. And I think I expected her to … I mean, I treated Sam as an adult who could deal with every major responsibility you could think of that was thrown on her within, like, a couple of months. You know – suddenly she became a parent. First she became a partner – the money was all dispersed between the three of us. You became a parent then didn't you?

Sam: Yes.

Jackie: Then she became a householder … and this was all from just leaving home …

Sam: I did it all at once.

Jackie: And I expected her to deal with it.

Most of the issues about money and domestic work have now been resolved. Jackie explains that 'now it's more about Jodie and the sort of dynamics of what goes on between the three of us'. When Jackie asked Sam to be Jodie's guardian, she took several months to decide that she would, but she now says that she cannot imagine life without them. Meanwhile, Jackie's attitude to family has changed since her relationship with Sam:

> if I was going to give them [families] a score out of ten, they'd score a one – or less. You know, I never held the family in any kind of regard at all. … Whereas now I see the family – me, Sam and Jodie, and my mum … I'd class her as part of the family. I feel I've got that, and … for the first time in my whole life, I've got a family that I want now.

Sam has come to regard herself as a co-parent to Jodie. In the past, she was undecided about whether she wanted children or not, but on meeting Jackie, 'I knew that if the relationship grew into anything it would involve Jodie.' She says that, 'I am starting to learn, now … this is a family unit and that we operate how we want it to operate – it's on our terms.'

These are just four stories out of many we could have chosen. They have been highlighted here not because they are special, but precisely because they are not. They illustrate a range of possible ways of living, and they have been selected because the various narrative strands are central to our perception of contemporary relationships. They are stories of identity and community; of love and loss;

of fear and safety; of individual choice and mutual involvement; of being yourself and being made aware of (often hostile) others; of friendship and parenting; of commitment and negotiation; of responsibility and care; of living together and living apart; of continuity and rupture. They are stories of interwoven lives. What can they tell us about the changing meanings of homosexuality, how we live with risk and uncertainty, and how we build the sort of 'unconditional love' that Peter (pp. 30–1), lauds? In response to such questions, we want to highlight what we believe are four key elements: (1) the variety of means that exist for 'doing family'; (2) the privileged position of heterosexuality in our culture; (3) the emphasis on agency and self-invention in these lives; and finally, (4) the significance of the key concept used in this book, 'life experiments'.

A 'queer construct family'

A striking feature of the stories of Peter, Rachel, Greg and Mark, and Jackie and Sam is their willingness to use the term 'family' to describe their core relation-ships. This clearly suggests a reflexive awareness of the newly circulating stories about what Greg calls the 'queer construct family'. Like many others, our narrators are incorporating into their own lives an awareness that the language of family is now part of the intricate texture of the non-heterosexual world. It is part of the developing meaning of what it is to be lesbian, gay, bisexual, transgendered or 'queer' in the contemporary world.

A useful way of interpreting this is to follow Morgan (1996, 1999) in analys-ing 'the family' in terms of a set of social practices rather than an institution. From this perspective, 'family' can be seen less as a noun and more as an adjective or, possibly, a verb. Morgan writes that, ' "Family" represents a constructed quality of human interaction or an active process rather than a thing-like object of social investigation' (1999: 16). This is a social scientific approach, which may not resonate easily with people's experiences, but it has an important implication for understanding non-heterosexual lives. It displaces the idea of the family as a fixed and timeless entity – whereby one is either a member of the family, or else excluded from it, left shivering outside its protective walls. We see it instead as a series of practical, everyday activities which we live: through such tasks as mutual care, the division of labour in the home, looking after dependents and 'relations' – practices which people like Peter, Rachel, Greg and Mark, and Jackie and Sam regularly engage in. Nor need family practices be confined to the home: we can also participate in them when we are at work or involved in leisure activities. Greg and Mark, and Jackie and Sam are constantly aware of their responsibilities for their children, and the likelihood of stigma becoming attached to them in their neighbourhoods or at school. Rachel and Peter negotiate their relationships through the filters of community or racial difference. For all of them, 'family' is about particular sorts of relational interactions rather than simply private activities in a privileged sphere. Instead of being an objective phenomenon, which we can measure against a Platonic image of what the family is or should be, we can now understand it as a subjective set of activities, whose meanings are made by those who participate in them. From this point of view, it is less important whether we are *in* a family than whether we *do* family-type things. In the language used by Judith Butler (1990) to talk about gender, family practices are 'performative', and families are therefore constructed through their enactment. We live family rather than dwell within it. This approach emphasises human self activity and agency: family is what we do.

This is an important way of thinking about what constitutes family today. It allows us to recognise and begin to understand the fluidity of everyday life practices, and the way 'doing family' is related to the ways we do or perform gender, sexuality, work, caring and the other activities that make up the totality of life experiences. Family life is a historically specific, contextualised set of activities, intimately linked with other social practices. From this perspective, there is no theoretical reason to exclude non-heterosexual everyday practices from the pantheon of family and kin.

Whether we do, or should, use the language of family is a different question, perhaps even a more political one. For the idea of family is, of course, more than a set of practices: it is also a loaded symbolic term, and the juncture between different concepts of 'the family' is where most people actually shape their lives. A major study of the contemporary meanings of family responsibilities and obligations in Britain (Finch 1989; Finch and Mason 1993) has shown both the strength of a sense of kinship among genealogical families, and the constantly negotiated nature of the actual relationships. On the one hand, Finch and Mason (1993) found that the extended family has a tangible reality in most people's lives. At the very least it provides a minimum safety net, especially in crises, and this is what constitutes a family for most of their respondents. Interestingly, this is very close to Greg's and Mark's minimum definition of what they expect from their family of choice. As Greg says:

> I trust members of the family, yes, including those that are friends rather than parents … you can be who you are – exactly who you are. [It means] that if you trust this person they accept you as you are, which was why I can say that I trust the members of the family because it's a mutual thing that you take them for exactly the people they are and they take you [for who you are]. And therefore there's an honesty that can come from that, and … it's not going to then be twisted and turned and used, or whatever. And that these people are going to be there. That we'll be there for them and that, you know, they're here for us. (M17)

Mark echoes Greg's sentiments when he says:

> They relieve, they soothe, they support. If you've got a problem you can phone up and say 'Help!', and there will be someone there to help. That's

important … My life doesn't [have] to revolve round those people, but it does because they're important to me. (M18)

The vast majority of people still expect this sort of sustenance from their blood relatives rather than from friends (Roberts and McGlone 1997; McGlone, Park and Roberts 1999). Family, in the traditional sense, still has a special meaning, and most people continue to distinguish kin from friends. On the other hand, Finch and Mason (1993) find that you cannot predict exactly what sort of support will be obtained from family of origin. While people have a strong sense of duty and obligation towards dependent children, they do not by and large see specific duties attached to *adult* family relationships, nor do they operate according to fixed rules. The situation is more fluid than this, and although people may carry 'moral baggage' about 'the right thing to do', they operate through a series of pragmatic guidelines. This in turn implies that commitments must be based on negotiation between consenting participants, not on tradition or lineage. Ties of obligation, based on blood relationships, are increasingly being displaced in adult relationships by ideas of commitments that have to be worked out day by day, week by week. 'Responsibilities are thus *created*,' Finch and Mason (1993: 167) state, 'rather than flowing automatically from specific relationships.' Again, as we saw in the individual stories at the beginning of this chapter (and see also Chapter 3), this is in significant ways very close to the patterns of non-heterosexual commitments.

A major argument of Finch and Mason (1993: 58) is that the family patterns they describe are in part based on a respect for the individuality of other members of the kin grouping. There is a search for a proper balance in relationships, based on the idea that no one should be too dependent on someone else. They relate this to a long tradition of individualism in English culture, even as they acknowledge the intricate power relations, especially of gender, that limit this. But the individualism, as we suggested above, has a new significance for many non-heterosexuals as they attempt to marry a desire for autonomy with firm commitment. For Jackie and Sam, it is important that their family is based on equality, support and love – not what Jackie calls 'restrictive love', but a love that allows people to 'do what you want to do and be what you want to be' (F05). This is the authentic message of the new stories. Individual autonomy is about identity and space, but it is also about intimate involvement. Through that you can become free.

The heterosexual assumption

Here, we are suggesting that there are many strong parallels in the meaning of family practices across the heterosexual–homosexual divide. Both the language of commitment and the doing of family are surprisingly similar. Whatever is happening on the ground, however, there is a profound ambiguity in the cultural and political response to family change, which in turn is a sure indication of the difficulties many people experience in fully coming to terms with the new culture of intimacy which is emerging. Essentially, this revolves around the continuing privileging of heterosexuality in our culture, the awareness of which dominates the life stories discussed in this volume.

The privileging of heterosexual patterns is vividly apparent even in the most liberal discussions of the family and sexual diversity. On the one hand, many politicians and theoreticians give verbal recognition to the variety of family forms, and shift their concerns to the quality of relationships, and to the care of children, whatever the formal links between parents or carers and children. This underlies the moves in various jurisdictions towards giving greater recognition to non-heterosexual relationships (though, usually, they specifically exclude rights to adoption). On the other hand, most western politicians, no matter how 'progressive', pay verbal obeisance to the need to bolster the traditional family, and the defence of family values has, of course, become a crucial element in the armoury of social conservatives.

In Britain and the United States, the growing self-confidence of lesbian and gay claims to equality has often been accompanied by a strong reassertion of 'traditional family values'. In Britain in the late 1980s, a number of legislative measures were introduced, which were designed to 'statutorily fortify a sexual hierarchy of families' (Cooper and Herman 1995: 162) by specifically emphasising the priority of heterosexuality. These included the Human Fertilisation and Embryology Act 1990, part of which was concerned with controlling access to the new reproductive technologies, especially donor insemination; Section 46, Education (no. 2) Act 1986, which asserted the need to prioritise heterosexuality in sex education; and Section 28, of the Local Government Act 1988, which effectively condemned 'pretended family relationships'. This experience has been echoed elsewhere, as noted in the Introduction, for example, by the rushing into US law of the Defense of Marriage Act in 1996 as a response to the Hawaiian judgment on same sex marriage, and by the outcry in France in the late 1990s when the Socialist-led government struggled to put into law an acknowledgement of the legitimacy of non-marital relationships, including same sex ones (Velu 1999). The eventual 'Pacs' law in France, which came into force in 2000, like most other initiatives on recognition of non-marital partnerships, specifically excluded rights to adoption or artificial insemination.

Even at the turn of the twentieth century in Britain, with a New Labour government committed to equality in the age of consent between heterosexuals and homosexuals, there remains a profound ambivalence. The Labour government's consultation document, *Supporting Families* (Ministerial Group on the Family 1998), is probably the most liberal intervention in debates on the family ever to appear from a British government (Weeks 1999). Its basic tone is one of pragmatic adjustment to the changing realities of intimate life rather than an absolutist defence of the traditional family. It is full, as the Home Secretary, Jack Straw says in his Introduction to the document, of 'sensible measures' to strengthen 'families'. The use of 'families', plural, is itself a nod towards the recognition of diversity. There are no proposals to positively discriminate in favour of marriage through the taxation system. There is no condemnation of non-marital relationships. On the contrary, the document states that: 'There are strong and mutually supportive families outside marriage and many unmarried couples remain together throughout their children's upbringing and raise their children every bit as successfully as married parents.' There is nothing in the document which explicitly excludes or devalues non-heterosexual relationships or parenting; in fact, the formal recognition of the existence of a diversity of families should allow it.

However, at the same time it wants to promote marriage. People do not want to be 'nannied', the document states, but 'we do share the belief of the majority of people that marriage provides the most reliable framework for raising children.' This led the British government to propose a raft of measures strengthening the institution of marriage, which ranged from the anodyne to the frankly unworkable. We are forced to ask, 'Why?' The reality is that the government was caught in an acute dilemma on this question. It correctly recognised that there had been a profound transformation of intimate life in the past generation, and did not want to interfere overly in people's private lives. It realised the futility of moral absolutism. It also recognised, which many moral conservatives did not, that many people were making a pretty good job of making up the new rules of intimate life as they went along. The government rightly wanted to concentrate its efforts where it mattered most, by providing support for good parenting. On the other hand, however, it could not quite bring itself to question the institution of marriage, or the primacy of the two parent (heterosexual) family, let alone explicitly validate non-heterosexual parenting. This was subsequently underlined when attempts were made to repeal Section 28 in 2000. The discriminatory nature of a law that banned the 'promotion of homosexuality' in schools, and which viewed it as a 'pretended family relation-ship', was fully recognised. A great deal of political capital was expended in attempts to push repeal through the Scottish and Westminster parliaments (with success only in Scotland). But it was judged appropriate to balance a liberalising measure with an explicit endorsement of teaching the importance of marriage in all schools (see Roberts 2000), to calm fears of homosexuality running rampant.

We would argue that this reflects the reality of a continuing institutional prejudice and discrimination against non-heterosexual ways of life. This has been variously theorised as 'compulsory heterosexuality' (Rich 1983), the 'heterosexual matrix' (Butler 1990), the 'heterosexual panorama' (Blasius 1994), or 'heteronormativity' (Warner 1993). We prefer to use the term 'heterosexual assumption' to describe an all-embracing institutional invalidation of homosexu-ality, and presumption in favour of heterosexuality. The term recognises the all-pervasive background noise which always privileges and shores up the heterosexual model as the norm, even as societies grow more formally accepting of difference.

As we have already observed, much has changed over the past generation, and the broad result is a greater social toleration of non-heterosexuality. But the increasingly recognised fact of sexual diversity has not led to its full acceptance or validation. This has inevitably structured the lives of non-heterosexuals, and can be accounted for by the continued impact of the heterosexual assumption. The anxieties expressed by Mark and Greg, and Jackie and Sam in their narratives about parenting are the most graphic illustration of the continuing impact of the privileging of heterosexuality. There are many other forms of discrimination which we chart in Chapter 8. As Blasius states, the simple truth is that

> The condition of compulsory heterosexuality, what Christopher Isherwood called 'the heterosexual dictatorship', makes simply living everyday a serious problem for lesbians and gay men. Laws, forms of culture (rituals, symbols, etc.), and the most mundane social expectations make one an alien in the world.
>
> (Blasius 1994: 187)

Our aim here is not to theorise heterosexuality in a general sense; there are many other studies which attempt this (for an overall summary, see the essays in Richardson 1996; also Katz 1995 for a history of the concept), and we return to the theme throughout the book. Instead, we wish to outline some of the complexly intertwined features of the heterosexual assumption which directly impact on our analysis: the naturalistic fallacy; gender and sexual binarism, and their hierarchical ordering; and the ideology of parenting.

To take the first point, the naturalistic fallacy is the most challengeable and the most pervasive belief: that heterosexual sexual behaviour is 'natural', linked to reproductive imperatives derived from our animal nature, and finds its inevitable culmination in the biological family. This means that the non-heterosexual, the non-reproductive, and the extra-familial are by definition 'unnatural'. In our current moderately liberal climate, few would put forward this view in such a crude form. But it is difficult not to believe that lurking behind every prejudiced phrase or act lies some similar assumption. The clearest expression of this assumption can be seen in our continuing uncertainties about gender and the binary divide between heterosexuality and homosexuality.

Over the past two hundred years, in western cultures at least, masculinity and femininity have in large part been defined by the absence of homosexual sexual behaviour. To be a real man was to be exclusively heterosexual; a masculinised woman, as lesbians were frequently seen as being, was not a full woman. As Connell (1995) has shown, the changing patterns of 'hegemonic masculinity' have not dislodged the continuing marginalisation of gay men, even as they partake of many of the privileges of their gender. Similarly, many lesbians have often found themselves locked into a gendered division of labour, especially if they have married, as a number of our female interviewees have at one stage of their lives. As Dunne (1999) remarks, when two genders coexist, they do what they are expected to do in interaction. It is difficult to escape dichotomous ways of being.

This in turn impacts on beliefs about parenting. The British government consultation paper on the family, discussed above, remains preoccupied with the importance of marriage as the best context for bringing up children, precisely because it assumes a firm commitment between a man and a woman is the best state for parenthood (compare Melanie Phillips' comments in Davis and Phillips 1999; and Phillips 1999). Other forms of parenting are by definition less satisfactory, no matter how 'good' or indeed committed the alternatives may be.

There is now an extensive scholarship that has analysed and deconstructed many aspects of the heterosexual assumption. And, despite the seductive arguments of recent social biologists about our animal-based behaviour, cross-cultural evidence refutes the suggestion that traditional western society is the best model. Theorists have argued for the performative nature of gender, and the historical formation of masculinity and femininity. Feminists and others have challenged the gender hierarchy, and historians have charted the historical construction of the rigid binary divide between homosexuality and heterosexuality. Yet it is noticeable that even as the contemporary family is deconstructed by such writers as Beck and Beck-Gernsheim (1995), little or no attention is paid in their work to the emergence of non-heterosexual patterns of relationships. The heterosexual assumption, despite everything, retains its seductive credibility.

Self-invention

Given the resilience of the heterosexual assumption, it is not surprising that non-heterosexual people rely on their own resources, in terms of both their self-identities and their relationship choices. The history of the past generation has been one of resistance and agency, in which the marginalised have sought to create viable ways of life within their specific circumstances, drawing on the communities of meaning in which they are involved, and rejecting, implicitly or, increasingly, explicitly, the heterosexual assumption.

The narrative of self-invention is a very powerful one among our interviewees, particularly in relation to self-identity and lifestyle. As Greg puts it:

> speaking from my generation ... discovering that I was homosexual meant having to invent myself because there was nothing there ... there weren't any role models. It may well be different for gay men coming out now. ... But there's still that element of self-invention. (M17)

Finding, or creating, a new identity, has been likened to finding a map for an unknown country (Weeks 1985). It provides a sense of direction, a sense of the various paths one can follow, and the likelihood of being recognised, and recognising others, along the route. Maps provide a shared knowledge, which has to be carefully constructed over time. There exists a rich literature pioneered by lesbian and gay historians and sociologists, which traces the construction of recognisable non-heterosexual identities over the past century (see Weeks 1977/1990 ; Bray 1982; Vicinus 1996). Identities are social creations, the labels we give to the different ways we are positioned by, and position ourselves within, the narratives that pre-exist us. But we now live in a world where the possibilities of self-invention are greater than ever before. As Beck-Gernsheim (1998: 57) has observed, though not specifically mentioning the non-heterosexual experience, 'the normal life-history is giving way to the do-it-yourself life-history'. Self-descriptions change as circumstances change, and new possibilities open up, paving the way for invention and reinvention.

Sometimes this involves a *refusal* of a fixed identity. In the following conversation between Sam and Jackie (F04 and F05), for instance, Jackie outlines her reluctance to employ *any* particular term to describe her sexual identity. We asked the question, 'what do you call yourself – lesbian, bisexual, gay woman or …?':

Jackie: I find that one hard. We talk about this don't we?
Sam: We do, yeah.
Jackie: I can't answer it.
Sam: Jackie isn't … you know.
Jackie: No. Because you asked me this exact question about a week ago and I said, 'Well, yes, in terms of being "right on" – okay, I'm a lesbian.' But I don't know. If, say, Sam died … and I was alone again, then I don't know what would happen. I can't answer that.

For Jackie and Sam, each in their first lesbian relationship, identity is inextricably linked with their relationships. Only gradually did they feel the need to 'plunge into' the wider lesbian world, which was in part a reaction to feelings of isolation. Their identities are being negotiated and reinvented through their experience and personal interactions – not least their daughter's clear ambivalence about lesbianism, as mentioned earlier. Naming yourself fixes you. But the awareness of the outside world forces people to draw on the available language, because without it they feel exposed, as this discussion between Sean (M37), a 42-year-old white gay man, and Arthur (M38), a 64-year-old black gay man, demonstrates:

Arthur: I don't know what to call myself.
Sean: Nowadays it's hip to be queer … being gay … only exists through homophobia. I mean if homophobia didn't exist then being gay wouldn't exist. … It's kind of like a reaction. … But I suppose just generally for the sake of everyday use, I'd probably say, yeah, gay. …
Arthur: I don't know what I call myself.
Sean: (*to Arthur*) You know, people have different names, different places at different times … from being homosexual to being … poofs or queers or gay or whatever.
Arthur: But I'll tag along with gay, that's all. Okay?

'Tagging along' with gay suggests an awareness that identity labels are never fixed or predetermined, but in certain circumstances they can still be essential (Weeks 1995). Joan, a 32-year-old white bisexual woman, has this to say:

I think it's quite important for me to identify as bisexual. ... Just because I think bisexual people are so invisible really. The issue is so invisible, so for me it's quite important to be as sort of loud about it as I can in all the situations that I can, so that then opens up possibilities for other people. (F32)

Similarly for Julie, aged 34, self-description is very important:

I would identify as queer or a dyke. ... I think the word 'dyke' is a ... reclaiming thing. It used to be a derogatory term, but ... to say it before somebody else does, or 'queer', it's all like, a reclaiming thing. (F14)

These reflexive accounts allow us to observe the extent to which cultural and even political motivations influence the kind of story about self-identity that people want to tell. The reality is of a complex coexistence of various personal (and collective) identities – lesbian and gay, but also a variety of 'queering' terms and identities marked by other dimensions of difference, especially those of race and ethnicity. The crucial point, however, is that the terms we use, the identities we assume, are basic elements in the creation of the self in a culture that still cannot bring itself to fully validate non-heterosexual ways of life.

But whatever the fluidity and contingency of identity, it is apparent that a sense of self is confirmed through involvement with others. As Simon (aged 32) puts it:

because I can't think of myself as being anything other than a gay man, having those friendships and support networks, I suppose, is extremely important. I think I'd be a very sad and pathetic person without them. (M05)

It is increasingly clear that narratives of the self and narratives of chosen families are being linked together. As Weston argues,

When cast in narrative form, the shift from identification of gayness with the renunciation of kinship (no family) to a correspondence between gay identity and a particular type of family (families we choose) presents a kind of collective coming-out story: a tale of lesbians and gays moving out of isolation and into kinship.

(Weston 1991: 212)

Through these narratives we can see the emergence of new ways of conceiving of family and intimate life, which emphasise simultaneously the realisation of individual needs and the reciprocity involved in patterns of intimacy and trust. Earlier, we quoted Greg (M17) on this theme, but his views are echoed in many other accounts. Coral (F13), a young lesbian, comments that a family 'should provide support, acceptance of who you are and what you want to do'. If the family of origin fails you, or even when it does not, alternatives are necessary to 'always be there to help you ... my friends provide that. ... That's what I think a family should be and that's what these friends are for me' (Coral). Through chosen relationships individuality and mutuality can be reconciled.

Many non-heterosexuals, therefore, stress the importance of creative choice in shaping their friendship patterns. For many non-heterosexuals, the idea of a *chosen* family is a powerful affirmation of a new sense of belonging, and an essential part of asserting the validity of homosexual identities and ways of life. This does not mean that non-heterosexuals deny parallels with heterosexual life, but that the achievement of alternative forms has a different significance. As Coral says: 'I get a hell of a lot of support and understanding [from friends] I mean, they know everything about me and they still accept me.' That acceptance, and the mutual recognition that goes with it, are seen as the defining characteristics of the chosen relationships.

The idea of choice is central to contemporary individualism, and is often portrayed as the triumph of individual need over collective responsibility (see Chapter 1). Our stories, on the contrary, suggest that for many non-heterosexuals, involvement with others is the precondition of a sense of individual satisfaction. The freedom to choose is, therefore, the necessary condition of responsible and reciprocal relationships, based on respect and care for others. This in turn requires recognition that relationships have to be based on a willingness to negotiate, implicitly or explicitly. In the stories at the beginning of this chapter, we can see the process of negotiation in action: the working out of sexual relationships, living arrangements, child care commitments, and so forth. In that process we can also see the limits of choice, as individuals encounter barriers of class and income difference, of racial inequalities, of sexual incompatibilities, and the myriad effects of a culture which finds it difficult to accept or validate non-heterosexuals' patterns of life. But the guiding assumption is that the chosen nature of relationships, and the process of negotiation that that must involve, open unique opportunities for more equal relationships than are available to heterosexuals.

Non-heterosexuals are telling two related stories: one which affirms difference, which roots their relationship patterns in a distinctive history; and another which asserts a claim to equivalence, equality and ultimately similarity. Both reflect what Blasius (1994) describes as a distinctive ethos, or what we prefer to describe as an evolving value system in which relationships are being explored, and new narratives are being elaborated.

On the one hand, there is a passionate affirmation of difference, based on a rejection of the heterosexual assumption. As David, a gay man in his early twenties, sees it:

> to me, the whole basis of lesbian and gay relationships are different from heterosexual relationships … I don't know whether it's good or bad, but I mean, that's a fact. It is blatantly different. And trying to tailor heterosexual laws and understanding towards gay relationships is bound to fail. (M12)

Rachel is equally strong in her affirmation of difference:

I do not, as a black lesbian, want to be seen as the same as a heterosexual couple. I do not want to marry my lover, nor do I want to do anything that even remotely looks like that. I don't want to make a commitment publicly. I'm quite content with the fact that I can make a commitment privately, and that's just as important. (F02)

On the other hand, there is an equally forceful assertion of equality, at least in the claim to rights. Coral is of the firm opinion that

people should have equal rights whatever, and it all comes ... under equal opportunities. Equal opportunities doesn't exist, particularly for gay and lesbian people ... I believe that [all] people should have them. (F13)

The contradiction between these two positions is more apparent than real. Overwhelmingly, our interviewees feel that being lesbian, gay, bisexual or queer opens opportunities for more equal and fulfilling relationships than are available to most heterosexuals. This is because non-heterosexual relationships can be based on choice, and because they can escape the rigid assumptions about gender which continue to confine heterosexual relationships. Many non-heterosexual people have consciously shaped their relationships in opposition to assumed heterosexual models, especially the power imbalance which seems to play such a significant role. Non-heterosexual relationships offer opportunities for co-operation and egalitarian relationships that do not require the institutional backing of marriage, the pinnacle of the heterosexual assumption (cf. Dunne 1997). As Rachel comments:

so far as I'm concerned, marriage or partnership rights, or whatever you want to call it, is about ownership – and I do not want to own another person. I don't want that at all. I'll be responsible for my own relationship but I will not own someone. And I think it's very strange that there are women who think that this is a good thing. Because marriage has never been in women's interests – ever. (F02)

We will explore the meanings of these statements in the following chapters; our purpose in quoting them here is to underline the argument of this chapter. Non-heterosexuals conform in many ways to what writers on the family see as broad-based changes in the patterns of intimate life. Non-heterosexuals feel they live the reality of these changes, precisely because they have rejected, or been rejected by, heterosexual norms. The resulting ways of life are seen as the achievement of self activity, of conscious human agency.

Everyday experiments

There can be no doubt of the potent meanings attached to relationship networks by many self-identified non-heterosexual women and men. As we have seen, they have the potency of family-type relationships, in either supplementing or displacing traditional forms. On the surface, at least, this lends credence to the idea that for many people friendships offer surrogate or 'pretend' families: substitutes for the real thing. This is not, however, how non-heterosexuals see the significance of their relationships, nor how these relationships are characterised in the recent literature on the subject. Bozett (1987), for example, sees lesbian and gay relationships as having all the significant defining features of biological families, and Nardi (1992a) has described friends *as* family (but see Nardi 1999). Weston (1991) has concluded that, in creating chosen families, lesbians and gays are neither involved in imitating heterosexual families, nor in necessarily replacing or substituting a family of choice for a family of origin. Like Weston's research, our own strongly suggests that for many non-heterosexuals the term family can be used to describe a variety of selected relationships, which includes lovers, possibly ex-lovers, intimate friends, as well as blood relatives. Greg (M17) and Mark (M18) bring out this complexity of meaning in the following exchange:

Greg: And what does family mean? It means a core of people that … [is] not tied by blood. … I mean, the family probably only includes, what, three heterosexuals? And two of those are the grandmas …
Mark: My family? At the moment my family are being a bloody nuisance. My bloody brother, my bloody grandparents!
Greg: [laughs] But that's just families, isn't it? That's what families are.

Of course, using the language of family is not the same as saying that networks of non-heterosexual relations *are* families. In a recent study of gay male friendships in the United States, Nardi (1999), while acknowledging the potency of the language, is notably sceptical of the usage. In particular, he notes the general absence of the age and status differentials that characterise most kin relations (though Greg's and Mark's 'family' certainly do not lack these), and concludes that:

> Structurally, friendship circles do not look like families: they certainly do not have the legal, ceremonial, or religious attributes that characterize the family institutions in American society. To say they are like family may serve, then, as a shorthand form of communication.
>
> (Nardi 1999: 68)

We would agree that families of choice are different from traditional families, and we also share the scepticism of a number of the people whose stories we tell in this book about the use of familial language. Our major concern is elsewhere, however: in what the use of the language of family tells us about changes in personal life. In Chapter 1, we argued that the public emergence of 'families we choose' signals an important shift in the preoccupations of the non-heterosexual world, and is part of a wider transformation of intimate life in which the idea of the family is itself changing. In this chapter, we have suggested that if we see family in terms of practices rather than institutional forms, of meanings rather than structures, many non-heterosexuals 'do family' in ways that parallel heterosexual patterns. The growing preoccupation with parenting among many non-heterosexuals, signalled in the narratives of Sam, Jackie, Rachel, Greg and Mark (and discussed in more detail in Chapter 7), underlines rather than undermines these parallels. 'Family' may be a shorthand, but it is a useful one to describe a shifting reality.

There are many historic echoes of the usage of family language, often by communities of marginalised or embattled people. The idea of fictive kin has been used to describe the way in which African-American, Native-American and white working-class families in the US expand their kinship networks by absorbing friends and neighbours into them (Stack 1974; Weston 1991) – and similar patterns can be seen in British working-class and minority communities. Rapp (1982: 178) uses the phrase 'continuous family' to describe such networks. There are obvious parallels with the lesbian and gay world, where friendship and sexual community provides some of the same elements of support as a working-class or ethnic neighbourhood, though not necessarily through geographical propinquity. However, the fictive kin concept still assumes the blood family as the starting point, whereas for many non-heterosexuals it is precisely the ambiguous relationship with family of origin that is the problem, and friendships instead become the core network of support.

The word 'network' points to the real significance of what is happening. A network is a complex system of interconnected strands. It also evokes the dense lines of communication of the Internet, which has no single focus but rather a myriad of different points of information and communication, with an infinite possibility of juncture and disjuncture, apparently random, but able to resist practically any attack on its integrity. Castells (1996, 1997, 1998) has discussed in depth the 'rise of the network society' as a consequence of the 'information age'. With only a touch of poetic licence, we can see families of choice as an example of the rise of 'network families'. Indeed, several of our interviewees use this image in a thoughtful way to describe their complex involvements. For Mo (aged 22), her immediate circle of friends, which she regards as her 'community', is explicitly part of a network:

> I have access to maybe a hundred people's names and addresses. … And they have access to other people's that … they would probably let know about what was going on. Therefore, if I have a problem, I maybe need only contact about ten people, and fifty people will get to know about it. (F43)

Mo may not directly know everyone in this tree of communication, but she knows there are links beyond her closest circle that she can draw on for possible support.

Such networks are the product both of changing patterns of communication and of the dense interconnections that exist among people. We suggest that the new language of family is an index of these shifting social possibilities in a rapidly changing epoch. Clearly, families of choice build on historical experience (see Chapter 3). But above all, and as theorists such as Giddens (1992) argue, they are examples of the 'everyday experiments in living' that people are required to undertake in an increasingly complex world. Non-heterosexuals feel they have more open possibilities for two reasons: first, greater choice and openness in their relationships, and second, the belief that they can escape many of the structural differences, especially those of heterosexuality, which limit traditional relationships. In the following chapters, we argue that no matter how difficult their achievement may be, these beliefs structure the everyday practices of many people: a powerful story has developed which is helping to reshape intimate life. For this reason, we agree with Giddens that non-heterosexuals can rightly be seen as 'the prime everyday experimenters' (Giddens 1992: 135). This is certainly how it is seen and expressed in the stories we have discussed in this chapter. As Paul (aged 36) says, he and his partner are

> constantly experimenting with just how far we want to go, and sometimes feel that we have some degree of mobility in a given situation. … It's not so much political flag-waving, it's just doing what we want to do and trying to push the boundaries a bit, to see how people cope with it. (M21)

He continues, 'it has first to be a fairly measured experiment because there are some situations where you just put yourself at risk'. But no matter how great the risks, what is apparent is the sense of new possibilities for shaping personally satisfying ways of life, against the social and cultural imperatives of heterosexuality. Stuart (1995: 28) describes non-heterosexual relationships, built around friendship rather than biological kin, as, 'a perfect example of people on the margins, travelling outside the domain of the dominant discourse, weaving a new tapestry, a new model with which to understand their lives'. When non-heterosexuals 'do family', they are creating life patterns which give new meaning to their relationships, which are being formed within a constantly evolving society. And central to these patterns is an ethic of friendship, the subject of the next chapter.

3 The friendship ethic

The power of friendship

The most commonly told relationship story among non-heterosexuals is one of friendship. There is a long tradition behind this. In the complex history of same sex desires, friendships emerge as a leitmotif. They are commemorated by the ancient Greeks (Nardi 1999), honoured in commitment ceremonies (among men at least) by the early Christian Church (Boswell 1994), underpin what Rich (1983) calls the 'lesbian continuum', and were the focus of celebration among the earliest advocates of homosexual rights from the late nineteenth century (Carpenter 1902). In the twentieth century, as new, more positive lesbian and gay and other dissident sexual identities asserted their claims, friendships became even more significant, the basis, as Nardi (1999) says, of 'invincible communities'.

Friendship is a key to understanding non-heterosexual ways of life, and the most important recurring theme among our narrators in this book. In this chapter, we explore the meanings of friendship: its history and changing forms, its significance at 'fateful moments', its complexity and diversity, and its implications for our understanding of reciprocity, commitment, care and trust. The non-heterosexual world, we argue, is sustained by the intricately woven but durable strands of a 'friendship ethic'.

Friendships exist in many forms, and have varying symbolic meanings in different places and at different times (Rubin 1985; Allan 1989, 1996; Nardi 1999). Of all our relationships, claims Sullivan (1998: 176), 'friendship is the most common and most natural. In its universality it even trumps family.' But friendships particularly flourish when overarching identities are fragmented in periods of rapid social change, or at turning points in people's lives, or when lives are lived at odds with social norms (Weeks 1995: 145–6). Friendships are portable, they can be sustained at a distance, yet they can allow individuals who are uprooted or marginalised to feel constantly confirmed in who and what they are through changing social experiences. They offer the possibility of developing new patterns of intimacy and commitment. All these features give a special meaning and intensity to friendship in the lives of those who live on the fringes of sexual conformity. In the accounts of non-heterosexuals, friends provide both emotional and material support, but they also affirm identity and belonging. Altman (1982: 190) notes that, 'what many gay lives miss in terms of permanent relationships is more than compensated for by friendship networks, which often become de facto families'. As discussed in Chapters 1 and 2, the difference with traditional families, however, is that friends are chosen.

During periods of social upheaval, like that of our present society, it is not surprising that heterosexuals and non-heterosexuals alike are emphasising friendship. The 'bridging ties' and flexibility provided by friendship offer valuable ways of negotiating risk and uncertainty (Pahl and Spencer 1997). Not all friendships are equally valid for this. There are friends, and then there are *friends*. Some may be friendly acquaintances or those who you socialise with on only a casual basis; others form part of an intimate circle, part of the intricate weave of your life – although, inevitably, that also changes over time. As individuals move through life there is a changing cluster of 'significant others', which Pahl and Spencer (1997) have likened to 'social convoys'. Members of these convoys may rarely meet together, except perhaps at important times – christenings, marriages, funerals – but they regularly maintain a sense of belonging which keeps the friendship intact. There is some evidence that the pace of contemporary life makes many of these links increasingly tenuous for many heterosexuals (McGlone, Park and Roberts 1999), but for non-heterosexuals they are much more significant.

For there is an important difference between heterosexual and non-heterosexual experiences of friendship, which can be found in their varying attitude towards kin. Most people still make a basic distinction between friends and kin in terms of obligation and commitment (Roberts and McGlone 1997), and this conforms with Finch and Mason's (1993) findings, that while a few of their interviewees said they would prefer to turn to friends in life crises, the majority would turn to relatives through blood or marriage. This is also apparent among some of the participants in our research. Mollie (F30), a lesbian in her early fifties, comments: 'I'm just a bit outdated with feeling there's a difference with blood relatives, who often aren't actually as reliable, in fact [as friends].' But for many other non-heterosexual people, friendship has a meaning and depth that goes beyond its conventional implications. As Jo (F43), a young lesbian says, 'for my part, I don't have friendships on the level that I think heterosexuals have friendships. I think my friendships are more intense.' That intensity is necessary as a counterweight to the assumptions of institutionalised heterosexuality.

In the lesbian and gay world, as Nardi writes, 'at the core of the concept of friendship is the idea of "being oneself" in a cultural context that may not approve of that self' (Nardi 1992a: 115). Friendships – sometimes linked to couple relationships, but often not – provide the space for the exploration of who or what you are, and what you want to become. This is true at all points of the life cycle, from the first tentative stages of coming out as 'different', through the crises of relationships, to the potential loneliness of old age – those 'fateful moments' (Giddens 1992) of a life, which force individuals to reassess who and what they are, and to find ways of adapting to new situations.

However, friendships are more than mere crutches for those who society barely acknowledges or accepts. They offer the opportunity for alternatives that challenge the inevitability or necessity of conventional family life. Michel Foucault, for example, has seen in non-heterosexual friendship a much more radically disruptive challenge to traditional society than the sexual acts which have historically defined homosexuality:

> Imagining a sexual act that does not conform to the law or to nature, that's not what upsets people. But that individuals might begin to love each other, that's the problem. That goes against the grain of social institutions. ... The institutional regulations cannot approve such relations, with their multiple intensities, variable colorations, imperceptible movements, and changing forms – relations that produce a short circuit and introduce love where there ought to be law, regularity, and custom.
>
> (Foucault, quoted in Halperin 1995: 98)

This insight underlines what the personal stories recounted in this book confirm. Non-heterosexual friendship, especially when the barriers between friendship and love are fluid, continues to disrupt radically the conventional boundaries and separations in everyday life. They make life experiments possible.

Patterns of friendship

As Foucault's comment above suggests, there are distinctive features of non-heterosexual patterns that speak for a separate history, a history intimately linked with the erotic. Not all, or even most, non-heterosexual friendships are sexualised; not all sexual relationships involve friendship or intimacy. Yet we cannot divorce the history of non-heterosexual friendship from the vicissitudes of desire, though the links are often complex, rarely straightforward. Clearly, people categorised and socially excluded by their sexuality are more likely to define their relationships through erotic attraction, but there is strong evidence of historic differences between men and women over this, as well as of considerable recent change.

Many historians have emphasised the importance of friendship in establishing links among women (classical accounts are provided by Faderman 1981; and Smith-Rosenberg 1985). From the eighteenth century, a widespread literature has documented and celebrated 'romantic' or 'passionate' friendships between women. At the time, they were generally assumed to be non-sexual and confined to the upper classes, and an effective training for later devotion to husbands (Donoghue 1993; Stuart 1997). Indeed, many of the women involved were married, though some struggled to be independent, and sometimes established domestic arrangements with other women. The recently decoded diaries of Anne Lister, an early nineteenth-century landowner, heiress of Shibden Hall, near Halifax in the north of England, reveal a story of scholarship and entrepreneurial skill coupled with a more or less secret lesbian life.

Lister was at the centre of a substantial lesbian network: she was searching for a 'marriage' with another woman, and had several long-term relationships, several of which could be considered almost dynastic alliances (Liddington 1999). The last, with Ann Walker, ended tragically in western Georgia in the Russian empire in 1840, when Lister died following an insect bite. It took Walker six months to bring Lister's body home for burial in Halifax. There can be no doubt today of the nature of their relationship, though it was cloaked in the language of the time:

> Miss W[alker]- told me in the hut if she said 'yes' again it should be binding. It should be the same as a marriage & she would give me no cause to be jealous. [She] made no objection to what I proposed, that is her de[c]laring it on the Bible & taking the sa[c]rament with me at Shibden or Lightcliffe church.
>
> (Quoted in Liddington 1993: 70; see also Liddington 1999; Whitbread 1988, 1992)

It appears that Lister's impeccably upper-class credentials allowed her a large degree of freedom in pursuing her passions, as long as she remained discreet and outwardly conventional. However, the language of affection and love deployed in the voluminous correspondence that survives of many other women is usually more ambivalent about sexual desire, and has led lesbian and feminist commentators to see in such effusions evidence of what Rich (1983) has called the 'lesbian continuum', in which the bonds of friendship among women transcended the mere sexual. The erotic content of these relationships has become the subject of much controversy. Smith-Rosenberg (1985) and Faderman (1981) have stressed the importance of intimate friendships among women, which are distorted by attempts to force a sexual definition on them. Some feminist and lesbian historians have argued that the possibilities of intense female friendships were inhibited by the efforts of sexologists to heterosexualise women, and to name, label and stigmatise lesbianism (for example, Jeffreys 1985). However, other historians, such as Vicinus (1996), have explored the separate development of lesbian sexual cultures throughout the nineteenth and into the twentieth century where friendship and a more explicit erotic content coexisted. There is evidence that there were strong suspicions of these relationships among contemporaries (Donoghue 1993; Vicinus 1996), but so long as they were not overtly sexual and did not disrupt the social order they were tolerated. So-called 'Boston marriages', intense but ostensibly non-sexual relationships between two women, were well recognised, and in fact, self-consciously survive as ways of life for some women today, without any necessary connotation of homosexuality (see Rothblum and Brehony 1993). What the evidence does suggest is that for many women involved in close relations with other women, intimate friendship was the route into whatever sexual elements emerged. In an all-female milieu, it was possible to explore sexual desire in a non-threatening way.

For men, however, the sexual elements have always been more salient. The evidence of what we would now call (homo)sexual subcultures in most western cities, from at least the late seventeenth century in England, and earlier in places such as Italy, is overwhelming (see summary in Trumbach 1998). These were not gatherings of 'homosexuals' in the contemporary sense, because the concept of homosexuality as a distinct experience did not exist, but they were places in which same sex erotic activities took place, and relationships could be nurtured outside, but combined with, conventional marriages. Until the eighteenth century, no clear distinction existed between 'homosexuals' and 'heterosexuals' (and the terms themselves, invented in the late nineteenth century, only came into general use gradually in the twentieth century. See Weeks 1977/1990). In the absence of a sexualised division, friendships were a central aspect of relations among men in the pre-modern world. There is evidence that the Church formally blessed them for over a thousand years, providing the basis of stories about the existence of same sex marriages at earlier times (Boswell 1994; Bray 1997). Because men and women occupied separate social worlds, friendships among the same gender often provided men with a stronger emotional commitment.

In his essay on male friendship in the early modern period, Bray (1990: 3) draws a contrast between friendships among 'sodomites', itself a vague category which cannot simply be equated with contemporary notions of 'the homosexual' (Foucault 1979), and more conventional male friendships. Both, he argues, involved physical closeness, including kissing and embracing, emotional bonding and mutual reliance. To be someone's 'bedfellow' signified intimacy, private conversation, support in the endeavours of life, especially for those in a position of power, but not sexual involvement. Intense male friendship was not seen as incompatible with marriage, by either men or women. On the contrary, in a society where marriage was a social necessity, but not necessarily or even generally a matter of personal choice based on sexual attraction or love, friendship among men, and among women, carried a meaning that transcended the often tenuous emotional links across the gender divide – between men and women.

By the early eighteenth century, in most western countries, however, this pattern was significantly changing. Trumbach (1998) argues that by the 1730s in many parts of England, a distinction was being made between a sodomitical minority of men, and the majority. The pattern of a categorical distinction between homosexual and heterosexual men, in a way we today take for granted as inborn and natural, was emerging; it was to be another couple of generations before the same distinctions between women began to develop. The idea of same sex friendship became increasingly tainted with the suspicion of untoward sexual involvement. But as long as the erotic remained repressed or discreet, same sex friendships could survive. It was only when male homosexuality emerged as a named phenomenon in the late nineteenth century – a looming threat in the expanding subcultures of the great cities, spoken of in an emergent literature, minutely dissected in sexological texts, and dramatised by a series of scandals culminating in the trial of Oscar Wilde in 1895 – that the fear of the erotic became a barrier. The journalist W. T. Stead, himself resolutely heterosexual, and through his newspaper exploits partly responsible for the campaign that effectively outlawed all forms of male homosexuality in England and Wales, commented to the homosexual Edward Carpenter that, 'a few more cases like Oscar Wilde's and we should find the freedom of comradeship now possible to men seriously impaired to the permanent detriment of the race' (quoted in Weeks 1977/1990: 21). In other words, the club environment of men was being threatened by the greater awareness of male-to-male desire.

Heterosexual male bonding has not disappeared from twentieth-century history, but in the cold climate of Britain, the emotional intensity of male friendship, which was characteristic of earlier periods, faded from view, with the stigma of homosexuality perceived as being the main barrier (see Sedgwick 1985, 1990). There is no doubt that from the late nineteenth century, the overlapping worlds of heterosexuality and homosexuality were pulled apart, with friendship assuming a new meaning. The erotic undercurrents of friendship became homosexualised. As Allan (1989: 73) has observed, the dominant images of hegemonic masculinity ensured that male friendship was about sociability rather than intimacy.

Paradoxically, however, the divide between friendship and sex was also a feature of male homosexual relationships, seen as part of a complex social situation in which a variety of sexualised and non-sexualised patterns co-existed. While the evidence of women-to-women relationships is generally within specific social milieux and class similarities (for example, the role of the spinster teacher; see Vicinus 1985), sexual relations among men frequently crossed class barriers, with the class distinctions offering opportunities for casual 'trade'. A separation developed between friendships among men of the same milieu, which were generally non-sexualised (though often highly eroticised), and casual sexual liaisons, frequently in public places such as toilets – 'cottages' (Weeks and Porter 1998). Oscar Wilde's taste for 'feasting with panthers' is one of the best-known examples, although the literary memoirs of the early twentieth century provide many others (see Weeks 1977/1990; Parker 1989). Friendship and sex were often separated, with casual sex a route into lasting friendship rather than exclusive partnerships. Close one-to-one relationships did develop, though they were often inhibited by the need for secrecy when homosexual activity was totally illegal, whether in public or private, but these often co-existed with a culture of casual sex. Although by the 1950s much had changed, these historically shaped elements survived in a distinction often made by many 'queer' men between friends and lovers. An 'incest taboo' prohibited sex with friends, who were frequently described as 'sisters'.

By the 1970s, however, there was a sizeable shift in the lesbian and male gay worlds. Both, it has been suggested, 'had begun to picture friends and lovers as two ends of a single continuum rather than oppositional categories' (Weston 1991: 120). There had been a shift from contrast to continuum, with lovers and friends overlapping (Weston 1991: 122; Verere 1982), although differences in relationship patterns between lesbians and gay men still remained. Gay men are significantly more likely to form friendships through an initial sexual encounter; lesbians, however, are more likely to sexualise a pre-existing friendship (Nardi 1992b). This is not surprising, since gay men, freer than most women to circulate outside the domestic sphere, are more likely to meet in a highly sexualised situation. On the other hand, lesbians tend to meet partners in more restricted friendship networks, or since the 1970s, in feminist political groupings. A major reason for this lies in the limited size of the lesbian scene, especially for the closeted (Stanley 1996). Weinstock and Rothblum (1996) note the vague distinction between lovers and friendship among many lesbians (for examples of erotic components of friendship, see Part II of their book). It has often been suggested that non-heterosexual men and women show some of the characteristics of heterosexual masculinity and femininity, with women finding sexuality through intimacy, and men finding intimacy through sexuality (see Gagnon and Simon 1974), and many of our narrators argue along similar lines. Yet it is also increasingly possible to see a subversion of this stereotype in the actual lives of non-heterosexuals. As Nardi puts it with regard to gay men:

> As men, they see sex as the way to intimacy. But as gay people, they develop a strong emotional intimacy with other men, unlike what research shows about how heterosexual men relate to other men … they subvert the norm of masculinity by showing that men can be intimate with one another at an emotional sharing level.
>
> (Nardi 1992b: 183)

Stuart (1995) similarly argues that only 'soft boundaries' exist between friendship and sexual intimacy among women, and goes further. She suggests, from a lesbian perspective, that we need to liberate sexuality from the privatised world of the couple relationship and put it at the heart of all relationships, as a force for social as well as personal transformation. Weinstock and Rothblum (1996: 15) also suggest that the greater freedom of lesbians from assumed roles may open up unique opportunities to question definitions of intimacy and sex, friendship and lover relationships. These issues are explored in greater depth in Chapter 6.

Underpinning these changes are several factors that have changed the possibilities of lesbian and gay life since the 1960s. The collective coming out experience of many self-identified lesbians and gays, and the creation of a sense of collective identity associated with developed communities of interest and identity, has opened new opportunities for personal experimentation in which friendship, intimacy and the erotic can more easily co-exist. At the same time, a 'domestication of gay sex' among men has taken place (Trumbach 1999), in part a result of the old association of male homosexuality with street life and prostitution having been displaced by a more partnership-oriented culture, where the relationship between love, commitment and sexual pleasure is being renegotiated (Weeks 1977/1990; Bech 1997; and see this volume, Chapters 5 and 6). This has been accompanied by an increasing eroticisation of the lesbian scene. As a result, some observers of contemporary non-heterosexual life have identified a major transformation of the meaning of friendship, with the emergence of what Blasius calls 'erotic friendship':

> an ethico-erotic relationship productive of equality; the participants (whatever they name themselves – lovers, ex-lovers, fuckbuddies, partners, etc.) are inventing themselves and become the conditions for such self-inventions of each other.
>
> (Blasius 1994: 221)

This perhaps overstates a more complex reality. While the erotic components of friendship and community are omnipresent, the new realities of the non-heterosexual world allow for a greater flexibility of friendship than ever before. Sexuality is only one element, though the one that continues to define the separate existence of a non-heterosexual world. The friendship patterns that emerge are circumscribed by a host of differences, and yet defined by one overriding factor: the continuing marginalisation of same sex activities and relationships in a world overwhelmingly shaped by the heterosexual assumption. Non-heterosexual friendships must therefore develop simultaneously as a focus for survival and self-actualisation in a hostile world, and as a framework for love, sex, reciprocity and commitment in building alternative forms of life. The friendship ethic, rooted in a hostile history, now forms the basis of increasingly complex sexual and social patterns.

Facing fateful moments

We can see the friendship ethic at work among contemporary non-heterosexuals, especially in confronting what we earlier referred to as 'fateful moments':

> times when events come together in such a way that an individual stands, as it were, at a crossroads in his [*sic*] existence ... There are, of course, fateful moments in the history of collectives as well as in the lives of individuals. They are phases at which things are wrenched out of joint, where a given state of affairs is suddenly altered by a few key events.
>
> (Giddens 1991: 113)

Friendships, regardless of sexual preferences or identifications, provide one of the key sources of support in such circumstances. As Rubin (1985: 13) observes, '[I]t is friends who provide a reference outside the family against which to measure and judge ourselves'. But for lesbians and gays, friends are not only an alternative source of support, sometimes they are the *only* support (cf. Stanley 1996). William, a 40-year-old white gay man, says one of his favourite quotes is: 'Friends are God's compensation for your relatives' (M03). So friends need to do more than simply provide 'pleasure in someone's company, new ideas, laughter, continuity' (Jenny, F21); they must also, as William observes, 'allow me to be weak' (M03). As many narratives make clear, people are seeking support, understanding and acceptance for who they are.

This is not a once and for all need: it takes place at all stages of the life story. The first tentative steps into the homosexual world can be the most difficult, as individuals must come to terms with their often confusing sexual desires in a society which they perceive as hostile. Coming out as lesbian, gay or bisexual to family can be traumatic, especially if relations with parents and siblings are difficult, or if they reject non-heterosexuality (Davies 1992; Marcus 1992; Benkov 1994). Similarly, not coming out to parents also can distance the non-heterosexual person from his or her family of origin (Cramer and Roach 1988; Driggs and Finn 1991), creating a sometimes unsurpassable barrier, involving evasion and lack of trust. Even when parents are accepting, there is still a need for emotional support that family cannot easily provide (Kurdek and Schmitt 1987). Simon, 32, vividly recalls his early experiences of coming out:

> where I've come from … was an extremely heterosexual environment to be in … if you were even remotely effeminate, or not masculine, then you were singled out and it was just real hard work the whole time to exist in that environment. And I formed very close friendships with people who were ostracised in similar ways to me, and I think that was the mechanism by which I became friends with a lot of gay men, because … we all gravitated towards each other. And I ended up being friends with about four other boys … who turned out to be gay as well. And that was, I suppose, the major … thing that made life liveable. (M05)

Simon's is a common story: of a sense of difference, accompanied by hostility from peers, and all too frequently from members of family of origin. There are many stories of rejection by families of origin, and stories of selective relationships in the family: with the mother, but not the father, with one brother or sister, but not others. And sometimes, relationships with blood relatives entirely break down. Coral (F13), for example, a white Australian lesbian, aged 26, felt the need to 'divorce' her family of origin, and moved to Britain in order to put a distance between herself and them. She has made friends in England, and they have become her 'adoptive family'. This is a common pattern.

As the individual moves into adult life, friends provide a sense of affirmation of who you are, which is often denied elsewhere (Weston 1991; Nardi 1999). Matt, a 22-year-old student, says:

> I couldn't live without close friends. I mean, I tend to see friends as being almost like a mirror. You see your personality reflected in someone else. … You can't really know who you are until you can see how you get on with other people. … And it's good for building up self-esteem, as well. (M10)

Sympathetic friends can provide a 'life-line', as Miriam (F44) told us: 'particularly as … my family don't offer that. I couldn't survive without my friends.'

Friends offer a barrier against hostility, a sense that you are part of an ongoing history, a school of manners and values, and a sense that there are others who are experiencing similar hopes and disappointments. Alan, 44 years old, divorced and gay, has this to say about friendships: 'Sharing is the obvious or first word that comes to mind – you know, somewhere to kind of share experiences – and to get support and to be supportive' (M39). Similarly, for Angela:

> I like to share ... I mean, I like the nice times with my friends – 'I've got a new job ...', 'I've started a new relationship ...' – that's really nice, as well as like the times when they're struggling. And we talk through a lot of our relationships, and wanting to leave relationships. (F28)

If you cannot share your most important life experiences with friends, especially the delicate joys and frustrations of desire, then what are they for? For William openness about your sexuality is the defining quality of close friendship:

> So far as I'm concerned, it should be one of the things people know about me very early on. The people I get to know well and care for – if they can't get over that hurdle, well then, forget about the next. What's the point of them finding out whether you prefer, you know, a lot or a little garlic in your spaghetti bolognese if they can't deal with your sex life, for God's sake! (M03)

Frankness about sexuality and relationships is a crucial factor in defining the difference between close friendships and family of origin. As Angela (F28) observes, who else but friends 'could you go to with that?' But, paradoxically, it is during periods of emotional and/or sexual pleasure or hurt that the image of friends as an alternative family is most strongly evoked. As Juliet comments:

> The way that I think about those people [my friends] is the way that, you know, generally, people would regard family. ... I share my thoughts, I share my feelings with them. I share lots of the aspects of my life with them, and they are the people I would go to if I was in trouble, or if I was sick, or if I needed money, or whatever. And I know that they would be there for me ... with an element of caring that my actual family I don't think would have. (F01)

Friendships are most important when they are ongoing, when they have been embedded in 'taken-for-granted' assumptions and patterns, when you are accepted for who you are. This is especially important if you are not part of a couple relationship, or when you live alone. In his 'post-AIDS' reflections on gay friendship, *Love Undetectable*, Andrew Sullivan (1998) makes clear that for him and many of his contemporaries, especially when confronted by the horrors of epidemic, it is friendship rather than romantic love or one-to-one partnerships which is the real guarantee of survival. One of our interviewees, Melanie (aged 52), argues much the same:

Since I've come out as a lesbian, and also I live on my own – that's generally speaking – I think I need that support from friends, because I could get quite isolated and quite lonely … if you just go to work every day and then come back home, and you're too tired to do anything, and go back to work and go back home – that can really get me down really. (F29)

Similarly, Paul, who is in a new (but non-cohabiting) relationship, stresses the importance of friends:

I have a lot of people I really like, and who are my friends, but there's a much smaller group who I feel even closer to, and in a much more recent and exciting way … it's partly to do with just knowing they are there, and there's a largely unquestioned loyalty I can expect from them, and support. … And it's not particularly riding on contingencies or contract, it's just taken for granted that that's the level at which we relate, which is a bit different to chums and acquaintances. They're essential. … Obviously, it's a bit different with a boyfriend because two months in it's wonderful, but [after that] who knows? (M21)

Much of the literature about gay/lesbian relationships has tended to concentrate on couple relationships as the exclusive focus of intimacy, and as we shall see, couples are indeed important (Chapter 5). However, for many individuals who are not in long-term relationships, as well as for those who are, friendships as families of choice are the prime focus of emotional support. Friends may change; new people may enter the circle. But friendship networks seem permanent – certainly, many individuals act on the assumption that they are. In contrast to the vagaries of one-to-one relationships, friends, on the other hand, are a focus of long-lasting engagement, trust and commitment. Joan, a self-identified bisexual, says:

Well, I *know* that with [my] very close group of friends, we've got a real deep commitment to each other that I see, and they see as well, as going on for – well, for ever really. I can't imagine what would happen such that the rela-tionship I've got with these people would deteriorate, because there is such a strong bond there that even if we fell out, we'd sort it out. … So, it's just a really deep sense of caring and commitment. It's commitment, really. (F32)

Without the commitment of friends, life would seem empty, and fateful moments would be even more difficult to navigate.

The complexities of friendship

Central to this reliance on friendship is the fact that friends are freely chosen, and offer a fundamental sense of equality. For Dan (M44), a white gay man aged 71, friendships have sustained him in a long life. Unlike most of his biological family, which 'sort of nurture you, or are supposed to nurture you, [but] they also stifle and cripple you', the chosen nature of friendship can allow for greater emotional possibilities: 'My emotional safety net, or whatever you like [to call it], is in my friends ... my emotional base. ... The difference is you *choose* your friends.'

Choice implies selection and distinctions. In general, no one chooses randomly, and there are limits to choice. In his study of friendship, Allan (1989) has argued that, far from being simply a matter of personal or free choice, friendships – heterosexual and non-heterosexual – are structured and patterned, like all other social relations, by factors that go beyond simple personal wish. These factors include social class, social mobility, occupational status, leisure interests, gender differences, ethnic and racial categorisations, age, and so forth. And although a common sense of identity often manages to bridge the divides, this does not automatically happen: friendships are not given, they have to be worked at. Malika, for example, is very conscious of the work that has to be done with friends:

> I have very high standards when it comes to friendship, right? And I'm not very good at having superficial friendships because I find them dishonest. So my standards are about honesty. And this is in friendships and relationships. ... Mutual honesty, mutual respect and mutual, sort of, caring and looking after each other. And I haven't found that with very many people at all ... and that means honesty so that it's okay to make mistakes, it's okay to get things wrong, it's okay that you end up hurting somebody. But a good friendship to me would mean you could work through that and move on from there. So the few people that I do think of as being my really close friends are people that it's taken a long time to work to that level of honesty and trust and caring. But now that I've got it – it just feels really good. (F03)

Friendships take time. Like Weston (1991), we found that the friendship networks of our interviewees had fluid boundaries and varying membership, as friends worked through their tensions and difficulties over a lengthy period. Friendship networks are necessarily dynamic, with members added or falling away as circumstances change. People do not consciously decide at a point in time that a given nexus of friends is close enough to be like family or not. Several of our interviewees refer to the gradual nature of developing relationships, which involves shared experiences, an intertwined history, a sense of continuity and some sense of permanence. The gradual process through which someone becomes a 'family member' might only be realised in retrospect. Jenny, as a parent, describes one way in which this happens:

> And it's sort of just automatic ... for instance, it's one of the kid's birthdays or something, those are the people who get rung up to say, 'Do you want to come over for birthday cake?', and things. And ... you know, I sort of looked at it recently and thought, 'God, the room's full of uncles' – it's that

sort of relationship, some of which just comes from years of knowing each other. (F21)

Thus, people make distinctions among friends: those who are social friends and those who are 'part of the family'. Jenny, again, describes the difference:

this is a weird answer, but I think it may be close to it. Almost a sense that we have some sort of connection with each other even if we don't see each other for a while or even if at some points we don't particularly like each other. And it isn't quite about obligation … it's when the commitment or the connection goes somewhere beyond just social things or somewhere beyond – I almost want to say somewhere beyond choice. Well it isn't just like choosing whether you're going to spend the evening with somebody or if – somehow there is more of an underlying connection. (F21)

When distinctions emerge, these connections can be complex. As Peter describes:

I can very quickly mark off who my close friends are, who I could spend almost infinite amounts of time with. And then there's another little tier of people who I am friendly with and I like going out with and I probably see, you know, once a week, once a fortnight – they're more sort of 'doing' friends. … But my close friends are more my 'hanging out' friends. … The people I can just drop in on are my close friends and then there's my organised friends and then there's acquaintances. (M11)

Sexual links add a particular element to friendships, which broadly differentiates non-heterosexual from heterosexual patterns. Like Weston (1991) and Blasius (1994), we found that our interviewees often included within their closest circles former lovers as well as current sexual partners. For example, Joan (F32), who defines herself as bisexual, remarks that the most important people in her life, apart from her daughter, are two men and three women, three of which she regards as lovers as well as her closest friends. The terminology of friendship and family is inadequate to grasp these complexities. As Joan notes, 'a lot of the time I want to describe them as friends but then I also feel … in terms of what most people understand friendship to be, it is actually more intimate than that'. But intimacy has a particular meaning here. One of her lovers lives half-time in the same city as Joan, one in another city in the south of England, and one in another country. Joan spends different amounts of time with each one: 'it's like having a family really – very much so. Just to know that we're going to sort of stick together, no matter what – which is a lovely feeling.' 'It's about me wanting to get away from sort of conventions,' she continues, 'and enable a kind of greater number of possibilities to exist.'

This sense of open possibilities is powerful, and it recurs throughout our interviews, leading to highly intricate patterns, like circles crossing over one another. This is especially the case when partners may have overlapping but different networks of friends. Edmund White has compared such patterns to 'the banyan tree' phenomenon, so-called because the banyan tree's branches send out shoots which then take root and form new trunks (quoted in Sullivan 1997: 133), while Weston speaks of 'ties that radiated outwards from individuals like spokes from a wheel' (1991: 109). But as these images, whether organic or mechanical, suggest, the patterns and possibilities are not really infinite. Choices are limited, not least by the impact of key developments in the non-heterosexual world since the 1960s.

One significant feature of our interviewees is the tendency for close friend-ships to be homosocial, or single sex, though this is by no means universal (cf. Weston 1991; Nardi 1999). A number of gay men who we interviewed claimed not to know many lesbians, and vice versa. We have already observed that, while there is an intertwined history between the two groups, the stories of male and female non-heterosexuals are often distinctive – legally, socially, culturally and emotionally. Among our interviewees, although there is little difference in attitudes to families of choice between men and women, to an important extent lesbians and gay men inhabit different social worlds. Many lesbians and gays do mix together in networks, but for others there is a barrier which separates them.

This partly stems from the fact that many lesbians and gay men have strong perceptions of their difference. Peter (M11), who has a number of lesbian friends, believes that '[lesbians] talk more and they understand each other's emotional intimacy more, so they get a better knowledge of each other'. Pat (F36) echoes this sentiment: 'I see women's level of commitment, or emotions, more intense in their friendships … [Men] talk about sex a lot [laughs], whereas lesbians don't.'

Although, as we have seen, there is a historical basis for this distinction, more often than not it comes from ignorance about each other's lifestyle. A significant number of gay men do not know any lesbians, and similarly many lesbians do not know, or do not want to know, any gay men. For some lesbians, this is a political decision – several of our women interviewees had gone through periods of their lives where they deliberately avoided relations with men, either gay or straight (see Dunne 1997). Sometimes, however, it is simply the fact of common sexual interests that shapes choice. Although most of Peter's close friends are women, he has this to say about his closest male friend:

> The reason that he's important to me is that I can – there's lot of things that I can talk about to my lesbian friends, but there's certain things that I need to be able to talk to another man about, in terms of relationships, but also … it's things around sex and cottaging and all that kind of biz. Where you just want to have a laugh about it. (M11)

Bisexual relations, one might assume, promise to remove these categorical distinctions, and are unlikely to be homosocial. Certainly, bisexuality rejects the absolute divide between lesbian and gay men that history and experience has often hardened (see Garber 1995). The reality, however, as some of our interviewees suggest, is of alienation from the conventional heterosexual world, without full acceptance in the non-heterosexual world. In her essay, 'Locating Bisexual Identities', Clare Hemmings describes the sense of 'dislocation' that flows from this:

> For example, I would say that I am closer to a lesbian feminist than to a male bisexual 'swinger' in many ways, yet at times I might ally myself with that swinger in response to biphobia from lesbian and gay communities. I am simultaneously located in terms of class, 'race', education and age.
>
> (Hemmings 1999: 198)

A sense of difference, especially when shaped around gendered experience, helps produce different social worlds, and makes conversation across the divide difficult. And yet, when confronted by the force of the heterosexual assumption, a strong sense of common interests occurs. Rubin (1985) notes that lesbians and gay men establish most of their close supportive friendships among other non-heterosexuals, and this is confirmed by other accounts (Hidalgo and Christensen 1976/1977; Tanner 1978), as well as by our own interviews. The accentuated separation of the homosexual and heterosexual worlds as self-identified lesbians and gays have developed quasi-ethnic identities (Altman 1982; Lewin 1998), have tended to shape a culture where friendship choices are often made entirely within homosexual circles.

Marian comments on how people differentiate between non-heterosexual and heterosexual friends:

> I suppose lots of it comes down to choices – lesbian women have thought so much about where they are and what they're doing, and hetero people avoid thinking [laughing] half the time, or seem to. (F33)

And here, Mo notes surprise when a relationship with a straight female friend goes well:

> with Patricia, the thing that particularly struck me all the time about her was how she's not bothered, how open to the whole situation she was, which you don't usually get from straight women, I don't think. (F43)

There can be no doubt that many of the taboos that have, for 200 years or more, inhibited close relationships across the homosexual and heterosexual divide are beginning to break down, as heterosexual life is itself reshaped by the impact of detraditionalising forces and the redefinition of friendship. This is certainly true of younger people (cf. Nardi 1999). Matt, aged 22, for example, is best friends with two straight men:

> I like to have a few close friends, that I can have, like, quite intense relations with. ... I mean, you've got your own private jokes ... and when you're speaking to them you know you're always on the same wavelength. There's

no room for misunderstanding because you know each other so well – you know where you're coming from. (M10)

This situation, however, is unusual among the participants in our research, and in Matt's case may be accounted for by his relative youth. The evidence suggests that as people become more integrated into the non-heterosexual world, it then follows that their closest friendships become rooted there. There is a strong sense that heterosexual interests diverge too easily from lesbian and gay preoccupations, especially when a love interest comes along. Mollie comments wryly:

You know – the way the heterosexual women I used to know would drop an appointment with you, so easily, for something coming up with a man. I don't find the lesbians I know with partners that bad – although they are not as good as the ones without. ... I do find that there are whole sets of different difficulties around non-lesbian friends. ... I find that they're more trouble to continue friendships with. They don't stick to things in the same way. I've found that they're not as ... reliable. (F30)

Marian expresses a similar view with regard to lesbian and heterosexual relationships:

There are a lot [of differences between heterosexual and lesbian friends], behaviour patterns – social lifestyles, attitudes, inhibitions are much more to the forefront with hetero groups ... There are difficulties in mixing lesbian couples with mixed couples, I've found. (F33)

Regardless of how liberal straight friends are, there is a sense that a different agenda is operating for many self-identified lesbians and gays. Only self-identified bisexuals, like Joan above, find themselves totally at ease with a mixed collection of friends, at the very least in terms of gender, if not sexuality. As Pat suggests in the following quotation, there is almost a difference of language, and a feeling of group loyalty which inhibits intimacy across the heterosexual–homosexual divide. She believes that lesbians and gay men

know what you're talking about; you don't have to explain everything. ... I always feel when you're with straight people, you can't ... run other lesbians and gays down ... but when you're with gay people, it's all right [laughs]. You can ... be horrible and get away with it, and it's okay ... because it's part of your community. But I feel you can't do that with straight people. (F36)

Pat's comments underline the broad sense of common identity that is shared between non-heterosexual men and women when faced with heterosexual assumptions. Many bisexuals, like Sarah (F23), for example, are suspicious of straight men, but feel gay men 'are part of the family'. Similarly, many gay men, however limited in their actual friendships with lesbians, feel a sense of affinity which does not apply to heterosexuals. Contrariwise, for those who have been closeted, the absence of like-minded friends can be a source of deep regret. Lilly, aged 67, whose long-term, but semi-secret lesbian partner is now dead, has very few lesbian friends, 'because,' she say, 'we were so damned secretive':

> I think that's been a great loss. ... I can't ask her [Mindy, her dead partner] now, but I think that probably was a loss to Mindy, certainly I realise more and more [it was] a loss to me. ... I think it's a sort of desperate search for understanding, which is a bit, pathetic, isn't it? ... That, understanding, and the fact that ... it's been one long guardedness. Guardedness, what you do and say. Maybe this is all imaginary – [but it] would have been nice, just to be with people, with whom [you could] just sort of let your guard down a bit. (F47)

Differences

Thus far, we have suggested that close friendship circles have a strong tendency to be homosexual, with many preferring homosocial friendships as well. We shall next examine how socially homogeneous they are in other regards. Several commentators have observed that the emphasis on friendships within homosexual circles can limit the development of facets of the self that a broader range of friendships might encourage (see, for example, Blumstein and Schwartz 1983; Rubin 1985). On the other hand, given that most lesbians and/or gay men will probably meet people like themselves in non-heterosexual circles, it is hardly surprising that friendships are likely to be formed around common emotional or sexual identifications. In this context, it is understandable that many friendships will transcend traditional divides. Blumstein and Schwartz (1983), for instance, have remarked that some couples are apparently mismatched in terms of social and class backgrounds because they met in places where the common denominator was sexual rather than shared leisure or intellectual pursuits.

Many of the friendships described by our interviewees are both cross-class and explicitly egalitarian in their values, precisely because of a shared sexuality. Far from being a disadvantage, this can be seen as a potential strength. As Stuart (1995: 43) puts it, 'friendship can break rank', though, inevitably, there are different perceptions of how easy this is to achieve. When probed, it is clear that common class, status or professional interests going beyond the purely erotic do often intrude. As Jill half confesses:

> we all enjoy the same things – we all like eating, we all like talking ... we share the same sort of sense of humour, the same outrages, etc. You know, it's something to do with [the fact that] most of us are professional, I suppose, as well. I don't know if there's necessarily anything significant in that. (F22)

Disparities of income and of power in relationships are factors that cannot be ignored (and are discussed in more detail in Chapters 4 and 5). As the non-heterosexual world becomes more embedded, secure and diverse, other common elements will bring people together, and possibly undermine the power of common sexual interests. At the moment, however, the evidence is mixed.

Of the potential divides, age is perhaps the most difficult to bridge, and generational differences can matter, especially when, as is often suggested, the non-heterosexual world, like the heterosexual world, is aimed at young people. Lilly, for example, who is 67, says she is 'too old' to feel part of the non-heterosexual community; she thinks it is for people 'not a day older than 50' (F47). However, for Jill, aged 46, age isn't seen as an issue:

> one of the nice things I like about the lesbian community is that you can actually get on with people of any age, and I don't think of Marie as 22. I mean, she's got a maturity and a way with her [so] that the age is totally irrelevant. And it's just, nobody bothers about it, as well, I don't think. I mean, maybe, if you're having a relationship with them they do, but certainly as friends, it's nice to have a wide variety. (F22)

The experience of child care clearly shapes experiences and perceptions. Amy (F27), aged 31, laments the fact that a lack of children means lesbian and gay friendships are too often uni-generational (cf. Weston 1991). And Marilyn does not feel part of the lesbian and gay community, this time *because* of parenting responsibilities:

> we're just emerging from a long period of younger children so we've been rather immersed in full-time work and full-time parenting, so we haven't had a huge amount of time for community and social life. (F33)

As these examples show, friendships are shaped by myriad common interests and experiences, but these do not dictate friendships. The experiences of people differ, depending on their specific circumstances, needs, and other identifications. Non-heterosexuals, as much as heterosexuals, live in more than one social world, and often choose friendships on the basis of their various identities, not simply on the basis of their homosexuality. This is especially true if they feel discriminated against on more grounds than simply their sexuality. For example, Angela (F28), because of her hearing impairment, feels part of the disabled community. She also considers that the lesbian and gay community offers a network of friends which the straight world cannot. But this leads to tensions between a lesbian and gay community that does not want to know about disabled people, and a disabled community that does not want to know about sexuality, which in turn can lead to tensions in friendships (cf. Shakespeare 1996). Similarly, Joan (F32), who identifies as bisexual, feels somewhat alienated from the lesbian and gay world because of its lack of interest, if not actual hostility towards, bisexuality.

Diverse sexual practices are often treated with hostility by those who are not involved, and can fracture friendship ties. Sue, who identifies as a queer sadomasochist, observes:

coming out as an S&M dyke, I lost a hell of a lot more friends [than she did in coming out as lesbian], and that hurt even more because we were supposed to have this thing in common. We'd all gone through the same experience of being kicked out by the general community. So, I guess, a lot of my friends I cut off at that stage. Well – they cut themselves off, really. (F15)

Sue and her partner Julie's main identification is, therefore, with a group of people organised around a particular sadomasochist club, who 'break all the rules and don't give a damn'. As a result, they are now involved with more men than ever before, and feel their 'family' is about eight women and men who they met through the club.

Race and ethnicity are perhaps among the most crucial elements when considering the possibilities, and difficulties, of friendship. Many black feminists have criticised the early feminist (and gay) hostility to the traditional family (see Mirza 1997), focusing on the fact that for minorities the family is an essential bulwark against oppression and a source of support (cf. Weston 1991: 36). But even when black lesbians and gay men break with their family of origin to establish their own ways of life, racism is a constant presence, disrupting any sense of wider belonging within the non-heterosexual community, while also alienating them from their community of origin (cf. Hall and Rose, in Weinstock and Rothblum 1996, on the racial tensions that shape and inhibit relations across the barriers). Malika, a 28-year-old black lesbian, claims she no longer feels fully part of a lesbian and gay world – she did when she first came out, but became more and more aware of racism:

> the more racism that I've come across from the lesbian community … the more I've felt not part of that community, and not wanting to be part of it, either … and there isn't such a thing as a black lesbian community that I can become part of, because there's too few black lesbians around to make it feel like a community, in terms of having separate space and autonomy, and places to go, and things to do, and people to socialise with. So, no, I don't [feel part of a community]. (F03)

An awareness of the continuing existence of racism in the white gay and lesbian world challenges the very heart of the friendship ethic. Frankie (F41), a lesbian of Afro-Caribbean background, feels she receives most of her support, not from fellow lesbians, but from straight people. But at the same time, since leaving her church four years ago, she no longer feels a member of the black community. For Frankie, and others like her, friendship is not a given; it is something that has to be struggled for against the barriers of difference.

The value of commitment

Friendships inevitably have to weave through these complex social relationships, reflecting an increasingly diverse social world. This makes it all the more significant that despite differences, and whatever the barriers, many non-heterosexuals have constructed common values and commitments around friendship, which make meaningful lives possible for them.

In friendship, Elizabeth Stuart (1995: 44) writes, 'women and gay men experience mutuality', that is, a sense of involvement with others which goes beyond their isolated individual lives without diminishing their individuality. This is a delicate balancing act, which has to be constantly negotiated and renegotiated if friendship ties are to work and survive. This is not a peculiarly non-heterosexual challenge. As Finch and Mason (1993) have shown, it is precisely a similar challenge which shapes more conventional kin relationships, as family members try to balance a respect for the dignity and self-respect of individuals with a commitment to ongoing responsibilities to one another. As we shall show, there are many similarities between the evidence offered by Finch and Mason and our own argument. There are very similar patterns in the way we negotiate responsibilities and in our commitments: nothing can be taken for granted, either in traditional kin relationships or in non-heterosexual lives. Relationships have to be worked at, and worked out, over time. Neither group works to fixed rules (Finch and Mason 1993: 166) – though heterosexual relationships do carry more latent assumptions, we would suggest – and individuals live by guidelines about the right way to proceed rather than referring to a fixed list of 'oughts' and 'musts'. And yet, despite a high degree of fluidity, individuals have a strong sense of moral agency and an implicit hierarchy of values in the way they conduct their everyday lives in interaction with others.

Many of these values are common to all forms of close friendship. However, as we have argued, there are crucial differences between heterosexual and non-heterosexual friendships. Perhaps even more important is the lack of legitimacy in non-heterosexual relationships – regardless of how stable or fulfilling they may be – compared to the recognised legitimacy of kin interactions – no matter how difficult or unsatisfactory they may turn out to be. This puts an extra burden on non-heterosexual friendships, since they must combine both the traditional delights of friendship and the weight of emotional expectation.

As same sex relationships are constructed and maintained outside conventional institutional and legal support systems and structures, they are less likely to be characterised by predetermined assumptions and past histories than traditional family relationships. In the absence of legitimation by either blood or law – traditionally seen as the key elements of family – alternative forms of legitimating commitment become necessary (Lewin 1998). Inevitably, ideas of choice, trust and love take on a new significance. A sign at the Gay and Lesbian March, in Washington, DC in 1987, proclaimed: 'Love makes a family – nothing more, nothing less.' Weston comments:

> Grounding kinship in love de-emphasized distinctions between erotic and non-erotic relations while bringing friends, lovers and children together under a single concept.

> (Weston 1991: 107)

In practice, we found that the very American rhetoric of love is largely absent from the stories of friendship currently circulating in Britain. At the same time, there is a strong sense of the value of 'good friendship'. Behind this lies an emphasis on the value of freely chosen and egalitarian friendship as the basis for ongoing commitment, what we earlier called an emotional democracy. The concept of 'good friendship' is, we argue, the main legitimising factor for non-heterosexual relationships.

As outlined above, the relationships most people want are based on the values of sharing, mutual support, openness, common interests and a sense of trust and ongoing commitment, where individuals can be themselves and yet feel a sense of belonging to a wider circle. We now turn our attention to the meanings that flow from this generalised ethos, to use Blasius' (1994) term, in relation to such values as obligation, duty, and mutual responsibility.

In recent years, there has been considerable discussion about the meanings of these terms in relationship to family life as a whole. Those writing about family values – usually about their decline – have emphasised, as we discussed earlier, the corrupting effects of rampant individualism on traditional ties. Sociologists have observed the thinning of old solidarities and obligations (Beck-Gernsheim 1998). Communitarian theorists, in confronting these changes, have tended, therefore, to emphasise the importance of rebuilding the links between rights and responsibilities (e.g., Etzioni 1995), and obligations and duties (Selbourne 1994). One of the striking findings of Finch and Mason's (1993: 166) study, however, is the general reluctance of kin members to use the language either of rights or of duty. People do not see specific duties attached to extended family relationships, certainly in adult relationships, and view the concept of duty as an inappropriate way of looking at mutual responsibilities where children are not involved. Nor do people have a sense of rights in family situations. On the contrary, responsibilities build up incrementally over time through quite complex processes of exchange relationships, less a product of specific blood relationships than of negotiation in certain social conditions:

> Through negotiation people create sets of material and moral baggage which gets carried forward, and which help to create the framework for future negotiations. Material baggage is perhaps most easily recognised … Moral baggage, on the other hand, is less tangible, but involves the moral identities and reputations of the participants also constructed through this process.
>
> (Finch and Mason 1993: 92–3)

Like Finch and Mason, in relation to kin we found that terms such as duty or obligation tended to be avoided by non-heterosexuals when discussing their closest relationships, especially those of friendship. Such terms have, as Alan (M39) observes, 'a negative connotation'. Duty is, for Jackie (F05), 'like some kind of moral code that people use to put on you. … I don't think I need that kind of external thing put on me.' We suggest this reluctance to use the language of duty has two roots. The first is a common belief among heterosexuals and non-heterosexuals alike that the language of duty and obligation is at odds with, and undermines, the subtle give and take which is necessary for human interactions, and which guarantees moral autonomy. It does not mean, however, whatever the pessimism of moral conservatives, that people do not have an acute sense of the right thing to do. It more likely signifies people's mature sense that the right thing to do cannot be taken for granted, but instead has to be worked out. Second, however, among non-heterosexuals, duty and obligation have other very negative connotations, of submission to the moral *status quo*, and to external rules which deny the validity of non-heterosexual desires and choices. It is for this reason, for example, that Foucault in elaborating the 'practices of freedom' eschews the idea of a new morality in favour of ethics, guidelines for appropriate conduct rather than rules of moral conformity (see Halperin 1995).

Terms such as duty and obligation are therefore rejected by our interviewees in favour of concepts of responsibility and mutual care and commitment. For Juliet (F01): 'Responsibility is something I decide to do and I keep to; obligation is when I feel I have to.' Similarly, for Dan:

> duty is something that is imposed on you … if you feel responsible for someone. I mean, being a parent, you're responsible for your children, then you do that because you feel you want to, not because somebody else feels you ought to. (M44)

There are exceptions, but they usually refer to inescapable relationships, especially where elements of dependency are present. As William (M03) says, 'I have a duty to care for my mother. And I feel I have a duty of care to [his lover] but only because that's what we've chosen.' Distinctions are carefully made, especially with regard to parents and children. As Peter notes:

> If my friends were ill, I wouldn't feel obliged to care for them, I'd want to. But my mum and dad don't have that [i.e., friends] … they did it for me when I was a bairn so, you know … (M11)

Parenting highlights important questions about obligation, commitment and responsibility. Many non-heterosexuals, men and women, are involved in parenting in one form or another, as biological or adoptive parents, or as non-biological co-parents (see Chapter 7). The resulting parenting arrangements can be quite complex, involving biological parents, lovers, even ex-lovers, in an extended family-type arrangement. Those involved tend to be very conscious of the wider cultural anxieties around such arrangements, and are acutely aware of the sensitivities of the child, and the responsibility it entails. Regardless of the means of birth, or who else is involved in the parenting, and no matter what social and personal hazards may exist, the care and well-being of the child remains the first and ultimate responsibility of same sex parents, over and above the adult relationship itself. This would seem to be the common thread across the diversity of parenting practices. Obligation and duty – though the terms themselves may not always be used – here override the discourse of choice.

Among adults, however, notions of care and responsibility are commonly, and strongly held, especially when applied to close friends, but they are seen as the result of mutual negotiation. The resulting commitments appear to be situational, dependent on the needs of parents and other relatives, as well as of friends, but the ideas themselves are potent, organised around notions of what Peter (M11) calls 'the right thing to do' (cf. Finch and Mason 1993).

Peer relationships carry fewer of the necessary responsibilities that looking after ageing parents or children usually entail, and might lead the unwary to believe that they are inevitably more fragile. Yet, it can equally be argued that the thinning of enforced obligations, a more sharply defined individualisation, and the greater contingency of relationships which results from this, has led to a greater emphasis on making relationships work. Silva and Smart (1999b: 6) argue that for many people, family ties have become more important for exactly these reasons. Our own evidence suggests that for non-heterosexuals freely chosen relationships have the potential to be both free of imposed obligations, and, therefore, more intense, as the constant reiteration of the importance of commitment in relationships underlines.

Commitment, as Finch and Mason (1993: 94) argue, is an accepted responsibility, one which has lasting consequences. Commitments developed for yourself, through negotiations over time with significant others, are likely to feel much more powerful precisely because they are not imposed from outside. Finch and Mason (1993: 94–5) also suggest that individuals make an emotional investment in their closest commitments, resulting in the creation of what they call, following Becker, 'valuables', which can be material or moral. These valuables become one of the elements of reciprocity in the relationships. However, friendship can be based on more than a simple exchange of 'goods'. This is illustrated by Amy, who was asked whether she had the kind of relationships where people can offer, and she in turn can offer, practical support or money:

> Yes, both those things. … There are many people who I've lent money to, or whatever, and it's usually this way round because I've usually been working and a lot of the women I know haven't been working, or they have kids and have a lot of expenses. … It's not just money or practical support, it's emotional support as well. … I try to do it without any ties [or expectation of repayment], because I think the power thing is important in friendship, around trying to be equal, really, around power. (F27)

In Amy's comments we see a strong sense of reciprocity, which is not dependent on a balanced exchange of 'valuables', but is at the same time acutely aware of delicate power imbalances, leading to a generalised but strong commitment to making the relationships work. The main 'valuable' here is moral rather than material: the value of the friendship transcends money. We suggest that this is emblematic of the friendship ethic which characterises non-heterosexual relationships.

We believe that this ethic is built on an intricate weaving of several reciprocal values: care, responsibility, respect and knowledge (Weeks 1995: 172–85). Care involves an active concern for the lives, hopes, needs and potentialities of others. It is a highly gendered activity in western culture, seen typically as the prerogative of women (Finch and Mason 1993, make this point). But from our evidence, it is as likely to occur in male as it is female non-heterosexual relationships. The response to the AIDS crisis provides a classic example of this, as we argue below. Responsibility as a voluntary act, revealing our response to the needs, latent or explicit, of others, and receiving in return the responsible behaviour of others, is a clearly expressed ideal of our interviewees. Respect, for one's individual autonomy, and for the dignity of others, is a motivating force of many of the friendship circles of our interviewees. Knowledge, openness to your own needs and the needs of others, defines a good friendship. These are all features of the friendship ethic at its best.

Such an ethic comes into play most strongly at times of crisis and need. For many gay men, and other non-heterosexuals, the experience of the AIDS crisis has confirmed the importance of a commitment to care and mutual responsibility (cf. Adam 1992). In the literature, AIDS has been widely located as a potential catalyst in expanding definitions of family to reflect the reality of contemporary life (e.g., Levine 1991). It has also been argued that responses to the epidemic have made non-heterosexual caring relationships visible (e.g., Adam 1992), and have allowed gay 'extended families' to demonstrate their strength and durability (e.g., Bronski 1988). It has further been suggested that such relationships may be stronger and more durable than traditional family forms, because they are built on support and respect and are chosen (Bronski 1988; Plummer 1995). We agree with all these proposals. But perhaps the most important legacy of the crisis has been to demonstrate the implications of friendship. As Sullivan (1998: 175) puts it, 'I don't think I'm alone in thinking that the deepest legacy of the plague years is friendship. The duties demanded in a plague, it turned out, were the duties of friends.'

Both gay men's and other non-heterosexuals' caring responses to the crisis are regularly framed in terms of commitments that flow from a sense of loyalty to friends and belonging to 'community' (Heaphy, Weeks and Donovan 1999). As Rob comments:

> This sounds really crass, but it was just simply that I wanted to go and do something about something that was happening to a community that I belong to. And yes, I wanted to be educated, I wanted more information, but I also wanted to do something positive … whatever I could do. That's it in a nutshell, really, I think, for me. (M06)

Jackie makes a similar point:

I think it's a feeling of being part of a community and ... I just see us as part of a group who are in a minority, and we need to support each other very, very much, and I would like to support anyone who was HIV or with AIDS. (F05)

Even for those who have not had direct experience of the effects of the virus and syndrome in terms of friends or family, the impact that it has had on the gay community as a whole has led people, at a very personal level, to engage with issues to do with caring commitments. As Amy (F27) here indicates, the repercussions on both the community and the individual are often closely linked: 'it does make you think about all those issues about caring. About what would happen if you became chronically ill. All that stuff about death ... all the taboo subjects.' Luke concurs with her sentiments:

> I am more aware of people, of feelings. I am more aware of the importance of friendship – of relationships. I am more aware of the need for trust, and being dependable. ... When people around us have died – you know, the people that we have known – the love has been there to start with. And ... when you've got that relationship with somebody ... there's something inside that tells you there is more love needed or less love needed. You need to be more involved or less involved. You need to be more supportive or less supportive. I think that's always been there, and I think that AIDS and HIV have specifi- cally made it more important so far as friends are concerned. (M04)

If community in the broadest sense provides a 'vocabulary of values' for those involved, as we argue in Chapter 4, it also gives rise to smaller worlds where friendships are engaged. As William (M03) says, 'it [AIDS] makes some relation- ships more intense because they are inevitably going to be foreshortened'. Severe illness makes one aware of one's involvement with and need for others. It also, however, threatens one's sense of absolute freedom to do as one wants. Here, Mollie discusses the dilemmas she would face caring for someone in a crisis situation:

> If I've got concerns around it [caring for someone], it would be of getting stuck into something that was too restrictive with the people I'm closest to, and that does frighten me very slightly. ... I would certainly go ahead and do it, I mean, I'd try and get other people to help so it wasn't too big a strain, and I would certainly feel responsible, definitely. But I would be worried how I felt about the relationship. I would worry in case I felt too tied down. I don't mean I wouldn't do it, but I do think it might make me miserable. And I'd be frightened they'd notice. (F30)

Reflexive honesty of this kind simply confirms that, no matter how altruistic someone is, we are not saints. What it also demonstrates, however, is a sense of what needs to be done in extreme situations, dramatised by life-threatening illness. This is simply an extension of what friends seek to do in ordinary day-to- day situations, as they work through the implications of what it is to be a friend.

The significance of the friendship ethic

We have argued in this chapter that a friendship ethic, based on notions of individual autonomy *and* mutual involvement, is the key feature of the contemporary non-heterosexual world. For many people, friendships are like a family, or are an alternative, chosen family. Others reject the loaded term 'family', while acknowledging the reality: the existence of a complex vocabulary of values which acts as the moral cement for non-heterosexual lives. We have argued two things simultaneously: first, that in many ways non-heterosexual patterns are similar to the broader patterns of kin relationships as revealed by recent research; but, second, that the value of negotiated relationships and emotional democracy is heightened for non-heterosexuals by their continued marginalisation. The result is an intricate and sophisticated set of beliefs and behaviour which provides the necessary underpinning for moral agency in an uncertain world. This is what we call the friendship ethic.

These values do not, of course, emerge spontaneously from each individual encounter. Each relationship, each friendship network, is inevitably different, but there are enough general features to justify Blasius' (1994) argument for the existence of a distinctive ethos among non-heterosexuals, which we suggest stems from a wider sense of belonging. As we propose in the following chapter, the friendship ethic has the reality it does because it is rooted in the values of community, and the 'social capital' which derives from community.

4 In search of home

The different meanings of 'home'

The heterosexual assumption has long informed expectations about how we, as individuals, live at given times in our lives. It has also underpinned the belief that there are two primary forms of home life: the one in which we grow up in with our family of origin; and the one we create as adults, through 'settling down' and forming a family of our own. This, of course, implies getting married and raising children. But contemporary home and family life have proved to be far more complex entities. Families break up, recombine, and recombine again. More people live alone than ever before, due to separation, divorce, bereavement or simply choice (Hall and Ogden 1997; Hall, Ogden and Hill 1999). The everyday lives of many people, both heterosexual and non-heterosexual, no longer follow established patterns. Increasingly, we have little choice but to forge our own ways of living.

If the concept of home once conjured up the security of a given place and forms of belonging, in today's more fragmented world it appears to many that the security this offered is rapidly being lost. The decline of 'the family meal', which 'helps to steady our lives in these chaotic times' (Alibhai-Brown 1999: 4), has come to symbolise the dispersed relationships that characterise our society. This invites the question: 'if families cannot eat together, can they stay together?' One would think not, if one were to listen and accept all the prophecies of gloom that are so often voiced. But like so many images hovering over the 'declining family', this is an overly pessimistic picture. New securities are also becoming possible – through the homes and belongings that are being created from scratch, through contemporary life experiments.

First home

Non-heterosexuals often have no choice but to create their own notions of home, which are inevitably coloured by their memories of their first home. Thomas, who is 29, white and gay, has memories tinged with the golden hue of nostalgia:

> I'd loved living at home so much and loved my family – you know, mother and father and what have you. Growing up was ... great. It was fabulous. You know, you always have memories of long hot summers ... which don't seem to happen any more, do they? ... [I] had a great childhood – fabulous. (M01)

Jill, who is 46, white and a lesbian, has very similar recollections:

> I grew up in [name of place] – very white, middle class. I'm the eldest of three. I've got a brother who's five years younger than me and a sister who's ten years younger. [I had] A very happy home life – *very* happy, I would say. [It] was a very traditional white middle-class background ... and we were very close. We still are ... It was a very traditional, sort of fifties, after-the-war family. And as I say, I was very happy. So much so, that when I went to college in '67, I was quite homesick for a time. (F22)

As these familiar images suggest, a particularly strong element of non-heterosexual narratives involves the 'first home' (Hall Carpenter Archives 1989a, 1989b; National Lesbian and Gay Survey 1992, 1993). These are generally concerned with the places and relationships that individuals have grown up in, most often the parental home. In stories such as Thomas' and Jill's, we are presented with key elements of the 'good' home and, by implication, the 'good' family. The emphasis is on a time that has past, where home meant the love of two parents, and the 'carefree' experience of childhood. This offers a picture of a 'normal' home life, and the 'normal' family which is implicit in this scenario.

Both Thomas' and Jill's accounts resonate with traditional notions of what ideal home and family life *should* be like: the provision of shelter, a sense of emotional and physical well-being, and loving and caring relationships (Johnston and Valentine 1995: 99). In such imaginations, home is a private place that offers individuals security, sanctuary and identity – a place of freedom, where individuals and family members can be nurtured and 'be as they are'. As with narratives of home in the broader society, however, 'idyllic' accounts are all too frequently matched by memories of the 'oppressive' nature of home (Cant 1997: 9). For example, Coral provides an account of home and family that resonates with another (increasingly familiar) story of home life – that of the 'tyranny' of life behind closed doors, and the hidden side of the family (cf. Straus, Gelles and Steinmetz 1981; Straus and Gelles 1990; McGee 2000):

> My childhood was not very good. I had a lot of problems ... physical and emotional abuse, and when I was about 20 ... I thought, 'No, that's it'. That was the first time I stood up for myself, I told her [the mother] what I thought and said, 'I didn't deserve that', and I just sort of needed to get away. And I'd also wanted to come to England [from Australia], but once I decided to go, I thought, 'Yeah, I'll come here', because I needed to get a load of distance, a very long distance between us. (F13)

Home has been valorised as providing a space for individuals away from the gaze and control of others – where the protective shields constructed to negotiate everyday public life can be relaxed. But as Allan and Crow (cited in Johnston and Valentine 1995: 100) point out, 'the public world does not begin and end at the front door'. For Paul, who grew up in a West Indian family, and lived in a predominantly white, middle-class area, 'family' means much more than a simple image of the family:

> Family life was fairly stable. I think I quite enjoyed it … family was more than family because of the racial element. Family was also about a different culture, it wasn't just, you know – the private thing. (M21)

For many groups in society, especially ethnic minorities (see Mirza 1997), family is a critical defensive element in resistance to a hostile world, an essential bulwark that links you to others in similar embattled positions. It offers a sense of comfort and security, but if you are a minority within a minority, then your feelings are necessarily ambivalent. Home is vital to your well-being and survival, but it can also trap you in a set of normative values that deny your identity. Memories of first homes may be deeply ambivalent, with love of parents, siblings and other relatives mingling with suppressed desires and fears of rejection. As Bruce Voeller (cited in Muller 1987: 140) notes: 'Nowhere has the hostility to homosexuality been more frightening to large numbers of gay men and lesbians than in their own families, forcing them to feel like a minority in their own homes.'

A diversity of expert and common-sense knowledges tell us that early home life plays a major role in shaping 'who we are'. In a manner that is described by Bourdieu's (1977) work on habitus, the private arenas of early home and family life have a key role to play in informing individuals with a sense of what are appropriate and inappropriate ways of being. First home is a strategic space where habits are learned and values instilled. As Paul indicates, family and home life are likely to follow modes of operation that are structured in line with particular social and cultural values:

> it was a pattern of a West Indian family; we had domestic, well, I had, as an older child, domestic responsibilities which meant that I had to look after [my sister] quite a lot. And I had to learn to do a lot of things in the house that I noticed a lot of my friends, you know – they'd come home from school and it was, 'Where's my tea?' and, 'Oh, I've got to do my homework and then play'. I'd come home and I had various things I had to do. And so there was a degree of resentment, not so much of my parents, just of the way things were. But at the time I was absolutely powerless to change things, so I just had to get on with it. (M21)

In contrast to narratives of adult life, which focus on negotiation of choices and working out issues of power in relationships (see section on 'Everyday practices', p. 98), accounts of first home point to a different time in the life of the individual (and often to a different 'historical' time). The themes of 'powerlessness' and lack of choice that are touched on in the above quotation by Paul, are also referred to in Rachel's story, where there is a recognition of the limited choices available to children. Rachel, who is also black, remembers that:

> living communally was very, very difficult. I found it very hard, to start with. ... So I had a lot of contact with a lot of, I suppose – odd people. Although most of them were very nice. Some of them weren't, but – I didn't have any choice. ... I think the strangest thing about it was that I had a lot of independence but very little choice about my life. Which isn't unusual for 14-year-olds. But, it kind of felt like I should have all or nothing. Rather than a bit of this and a bit of that. But I did have a lot of independence and I liked that a lot. (F02)

Whether they are about exceptional or unexceptional experiences of growing up, narratives of first home concern particular notions of appropriate ways of living. They also concern the diversity of ethics and values that can underpin these. While they indicate a multiplicity of experiences, they also point to some common experiences among non-heterosexuals – not least the experience of growing up in the shadow of the heterosexual assumption. As Sam recalls:

> My family had very fixed ideas, I suppose, about what would happen when you did grow up, i.e., you grow up, you meet someone, you get married and have kids and a mortgage ... and all the rest of it. And I think ... subconsciously, that was what I was perhaps working towards. (F04)

The heterosexual assumption plays a key part in shaping a sense of what are 'appropriate' and 'natural' ways of being in the world (cf. Rich 1983; Connell 1995: 103–6; Dunne 1997: 11–18). It is not simply that individuals are 'conditioned' in line with the prevailing belief that heterosexuality is the preferable option. Rather, various processes, including socialisation in home and local community life, present heterosexuality as the only option: the commonsensical inevitability. It is rarely the case that individuals grow up with an unproblematic sense of the possibility of being non-heterosexual (Davies 1992). Home, family and community life usually assume a heterosexual outcome. Even for those who find themselves consciously at odds with the idea that they *should* be heterosexual, there are significant pressures to perform heterosexuality (Blasius 1994). This was the case for Luke, where 'home' referred to a set of relationships that included both family of origin and a broader religious community:

> I got engaged and it got to the point where I was either having to deny what I was and continue to feel as bad as I felt, and run the risk of spoiling Nicola's life. So I chose to leave [his town], basically because I went back to the church and I told the bishop how I felt and he told me I had a choice,

either to leave or be excommunicated. And so I chose to leave – and leave [his town] because if I had stayed in my home town, my parents would have known that I was not going to church. And they would have wondered why and it was only a matter of time before they got to know. So to protect them, I left and came to [the city] and that was distance enough between us to allow me to live my life, and be happy and protect them from the realisation of me being gay. (M04)

Silence and invisibility are recurrent themes with regard to the possibilities of living as non-heterosexuals (Hall Carpenter Archives 1989a, 1989b; Weeks and Porter 1998). Luke's story describes the pressures at play to publicly perform heterosexuality through marriage, or to maintain the 'heterosexual panorama' (Blasius 1994) through the silence and invisibility that would result from his absence from home. Not surprisingly then, there can exist a sense of 'crisis' when the individual's sense of who they are is at odds with the expectations of those around them. As Davies suggests:

the man [*sic*] on the brink of coming out … inhabits a social matrix, a social structure which assumes, expects, and enforces heterosexuality … the individual is faced with a psychic dilemma: the contradictions between the expectations of society and its creation: himself.

(Davies 1992: 76)

The power of the heterosexual assumption is partly based on the degree to which silence can breed silence, and the extent to which the problem of non-heterosexual desires are generally not a topic of discussion. As Juliet recounts:

there were not any positive role models at all … images of lesbians and gay people generally were very stereotypical and were not something I identified with at all. So, basically, I thought I was a boy [laughs]. I thought I should have been a boy. And that kind of went on, I think, until maybe I was about 16, 17, 18, by which time I realised that clearly that wasn't the case, and that I was a lesbian – although I kind of struggled a lot with that for a long time. … So, basically I had a bit of a kind of struggle, again with that. But – you know, it was kind of internal upheaval – I didn't discuss it with anybody. (F01)

Where the values in operation in first home are in tension with 'who' the individual is becoming as an adult, there can exist a strong incentive to leave. Cant (1997) suggests that moving away from the family home is most acutely experienced as freedom when the relationships and the values that reside there are experienced as a prison. At its most extreme, the desire among young non-heterosexuals to move out and move away can be informed by the need 'to escape the shame which you believe your homosexuality will bring to you and your family' (Cant 1997: 6). A variety of other factors that are unrelated to one's sexual identity can, of course, inform the decision to leave home: to seek employment; to attend university; or simply to be independent. Even for those who come out at home and receive a degree of acceptance, leaving can still be the attractive option. Irrespective of the nature of family and community relationships, and the reluctance or desire that individuals might have in leaving home, this event can often mark the opening up of new choices.

Moving out, or moving away, can be a key step in seeking new horizons (Coyle 1991; Davies 1992). It can provide the opportunity for the freedom to shape a new life. For individuals like Luke, this can be the freedom to begin to create a new home with others who can become a new family. In short, this can be a time for developing new ways of seeing the world, new relationships with others, and new ways of seeing oneself. As Jackie recounts:

> I went to London and then life changed completely … I suddenly realised these were different people and I could talk to them – and I'd never talked to anybody on that level in my whole life. I mean, never, never, never, never. And I was 19 then. And then this Japanese girl wanted to go off travelling so we went off for ten months. We went to Australia and all over Europe working and, you know – just going all [out] … And that sort of changed me, really. I came back ten months later and I was just a very different person.(F05)

Away from the everyday scrutiny of family and community of origin, the new (social and/or geographical) location can offer the opportunity to experiment (Weston 1991). As Peter recounts:

> [I] came away to college and that was it – I just went completely mad and went out with this very nice bloke called Archie for a little while and got into gaysoc and that was it – I was up and away. (M11)

Leaving first home is often (though not always) a key moment in the coming out process. On the brink of coming out few individuals live in homes or social structures of their own choosing. However, as Davies (1992) suggests, they can and will change familiar structures through a process of social relocation to different places, different social networks, and different social and sexual contexts. Through social relocation, opportunities exist for rethinking the values that individuals have grown up with, including those that underpin heterosexual ways of being in the world (cf. Weston 1991; Dunne 1997; Heaphy, Weeks and Donovan 1999). Leaving first home, then, can be one crucial step towards becoming '*in a real sense, a different person*' (Davies 1992: 77, emphasis in the original).

Tales of the city

Migration from home has long brought opportunities for the development of non-heterosexual identities (Chauncey 1994; Weston 1995; Bech 1997; Cant 1997). But as Cant suggests, it can also confront individuals with 'a major

responsibility to create new ways of living for themselves and to invent identities
that are sustainable in a world of flux' (1997: 100). A common story among
many non-heterosexuals is that of moving to what can be termed the 'queer city'
(Hall Carpenter Archives 1989a, 1989b; Cruikshank 1992; Bech 1997; Cant
1997; Weston 1991, 1995). For some this has meant a significant geographical
move; for others it can imply a new engagement with different social spaces
within the cities where they grew up. The city has a key role to play in lesbian
and gay folklore. Historically, it has provided the space for the formation of non-
heterosexual selves, and of homosexual forms of socialising (Chauncey 1994;
Bech 1997; Higgs 1999; see also Adam 1992: 175–7). As Weston (1995: 262)
points out, since the Industrial Revolution, a symbolic contrast has been
constructed between the rural and urban: whereby the city is castigated 'for its
artificiality, anonymity, and sexual license', and the country is lauded as the
location of 'nature, face-to-face relations, and "tradition" '. Commenting on her
own research, she recounts:

> In their stories, gay people who had migrated to the city often recapitulated
> this contrast, but they were also quick to revalue its terms. As they began to
> reposition themselves as lesbian, gay, bisexual, or queer, the city as a locus of
> iniquity became something that appeared to work *for* rather than *against*
> them. Its reputation for sexual license promised room for experimentation,
> its anonymity a refuge from the discipline of small-town surveillance … For
> people exploring same-sex sexuality in the years following World War II, the
> city became the place to be, not the place to flee.
>
> (Weston 1995: 262–3)

For non-heterosexuals, the city offers a laboratory for experimentation
(Castells 1983; Levine 1979; Herdt 1992). As Cruikshank suggests, the exodus of
gay men and lesbians from cities and rural areas all over the US and their
relocation in San Francisco in the 1970s showed that gay identity could be the
centre of one's life (Cruikshank 1992: 134). While the American and British
experience are significantly different in this regard, the 1990s have seen the
growth of key queer spaces within British cities, such as London and Manchester
(Eisenstadt and Gatter 1999). Living or socialising in these areas can allow for a
strong sense of belonging in a safe space. For example, James believes that:

> in [name of city] I think we're spoiled because there are places that we go
> in; there's a community, there's a group of friends, there's a network. That's
> important. And we live a gay relationship – almost in a completely different
> culture – which I think people in that sort of environment do. (M02)

People quite simply adapt to their queer neighbours, as Luke explains:

> [The heterosexual] neighbours haven't expressed any dislike or dissatisfaction
> with having two poofs in the street, but considering that there's two poofs,

there's two sets of lesbians, there's a gay household of students and there's a transsexual in the same street – you know – it's like *Tales of the City*. (M04)

There is a strong argument that the emergence of 'the homosexual' as a distinct type of being (Weeks 1977/1990) would have been an impossibility without the city. Bech (1997) has suggested that the moment the (male) homosexual steps out of the heterosexual social world in an effort to 'realise himself', he steps *into* an urban form of existence:

> The city is the social world proper of the homosexual, his life space; it is no use objecting that lots of homosexuals have lived in the country. Insofar as they wish to be homosexual, the vast majority must get out into 'the city' one way or another.
>
> (Bech 1997: 98)

This is a 'truth' that is confirmed in the stories of many non-heterosexuals who live in urban areas. In these stories it is not merely that the city offers a place of anonymity – away from the oppressive and limiting gaze of others – but also that it offers possibilities for places and spaces to meet and socialise with others, and to develop a diversity of relationships. For some it also offers a sense of the possibilities of building a protected space, as James highlights:

> I think actually that the [couple] relationship – our extended circle of friends – and living where we choose to live – is a haven. If we were to be dumped ten or twenty miles out of [this city] into a little village, I think we'd be aware of what we have – because what we've constructed around us … is a society that is a haven. And … when I'm away I realise what I'm miss-ing. Because I'm in an exclusively heterosexual environment then. (M02)

Non-heterosexual spaces within cities can provide the places or 'scenes' that can be important to the individual's sense of belonging. These play a crucial role in facilitating the formation of sexual involvements, friendships, partnerships and social networks, and can offer the promise of a new and 'freer' life. They also, however, have the potential for a different sense of isolation. As Binnie (1995: 196) notes, the development of gay spaces in cities such as London are a significant moment for queer cultural confidence, but are off limits to those who cannot afford them, or do not buy into a certain conception of what constitutes a 'gay lifestyle'. While the queer city may be sought out for the new connections it promises, great expectations can lead to significant disappointments. As Jonah, age 30, recounts:

> sometimes as a gay man, especially in London, you find … there are labels and there are ways of saying things amongst the community of men them-selves and sometimes that can be very hard to deal with, you know, that can be very lonely. Because if you find you don't fit that slot, well then, you don't

– you can't operate in that world ... if you're not visible ... if there are things that interest you more than what it is you should be interested in as a gay man. (M41)

The urban queer lifestyle is not to all tastes. And, despite Bech's (1997) polemic about the significance of the city, it is not *only* the urban environment that offers itself as home to non-heterosexuals and queer networks. Knopp (1995: 149) suggests that because the density and cultural complexities of cities have led to an understanding of sexual diversity as being a particularly urban phenomenon, this has meant that the existence of different sexualities within small towns and rural environments has been ignored and under-researched. In a similar vein, Kramer (1995: 213) suggests that the academic and research literature on the particular circumstances of homosexuality in rural and non-metropolitan areas has been underdeveloped. This has implications for our understandings of how rural and non-metropolitan spaces are negotiated by non-heterosexuals, and the gaps that might exist between rural and urban experiences. As Kramer (1995: 212) notes, rural and non-metropolitan lesbians and gay men can be more hindered in their search for identity and community than those living in urban areas. However, in a concluding discussion of his own research on rural homosexuality he states that, 'while a gap still exists between non-metropolitan lesbians and gay men and their urban counterparts, this discrepancy may be narrowing, thereby providing them with expanded choices concerning the environments, identities and lifestyles they wish to adopt' (Kramer 1995: 213).

In practice, many possibilities do exist, as Pat, a 34-year-old lesbian who lives with her lover in a small town, indicates in describing non-heterosexual life in her area:

> there are quite a few gay people living here – some who are totally closeted and others who aren't. Yeah ... I would say it's a very small ... a very, *very* small community [laughs]. But there are a few of us about and it's good to know that we're there ... there's Laurence and Liam who live just along the road, who are [her son] David's dads, and Justin who lives just further on ... [and] Ally and Beth, you know, we all seem to be living along here at the moment. But there are other people, as well, in [town] ... But there's nothing structured. (F36)

Even the most remote geographical areas can have informal non-heterosexual networks in operation. Although major cities appear to have much more to offer for lesbian, gay, bisexual or queer life, for some, the images of anonymity, loneliness and artificiality they can conjure up are far from attractive. Non-metropolitan and rural environments increasingly offer the opportunity for belonging and the formation of non-heterosexual networks or communities, but also for forms that transcend heterosexual/homosexual dichotomies. In an era of increasing queer confidence, some rural areas are witnessing the emergence of identities and communities that were historically formed in the city. This can be the result of an effort by individuals to be accepted for 'who they are' in their communities of origin. As Cant suggests:

> The identities which the contributors [to his book] have invented for themselves are the products of both the community into which they were born and the lesbian and gay community. They cherish, to varying degrees, the fact that they belong to these two communities. Their refusal to deny their sexuality in the community of origin and their refusal to deny their origins in the lesbian and gay communities is an enriching element for both.
>
> (Cant 1997: 15)

If a key historical challenge facing non-heterosexuals has been to build community places and spaces that were *separate* from the heterosexual world, and that could be a haven of safety, another challenge in the contemporary world is about experimenting with the possibilities of 'merging' communities. Acknowledging the importance of different forms of belonging (either related to sexual identity or not), and that they are *not* necessarily mutually exclusive (Cant 1997), can bring new demands and new challenges to the fore. The tendency has been to locate non-urban locations and communities as the places where repressive heterosexuality is strongest, and where the heterosexual assumption is most effective in silencing and making invisible the reality of non-heterosexual existence. It would appear, however, that some non-heterosexuals are prepared to take 'new' risks in openly creating homes in the heart of heterosexual spaces. As Rob indicates:

> We've always been open ... We're talked about in the village, we know. But we've never had any problems whatsoever. God knows what they say about us! But that doesn't bother me. ... I mean, we've been round [to the local bar] with very camp friends and been absolutely pissed, and I dread the next time I go in there. You know, Owen shouting, 'Diane, when are you going to open it up as a gay bar?' ... And all these very naff straights around. It doesn't matter when you're pissed, does it? But we're very close with the people here. (M06)

What makes the risk possible is the sense of confidence that comes from the identification with a wider sense of community.

Reflexive community

In relocating and coming out of the heterosexual selves they have been allocated, non-heterosexuals *come into* new communities (Blasius 1994; Weeks 1995). Community can refer to a broad range of relationships with other lesbians, gay men and bisexuals, and for some it has a solid geographical base (Dunne 1997; Eisenstadt and Gatter 1999). Many individuals share Peter's (M11) feelings as outlined in Chapter 2 – that they exist and operate within strong local lesbian and gay communities. Like Peter, they are at pains to emphasise that these are not merely imagined, but, instead, have a 'real' existence in particular geographical spaces. Angela similarly recounts:

> I moved to an area where I knew people who were lesbians. … And this area's quite a lesbian and gay friendly area, there are quite a lot of us live round here. So yeah, I moved into an area where I knew people. And since then, now other lesbian and gay men have moved into these blocks of flats and this area. … You all get to see each other quite frequently, even if it's just calling in for a cup of tea on the way home from work, you know, rather than a date or anything. (F28)

For others, community conjures up a broader set of relationships, embracing a positive idea of belonging and a sense of loyalty – 'the fact that we share a lot of discrimination and there's a bond I can't describe', says Pat (F36). This makes for a sense of excitement, as well as a feeling that there might be allies in unexpected places. As Jill indicates:

> you could say that the lesbian and gay community [in Jill's town] is family in a funny way too – they can be family. There are times when, you know, you feel this is where you want to be and those are the people you want to talk to and be around. … When you think that you're the only one out there and there's not many others, and then suddenly you discover there are loads – that's a great feeling and you want to encompass it in some way. (F22)

There are strong overlaps between narratives of community and narratives of family, friendship and political affinities. The friendship ethic (see Chapter 3) in particular, is often seen as a basis for community. As Bev Jo (1996, in Weinstock and Rothblum 1996: 288–91) put it in the title of an article, 'Lesbian friendships create lesbian community'. Kitzinger (1996: 298), also referring to women, argues that 'friendships (like relationships between lovers) are much more than simply individual private affairs: they are the building blocks of lesbian communities and politics'. Stanley (1996) concurs, suggesting it is a unique feature of lesbian life that women come together across the bounds of difference to create a community. For many, what Raymond (1986) describes as a 'passion for friends' is the very essence of a feminist politics. Similarly, Nardi (1999) sees gay male friendships as the basis for both community and political mobilisation among gay men. Our own research participants frequently acknowledge the significance of this empowering energy, but also signal that it goes beyond politics. Sue, who is 28, observes:

> Well, Greek women running around throwing themselves off cliffs and, you know, [the] feminist part, which is all very good, and it is a very important part of the history of lesbianism and what have you, but it's just sort of moving on from there and defining your own space and where your head's

at. And although I'm still a feminist, you know, that's the past and we're sort of, it's moving on from there really. (F14)

Similarly, for many men, friendship, community and political activity blend in a seamless whole, especially when the achievements of recent years seem threatened. What some have called the 'communities of the night', that is gay men linked by casual sexual interaction, have been central in the fight against AIDS (King 1993).

However, as the earlier comments by Peter (M11) suggest, the idea of a lesbian and gay community is a contested one. For many writers it is a myth. In Alan Sinfield's (1999) book *Gay and After*, for example, under 'community' in the index, it states 'see subculture', implying that this sociological term sufficiently encompasses the idea of community. But as his text actually suggests, the idea of community has a much wider salience for non-heterosexuals than simply a series of meeting places and networks in the interstices of a wider society. The importance of a sense of community built around social networks and friendships has been well documented as one of the major factors giving rise to the lesbian and gay movement in the US from the late 1960s (D'Emilio 1983), and this has been traced elsewhere, among women as well as men. Schuyf (1992) suggests that Gagnon and Simon were the first to use the term 'lesbian community' in 1967: 'by which they meant not actual spatial communities but loosely organised groups of lesbians whose prime function was mutual support' (1992: 53). In the Netherlands in the 1950s, lesbian communities were organised as cliques of typically ten to fifteen members, varying according to lifestyle, for example butch-femme, bar dancers, ordinary people, romantic friendships, intermittent lovers of women. Even in an embryonic form, we can see here the complexity of friendships and patterns of life that characterise contemporary non-heterosexual spaces. But in thinking of non-heterosexual communities it is perhaps more useful to think of community as a wider sense of belonging, containing a variety of smaller overlapping social worlds (cf. Jamieson 1998). Weeks (1996) has argued that:

> the idea of a sexual community may be a fiction, but it is a necessary fiction: an imagined community, an invented tradition which enables and empow- ers. It provides the context for the articulation of identity, the vocabulary of values through which ways of life can be developed, the accumulated skills by which new possibilities can be explored and hazards negotiated, and the context for the emergence of social movements and political campaigns which seek to challenge the existing order.
>
> (Weeks 1996: 83–4)

Blasius (1994) has similarly suggested that the lesbian and gay struggles since the 1960s have produced a sense of identity and community which provides the context for moral agency, and hence for the emergence of a distinctive lesbian and gay ethos enacted in everyday life. Non-heterosexual communities, we would argue, can be best understood as forms of what Lash (1994) describes as 'reflexive' communities:

> first, one is not born or 'thrown', but 'throws oneself' into them; second, they may be widely stretched over 'abstract' space, and also perhaps over time; third, they consciously pose themselves the problem of their own creation, and constant re-invention, far more than traditional communities; fourth, their tools and products tend not to be material, but abstract and cultural.
>
> (Lash 1994: 161)

For Lash, community is first and foremost 'a matter of shared meanings'. But reflexive community is also about shared core concerns – which include the generation of resources for living (Heaphy 1999). A key set of resources provided by non-heterosexual communities are those which enable the development of non-heterosexual forms of living. In coming out, non-heterosexuals choose to reject the heterosexual assumption, and in so doing become involved in creating new knowledge of how it is possible to be in the world. Indeed, in recent years there has been a dramatic expansion of local knowledges about what it means to be lesbian or gay. To come out in present-day western societies is to encounter a wealth of local knowledges on *how* it is possible to be as non-heterosexuals. These are available in a broad spectrum of arenas where non-heterosexuals have been active in producing knowledge about themselves and their ways of living. In effect, they concern the negotiation of the question of who and what 'we' are, and how 'we' can be. They can come in various forms, including: academic research; fiction; self-help guides; the visual arts; and other forms of popular culture. While they can be of an overtly political nature, they are also of a life political nature, such as: guidebooks on coming out; texts on relating in same sex couples; manuals on negotiating parenting; guides on health management, and so on (see Blasius 1994: 212).

What is crucial is that these local knowledges represent a form of knowledge about what 'we' are and can be, and as such are distinct from other 'expert' knowledges on living that shore up the story that heterosexuality is the only way of being (Giddens 1991, 1992). Indeed, these have developed historically in opposition to various expert knowledges that proffered the notion of heterosexuality as *the* appropriate way of being, and that have told the story (to homosexuals themselves) of the problematic nature of homosexuality. These are narratives of how 'we' know it can be, and are a crucial resource in informing individuals' visions of what they can become. Also, as Plummer (1995) has outlined (see Chapter 1), *personal* narratives have a central role to play as resources for developing non-heterosexual ways of living. For Plummer (1995: 87–91) the power of personal narratives, such as coming out narratives, is that they are bound up with the making of identities and communities. The reflexive nature of storytelling means that these narratives are both influenced by, and influence, the localities they come from and are told to. Personal narratives, in this scheme, need communities to hear them if they are to become strong stories, but communities themselves are built through such storytellings. Strong stories, Plummer (1995: 174) argues, gather people around them and attract audiences who themselves become storytellers. Through the 'telling of the tale' there exists the possibility of building commonalities in terms of perceptions, languages and ways of existing.

The issue of AIDS once again can throw a piercing light on this process, revealing the degree to which reflexive communities, such as non-heterosexual communities, can provide the context through which a broad diversity of (economic, cultural and social) resources can be accessed and generated by its members (Weeks 1996). This, and the 'vocabulary of values' which underpins non-heterosexual communities, are evident in both gay men's and lesbians' caring responses to the crisis, which are regularly framed in terms of commitments that flow from a sense of belonging to 'community' (see Chapter 3). As Weeks (1996) has suggested, responses to AIDS by the group most affected in the West have validated reflexive community as a crucial resource for affirming, supporting and sustaining identities. They have also indicated a significant accumulation of social capital by these communities – evident in caring and political responses. Social capital refers to key social skills that exist in the various communities which make up an increasingly complex and pluralistic society (see Fukuyama 1995; Wan 1995; Weeks 1996). These skills, which are deployed in a variety of community-based activities, have been central in enabling lesbian and gay communities to assume significant control over the threats that AIDS represented to them in the mid-1980s. While these threats included illness and death, they also included the possibility of a remedicalisation, and new marginalisation, of non-heterosexual sexualities. While reflexive communities may be imagined communities, responses to AIDS indicate that they can facilitate empowerment and transformation. Blasius has suggested that:

> The politics of AIDS has shown how the institutions of the gay and lesbian community ... have empowered lesbian and gay community through grassroots mobilisation, institution building, and advisory participation in public and corporate decision making. ... As an assertion of lesbian and gay rights, the politics of AIDS is framed as the 'third moment' of contemporary lesbian and gay politics: that of equity.
>
> (Blasius 1994: 170)

To a significant degree, this is due to the social capital a sense of community generates, and the ways in which this builds on and further generates other forms of (economic and cultural) capital.

Multiple belongings

Community for non-heterosexuals, we have suggested, can be both a place and a practice (Eisenstadt and Gatter 1999). Jill (F22), for example, feels part of a gay community in two ways: the wide sense of community represented for her by the annual lesbian and gay Pride celebrations, embracing the idea of the gay community as a whole as 'family'; and in a more particular sense in the town where she lives, and where she works on the local lesbian and gay help-line. But achieving a sense of community is not always possible. Coral (F13), for example, shares the values but feels cut off from the physical community living in the suburbs. Others are alienated from the community because of an awareness of its own discriminations, as we saw in Chapter 3. The non-heterosexual communities, despite their best aspirations, are bisected by the same forms of prejudice as wider society: in terms of class, race and ethnicity, able-bodiedness, and age. Lilly, aged 67 (F47), as described in Chapter 3, thinks she is 'too old' to feel part of the community. At the end of the 1960s and in the early 1970s, she and her partner were immersed in the rather 'less salubrious' aspects of the lesbian community in her home city, as she describes it, but after some time decided to discontinue their involvement. Her sense of involvement in the wider non-heterosexual world continues through participation in the Quaker lesbian and gay fellowship and the lesbian and gay Christian movement.

The reference to 'less salubrious' parts of the non-heterosexual social world reminds us that the community is not free of its own divisions on questions of sexual practice. Sue, who identifies as a sadomasochist, observes:

> I do find that I've been judged down by the wider [lesbian and gay] community and that my *personal* sexual practices give them something to judge me for. And for me, that experience is exactly the same as coming out within the heterosexual society – it's the same kind of judgement – in that what I do in my private time, and how I express myself sexually, is an area for wider judgement. Even down to lesbian strength marches, where S&M dykes weren't allowed to march. It goes back a long way. So I guess, in that way I don't feel part of the wider community. (F15)

Annie (F40), on the other hand, has become alienated from the gay community *because of* what she sees as its acceptance of sadomasochism and its defence of male cruising.

There are communities within community, reflecting diversity but also divisions. Community values can make many people feel trapped as much as empowered, and they seek escape (Weeks 1995). Or they have to live with conflicting loyalties, as the example of religious affiliations suggests. Faith communities can play an important part for many non-heterosexuals, both within and outside, or even against the lesbian and gay community. Many Jewish lesbians and gays have found solace within their faith, and spaces within organised Jewry for exploring both their sexuality and their beliefs. Similarly, Christians of various denominations find their faith an essential component of their identities. Quakers especially have found fellowship and acceptance with their own, and have made use of Quaker blessings of one-to-one relationships. Both Lilly (see above) and Dan (M44; see Chapter 5) have gained support and strength through their Quaker involvements. Other denominations are, however, more conflictual: in 1998 the world-wide Anglican Communion voted to reaffirm traditional Bible-based teaching against homosexuality. Backed by strong African and American conservative theology, the titular head of the Anglican Communion, the Archbishop of Canterbury, reaffirmed his belief that there was 'no room in the holy Scriptures for any sexual activity outside holy matrimony of a husband and wife' (quoted in *Guardian*, 6 August 1998). Yip's (1997) study of gay couple relationships demonstrates the complex intertwining of continued commitment to the Church and dissidence within it. Yip quotes Robert, a gay Church of England priest: 'I think it is important to me that God is part of the relationship, especially because psychologically speaking, there is so much to undermine your security' (Yip 1997: 13). Ironically, a large part of the insecurity seems to stem from his own church.

On the other hand, lesbian theologian Elizabeth Stuart (1995) has argued that the lesbian and gay community provides models of friendship that undermine the Christian emphasis on heterosexuality and marriage. Lesbian and gay people, she argues:

> may have some important insights to contribute to creative theological reflection of that crisis [of the family] – most notably in the expansion of the understanding of friendship to include our most intimate and commit-ted relationships.
>
> (Stuart 1995: xii)

Stuart sees a model of friendship in the life of Jesus, and a continuous thread of 'sexual subversion' that goes through the Hebrew scriptures 'like an underground stream that bursts to the surface in the Christian gospel, sweeping away dominant models of relating and replacing them with models based on friendship' (Stuart 1995: xiv; see also her comments in Stuart 1997). A strong spiritual element does indeed underline the move for commitment ceremonies and religious blessings of couple relationships, which several of our research participants have either contemplated or undertaken (see Chapter 5; cf. Goss and Strongheart 1997). Yet many individuals continue to experience a genuine conflict between different senses of belonging as a result of their faith. Sarah, aged 31, identifies as bisexual, and because she is deeply religious, struggles with this. Her priest believes homosexuality is wrong, and Sarah (F23) thinks that 'ultimately he's right … my own personal faith would agree with him, but my own personal sexuality disagrees with him'. As a result, she has to juggle her sexual life with her faith.

The notion of community is clearly powerful, offering a context and a wider sense of belonging in which friendships can flourish. However, it is also a potential site of conflict, in which different senses of belonging clash. Relation-ships inevitably have to weave in and through these complex social relations, reflecting an increasingly diverse social world. It is perhaps not surprising, therefore, that many people regard the idea of community as a myth. Our own participants, however, demonstrate the power of the narrative of community belonging. Even when it is rejected as a reality, the ideal remains the basic point of reference. What many people seem to want is the ideal of community as a resource: as a focus of identity, as a repository of values, as accumulated social resources through which the necessary skills for survival are acquired, and as a basis for political mobilisation as and when necessary (Weeks 1996).

Ways of living

Community, we argue, can provide a sense of belonging, but it alone cannot provide a new home in the practical sense of the term. Home-building can draw on the social capital and skills acquired in the non-heterosexual world, but each individual, couple or group necessarily does it in their own way, in the practices of everyday life. Experiences of early home life, negative as well as positive, matter. Far from being 'a medium of expression of individuality, a site of creativity and a symbol of self', the parental home is often the site where non-heterosexuals first learn of the necessity to 'pass' and become skilled in the performance of heterosexuality (Voeller, cited in Muller 1987: 140). Performance as a non-heterosexual, however, requires new practical resources. Bell (1991: 325) reminds us that the housing designed and built in the nineteenth and twentieth centuries was constructed for the heterosexual family. Home, as a place or set of relationships, is infused with, and shaped by, the heterosexual assumption – in 'doing' home there are multiple and constant pressures to 'do' heterosexuality. As Johnston and Valentine's (1995: 104) discussion of the home life of lesbians indicates, for the majority of non-heterosexuals, 'the freedom to be at home' is best met when they create and manage their own domestic situations – but this often involves quite difficult practical choices.

If non-heterosexuals' narratives of first home concern both the idyllic and the oppressive, this is also often the case in stories of the domestic environments which individuals create for themselves. Themes of security and belonging, therefore, consistently re-emerge. Mark (M18) and Greg (M17), for instance, strongly emphasise this:

Greg: Yes – it's somewhere safe. This is home, and this is our home, so no matter what goes on outside …

Mark: It always feels safe and secure, and you always feel wanted.

Greg: So yes, to that extent the home and the relationship is a haven, because it doesn't matter what you have to deal with out there, you can actually come back and unload it on to the other person and share it, and deal with it, and sort it. Rather than coming back ratty.

Frankie (F41) and Annie (F40) are of a similar opinion:

Frankie: It's home when – like you've got everybody around you that you care about.

Annie: It feels safe. I mean, the house before this [one], where I was sharing [never felt safe]. I never realised that until I moved to a place that was safe and then I suddenly realised I'd never been safe before. So that place felt like home for a few years and then things changed. And now this feels [safe]. And then Frankie is here as well.

Home can be thought of as a sanctuary, particularly for those who are not publicly open about their sexuality: 'You feel you've been, you know, creating a war out there. And it's so nice to come back here and think, "Oh, thank God I'm home" ' (Sam, F04). This is not to suggest that safety and sanctuary are a universal theme. As Annie (F40) indicates, for some individuals major insecurities can be caused by the hard facts of housing tenure, such as short-term rental agreements: 'I've been living like that for eighteen years, so ... I'm actually finding it really hard now.' For others, such as Coral (F13) who lives in a hostile area, the surrounding environment can be threatening. However, even for those who have little choice about where they live, and who are not at ease in their geographical surroundings, a sense of home can be created in a hostile (or even homophobic) environment. Jane (F07) and Dee (F06), for example, feel this way about their home:

Jane: Well, after – I mean, even after saying that we're not happy living in the place that we are [in] – it is our home, and it does feel like home. We've made it our home.
Dee: When we go away we get really excited about coming back again! We go, 'Oh! Our house again', and we run round. Even if it's just been a day, we just can't wait to get back. I mean, I really like it when I come back after I've been on holiday.

Of course, for those who can afford to choose where they live, and those who have secure accommodation through public housing, there can be an added sense of security in 'knowing that you actually have a home of your own' (Sue, F15). But the lack of automatic partnership rights can work against 'family' security, as Mark (M18) and Greg (M17) discuss:

Greg: At the moment it's in my name [the tenancy] because I was the person who moved in.
Mark: You did try and change it, but they won't ... see us as a couple. ... And I'm down as living here but I'm a non-dependant ...
Greg: If we'd been together at the time of getting the flat we could have been joint tenants. But at the moment it's just down as my name.
Mark: Not that we haven't tried.

A different sort of insecurity can arise with regard to home ownership when only one partner in a couple is the official home owner. Johnson (1990: 63) suggests that buying a house is a particularly important marker for practical commitment in same sex relationships. Individual ownership can lead to tensions about tenure and commitment. Rob (M06) and Scott (M07), for example, have had discussions about joint ownership, but Rob is reluctant to apply for a joint mortgage due to the possibility of being interrogated about his HIV status:

Scott: I don't think about it as much now, but it was a problem for me that it was only in Rob's name, and it's not the main reason I want to move, but I want to ... I want a house that's ...

Rob: This is your home but you still sometimes look upon this as my house.

Scott: That's right. ... So, you know, it's important for me. ... And it would be nice to get those things from the building society with both our names on.

Both for those who can afford to choose where they live and for those who cannot, making a home can require significant creativity and the negotiation of a diversity of choices (see McRae 1999). In the first case, decisions must be made about how to live – as a couple, alone, with friends, and/or as a family. While the focus here is on the living arrangements of our research participants at the time of interview, many of these individuals had already experienced – or experimented with – living in a variety of domestic formations. These arrangements are likely to be structured by the contexts in which individuals operate at particular times in their lives, and are related to such factors as employment, length of time in an area, age, relationship status, and so on. Given the diversity of possibilities available, it is surprising that the majority of work on non-heterosexual living arrangements has tended to focus on the male or female *couple* living together (see Weeks, Donovan and Heaphy 1996).

In reviewing the literature on lesbian and gay relationships in the early 1980s, Peplau (1982) suggests that female couples are more likely to live together than male couples (see Kehoe 1988; Johnson 1990). For both female and male couples, however, the period before living together can be seen as the time of dating and courtship (Tanner 1978; Berger 1990). Since there are no officially sanctioned events, such as weddings or engagements, to mark the beginning of same sex relationships, moving in together may have particular significance (Berger 1990). While many non-heterosexual men and women do not live with partners, others can rush into shared living in an attempt to solidify the relationship without considering questions of compatibility (Tanner 1978; Berger 1990; Johnson 1990). This was the case for Coral:

It was that quick, – I look back now and I think, "Oh God! You stupid idiot!" I thought I was more intelligent enough to know, but it was a very weird period that I went through. But, I would say, the good thing was that I learnt a lot about myself from that relationship. I learnt a lot of things that I wouldn't do next time. (F13)

According to some writers, the supposedly high 'divorce rate' in same sex relationships is explained by the lack of demarcation between 'choosing to commit to a partner' and 'sampling potential partners' (Johnson 1990: 74). Indeed, for some individuals the desirability of living together can be a device for demarking the potential that a particular relationship offers. Pat explains her feelings:

> Well, I knew I wanted it to be a relationship and not just sex, because of what we'd talked about beforehand. ... I felt that I could really live with this person. I mean, it was as strong as that. I could live with this person and be with this person for a long time. Well, it wasn't like, forever, but a long time. I just knew it and there's no concrete stuff, it was just a feeling. I just knew it. I don't know whether it was ... that strong for Carrie, but certainly, it just felt right. It just felt right. (F36)

Johnson (1990: 63) has argued that creating a home together 'is a particularly emotion-laden expression of practical commitment'. Over the course of developing a relationship, the decision to live together and/or to buy a house together is often of great symbolic significance (Berger 1990). For many same sex couples this is a commitment that is not entered into lightly – but practical and emotional motivations can come into play after the 'solidity' of the relationship has been established. Darryl (M19) and Sam (M20), for example, who have lived together for fifteen years, moved in together after three years:

> for me, it just seemed obvious that we should try to live together in one place, because running two places when you're together seven days a week is really stupid – financially, let alone anything else. ... And it did feel important. So when the council offered us a two bedroom flat – as a couple [we accepted]. (M19)

While much of the self-help literature on forming and managing same sex relationships acknowledges the diversity of possibilities available for domestic arrangements (e.g., Marcus 1992; Marshall 1995), in many cases it is implied that successful cohabitation is an indication of the mature or 'real' couple. Elsewhere, the authenticity of this form of relationship is enshrined in the value afforded living together through domestic partnership policies and legislation (Waaldijk 1994). This underlines the continuing strength of traditional heterosexual models of relationships. While McWhirter and Mattison's (1984) study of gay male couples was solely concerned with relationships whose 'birth' was usually recognised and marked by choosing to live together, the authors acknowledge the existence of couples who do not live together for a variety of reasons. The examples they give of such arrangements include: couples who live apart because of their jobs, family sensibilities, and mutual independence; couples who live in different geographical locations, such as cities or countries; male couples where one member is in a heterosexual marriage; and brief relationships between people which last less than one year. But even here, there is a sense of the 'inevitability' or desirability of cohabitation if individuals have free choice. Living alone, however, can make sense for a diversity of reasons. Juliet, who is not currently in a relationship, comments that,

> I moved into this house, and ... one of the things as well is spending a lot of time and energy on the house, decorating and doing various bits of DIY. And kind of – putting my own stamp on it, really. It feels very important to me, and I think I would find it very difficult to be in the position of negotiating or compromising with another person. ... I certainly can't imagine living with a lover, because I think that when things go wrong it's important that you have a stable base. (F01)

An important point here relates to our earlier discussion about the broader contexts (family/friendship/community relationships) in which people live. While Juliet talks about the joys of living alone, it is in the context of feeling part of a wider local network and not feeling 'isolated'. She says, 'although I live on my own I do like to feel in [a] kind of community residential as well'. Further, as Juliet suggests, the existence of a partner would not necessarily compromise her desire to live alone. Many people in long-term relationships choose *not* to live with committed partners. There are various benefits to be had from such arrangements – particularly in terms of maintaining independence. As Rachel (F02) states: 'it would be really difficult, if we lived together, to keep some kind of separateness about our lives and our identity – well, identities! – individuality'.

Living alone is not necessarily about being single or not in a 'permanent' relationship. As Hall and Ogden's (1997) research has indicated, this is also the case for heterosexuals. Living separately from one's partner is a choice that is increasingly being made. This has been influenced by the tendency by more young people to purchase their own homes within metropolitan cities. Equally, the choice to live alone is increasingly a more diffuse non-urban phenomenon (Hall and Ogden 1997). Unfortunately, studies such as Hall and Ogden's do not explore sexuality as a motivating or structuring factor in decision-making about living alone.

For many non-heterosexuals, living with friends can have much to offer as an example of a 'good relationship'. This is consistent with the degree to which friendship is often identified as the most 'stable' or long-lasting form of relationship (see Chapter 3). As Jonah (M41) states of his cohabiting friend: 'I mean it feels very natural – it feels very good – he's very supportive of me, you know, we have a really good relationship. It's been really important to me.' Living with a friend (or friends) can provide many of the 'goods' associated with living with a partner: love, stability, emotional support, and an equal and reciprocal relationship. But it can also require significant labour in working out the nature and boundaries of the commitment – and in resisting the broad tendency (and pressures) to equate domestic cohabitation with coupledom. As Colin (M08) and Ed (M09) explain:

Ed: A lot of people were saying … what a wonderful couple we make. And there's an awful amount of pressure suddenly came on us – to be a couple.

Colin: Yes, there was.

Ed: And we were sort of like – you start thinking then, yes, maybe you should be a couple. And then we realised just how different we were, in areas which would mean that the relationship just could not work.

Due to the intricacy of chosen kin relationships, domestic arrangements can be complex. Roy, for instance, has set up home with many of the most important people in his life: his female ex-partner, their biological and non-biological children, his ex-partner's male lover, and the latter's mother:

> I live with Anna … with Trevor, who's Anna's sexual partner – as it were, and who's someone I love. … Penny lives [here] – Trevor's mum. … And then Leslie – Leslie is our youngest, our adopted one. … And that's the household. Although we've [also] got Brad, he's the middle son who's about to go off to the States for a year abroad. You know, there's all that kind of thing. I mean, we're a very middle-class family. We're an incredibly privileged family – *families*, group of. (M30)

As Roy indicates in his comments above, co-living as a 'family', or a group of 'families', involves tensions and negotiations, even 'risk', but brings with it the benefit of positive choice. The following are comments made by one member of a household that consists of two lesbian couples and a female child:

> I believe in taking risks, and I decided, along with everybody else, to buy this house and live together. No, we – I decided, as did the other three, that we would choose our own family. And this was the family that we would choose outside of the families that we are already part of. And families have to live somewhere, and this family wanted to live in the same house. And so we bought this house. (Elisabeth, a member of one of the discussion groups)

Everyday practices

For those who are in same sex relationships, living together can mean a particular set of challenges. The everyday operation of the domestic relationship requires significant working out. It is not merely household organisation that is at stake, however, but also a whole set of values related to the heterosexual assumption. Morgan (1999: 16), as we have noted, suggests that conceptualising family in terms of practices ('doing' family) can allow for a more dynamic sense of the degree to which family is an active process. Elsewhere, Butler (1990) has directed our attention to the degree that we 'do' gender and heterosexuality through performance. The home is a crucial site where the tie between the doing of family (or the couple) and the performance of heterosexuality are linked. De Vault indicates what is at stake by focusing on 'doing gender' through domestic labour:

> Through this ongoing process, activities such as feeding, which members of society have learned to associate strongly with one gender, come to seem like 'natural' expressions of gender. This observation does not simply imply that all women engage in such activity. Some choose not to do feeding. Others improvise and negotiate, developing idiosyncratic versions of this 'womanly' work. And, of course, some men do feeding work and remain recognisable men. But as long as feeding is understood, collectively, as somehow more 'womanly' than 'manly' the work stands as one kind of activity in which 'womanliness' may be at issue.
>
> (De Vault, quoted in Benjamin and Sullivan 1996: 228)

In recent research on heterosexual home lives, there is an overriding emphasis on unchanging gender 'roles' and inequality (for exceptions see Finch and Mason 1993; Van Every 1995; Benjamin and Sullivan 1996). In contrast, the research on non-heterosexual lives, as we discuss in detail in Chapter 5, emphasises the possibilities available for egalitarian relationships (see Peplau, Venigas and Miller Campbell 1996; Weeks, Donovan and Heaphy 1996; Dunne 1997; Heaphy, Donovan and Weeks 1999). In the everyday operation of the domestic sphere, non-heterosexuals are often involved in negotiating tensions about traditional (heterosexual) values, and actively 'doing' non-heterosexuality through a rejection of gendered roles. This is particularly visible in issues related to the domestic division of labour and finances. The dominant tendency in organising domestic tasks is towards questioning traditional, highly gendered divisions of labour. This is a crucial issue in understanding the doing of non-heterosexuality within the home. As Jackie comments:

> That's what I've found incredibly easy with Sam, where I've never found with the men in relationships. ... We've fallen into a little routine which I have never experienced before, but I assume all households fall into [a routine] – but certain people do tend to do certain jobs. But they're not divided along traditional [gendered] roles. (F05)

In doing non-heterosexuality within the home, individuals are disrupting gendered assumptions which structure the heterosexual assumption. A key issue is the degree to which those in non-heterosexual domestic arrangements do gendered domestic tasks in an inconsistent manner. Even over time, where 'favoured' tasks can be allocated to individuals (McWhirter and Mattison 1984), these are likely to be mixed clusters of gendered tasks, as Rob notes:

[if] you said, 'Okay Rob, you do all the mechanics, you do the painting and decorating'. [Or] if it needed a washer on the washing machine or the taps, I would do that, because, yes, I'm very good with my hands. [Equally, you might say:] 'Oh, I see that you do cross-stitch, Scott – you do the sewing'. So this looks like real male–female role-play. But if there's a noise when we're in bed, Scott's straight downstairs – because I'm quivering under the sheets. (M06)

As Dunne (1999) remarks, a performative conception of gender as a socially situated accomplishment implies an audience. In other words, the gender of the person we are doing our gender with/for and who does it with/for us matters. It is not, she points out, that same sex relationships escape gender altogether, rather, they are formed and experienced in a different gender context to that of heterosexuals. The alternative gender dynamic underpinning same sex relationships within the home is an important factor in enabling the doing of non-heterosexuality. However, this is not to imply that there are never 'gender' conflicts. Such conflicts are most likely to occur where the relationship most closely approximates traditional heterosexual forms (cf. Finch and Mason 1993). Thomas' (M01) and James' (M02) relationship, for instance, is one of the few relationships in our research where one partner was the primary wage-earner:

James: The burden of responsibility [around the home] is on Thomas. But it's only because of the hours I work. We do talk about it, but now and again we have big arguments and then I re-adjust what I do.

Thomas: Well, it's a case of we argue about it and James says, 'Well, who's the breadwinner? So you should … do the cooking, shopping and ironing', and what have you. And I tell him, 'Well, if you want a wife – go away and marry someone'.

Even here, however, where there is a clear demarcation of the 'breadwinner', it cannot be assumed that the financially dependent partner will take on certain domestic tasks. In this case, Thomas employs conflict as a key means of disrupting the heterosexual assumptions that inform James' position.

In the majority of cases, people living together, whether as couples or as friends, have worked out clear guidelines for the management of finances. Finances have the potential to be a major issue of tension (Blumstein and Schwartz 1983; Peplau, Venigas and Miller Campbell 1996). Traditionally, the merging of finances has been seen as a marker of commitment, but separate financial lives can be symbolic of the ethic of co-independence which underlies the operation of same sex relationships. As Simon (M05) explains, in response to a question about having joint bank accounts with his ex-partner: 'No. No. That was too heterosexual.' Others, such as Darryl (M19) and Sam (M20), claim to have never thought about it:

Darryl: No. No way [laughs].
Sam: That would never occur to me to have a joint bank account – no.

While a few couples, like Rob and Scott, have 'merged' everything in a joint bank account, the most common approach is to make equal contributions to the upkeep of the household, and to manage the remaining finances individually, as in the case of Greg (M17): 'All of the ... electricity, the gas and that sort of thing are in my name. But the money and the amount needed to go out every month is totalled up and we split it fifty-fifty.' Like everything else in the non-heterosexual home, whether it is organised around a couple or friends, negotiation is a prime determinant of a successful relationship.

Home, community and care

In Chapter 3, we discussed the significance of concepts of mutual commitment among non-heterosexual people, involving complex practices of negotiated responsibilities. Central to these are the ideas of mutual care: care for the self, and care for others. The notion of the caring environment is intrinsic to popular conceptions of home. For many people living together, the doing of non-heterosexuality (and doing gender differently) can mean the conscious endeavour to create an ambience of care. Darryl (M19) says of his home that, 'friends [who] have come here say they find it a very loving and caring place and they feel very comfortable'. Making a 'very loving and caring place' might seem a quintessentially 'female goal', but here – and there are many similar examples from our interviewees – it is also among men that the objective is clearly articulated. The extensive literature on care has rightly tended to concentrate on its gendered nature, with women traditionally seen as the designated carers (Finch and Groves 1983; Dalley 1988; Graham 1991). A female ethic of care is frequently counterposed to a largely male ethic of justice, implying that men tend to be more instrumental, and women more alive to responsibilities to others (Gilligan 1982). This distinction is overwhelmingly refuted by the evidence of our own interview material. A sense of the injustices in the outside world fuels the quest for care and mutual responsibilities in the private world of the home – equally for men and for women.

As indicated throughout this chapter, however, home is more than a private place – it is often about broader communities and a wider set of belongings. Like home, the notion of community also conjures up the notion of concern for others. As we have argued above, for many non-heterosexuals and their networks, the links between home and community as the location of caring relationships have been given new credence through responses to AIDS (Heaphy, Weeks and Donovan 1999; see also Adam 1992). As Luke indicates, caring responses to the crisis of AIDS are often focused on the home:

> we both have friends who have been very ill and friends who have died – of AIDS. And we've actually discussed it with them, that we would be quite happy for them to come and stay with us. (M04)

Further, the ethic of care that informed spontaneous responses to AIDS often blurred the boundaries between community and private caring relationships, as Frank notes:

> he has taken younger boys under his wing ... and he's had three AIDS sufferers whom he's taken into his home and looked after, and he's got one at the moment. I mean, he's not there all the time but you know, he more or less says, 'feel free to stay here whenever you want, whenever you need to. Whenever you need peace and quiet or whatever'. (M36)

AIDS has raised the question of care for others, but as the following quotation from Luke (M04) demonstrates, it can also highlight the issues of care for the self:

> that extended to what would happen if it was one of us ... We'd probably be able to have a nurse or somebody to come in during the day – but we'd be at home and we'd care for each other. (M04)

However, AIDS is only the most dramatic example of the ways in which ideas of home and community are inextricably linked to caring responsibilities. Though many of those within couple relationships tend to negotiate the possibilities and practicalities of care for one another with partners (see Chapter 5), wider friendship circles or families of choice still figure highly in accounts of potential providers of care. For both heterosexual and non-heterosexual populations, questions relating to home and care arise sharply in terms of getting older. Phillipson *et al.* (1998, 1999) suggest that society has seen a shift, whereby old people, who would have once lived in a family environment, are now living alone or with married partners. Interestingly, they suggest that 'personal' communities are becoming more important for older people as alternatives to kin and neighbours – in short, that friends matter more. Grundy and Glaser (1997) point out that for the ageing generally, the risk of moving to an institution has substantially increased over time. For Bob, who is in his sixties and HIV positive, moving to sheltered housing has meant a significant break with the chosen relationships and community that had sustained him:

> I have to say I'm not very happy. And I think there's a variety of reasons for that. One is I miss Jamie, my alcoholic friend. The other is that I'm very much on my own. Perhaps, – you know, I said I liked my own company and all the rest of it – but perhaps I get too much of it here. And I'm aware that I'm probably rather isolated from the HIV point of view. ... I find it difficult to know quite what I am doing down here. Maybe it's just that I haven't made enough social connections, learned to identify with the place. But I feel very alien at the moment. Alienated. (M43)

Ill health and ageing can test to the limits the strength of home and community connections (see Dowsett 1996). For the younger generation, the combined issues of ageing, home and care require forethought and planning. Several women we interviewed refer to their perceived need for an 'old dykes' home'. The plans developed for these contingencies are likely to be consistent with the structures of relationships that individuals currently inhabit. Angela (F28), facing a hysterectomy while living on her own in a second floor flat, made a rota of friends who could support her during her recovery: 'That worked all right. That was nice because people did [quite a lot]. It was quite complicated, I had keys made for everyone.'

Planning for the future involves making commitments to others; it also highlights the value attached to caring 'for ourselves'. However, implicit in this is the desire to continue (and protect) the forms of living – and home and community lives – which individuals and networks have forged over time. Together with the risks of institutionalisation that face the ageing generally, non-heterosexuals are also faced with the risk that their ways of living can be negated by traditional caring institutions infused with the heterosexual assumption. Many of our interviewees feel they have much to lose – not least, the distinctive forms of existence which they have created for themselves.

Individuals need a sense of home and belonging most when they are vulnerable – through illness, as they grow old, when they suffer loss. But examples of need when people are vulnerable simply underline the message of this chapter. It is through the subtle ties of friendship, community and home that individuals become more than isolated atoms. The bonds that people create are essential to a confident sense of self and of mutuality, which in turn defines a meaningful life. This is true whether individuals, by choice or by circumstance, live alone, with friends, or as part of couple relationships.

5 Partnership rites

Couples

At the heart of the new narratives of family, friendship, community and home are stories of couple relationships: accounts of partnerships, the striving for equality, love, intimacy, commitment, and increasingly of same sex marriages. Here, in Plummer's (1995) phraseology, we see the greatest proliferation of new stories, and an audience who is increasingly keen to hear and tell them, recirculate them, and incorporate them into their own personal narratives – 'creating the stories of our own lives', as Paula Martinac (1998) puts it in her book, *The Lesbian and Gay Book of Love and Marriage*.

Martinac's book is just one in a growing number of texts on same sex relationships that are pouring from the printing presses, largely in the US, but increasingly from elsewhere as well. Consider these titles plucked at random off the shelves: *Lesbian Couples: Creating Healthy Relationships for the '90s* (Clunis and Green 1993), *The New Right to Love: A Lesbian Resource Book* (Vida 1996), *Intimacy between Men: How to Find and Keep Gay Love Relationships* (Driggs and Finn 1991), *The Male Couples' Guide: Finding a Man, Making a Home, Building a Life* (Marcus 1992), *Gay Male Christian Couples: Life Stories* (Yip 1997), *The Two of Us: Affirming, Celebrating and Symbolizing Gay and Lesbian Relationships* (Uhrig 1984), *Lesbian and Gay Marriage: Private Commitments, Public Ceremonies* (Sherman 1992), and so forth. Prescriptive or descriptive, self-help or confessional, psychological or sociological, they all have something in common: they seek to affirm the reality and validity of same sex partnerships, and to explore the subtleties and complexities of non-heterosexual relationships.

This public affirmation of same sex coupledom is relatively new, though of course non-heterosexual one-to-one relationships are not. Until recently, it was conventional to play down or ignore the relationships of homosexual men: a stereotype of predatory promiscuity was prevalent in the literature and in popular perceptions. By contrast, lesbians were seen as more likely to form couple relationships, and this difference was strongly related to assumptions about different male and female sexual and emotional needs (for a discussion of this, see Gagnon and Simon 1974). There was also a prevalent stereotype about the inegalitarian nature of many homosexual sexual and emotional involvements, defined or fractured by generational, class, racial or domestic inequalities. The butch-femme model, with the (often incorrect) assumption that it simply echoed the heterosexual pattern, dominated public consciousness, and many individual lives. But the evidence of this burgeoning literature, and of our own research, decisively refutes 'conventional' assumptions. The couple is widely seen by non-heterosexuals as a crucial, though not exclusive, focus of love and mutual care, as well as of sexual involvement. The dominant ethos among lesbians, gay men and bisexuals is of egalitarian relationships. And although there are continuing differences between male and female same sex relationships, these are less important than the similarities. Non-heterosexuals do not have the pre-given institutional framework of formal commitment via marriage that blesses or blights heterosexual life. Britain and many other jurisdictions at the time of writing, have few formal means of affirming non-heterosexual relationships. Yet, in spite of this, there is plentiful evidence that non-heterosexual men and women have developed strong narratives of love and commitment, with one-to-one partnerships forming a central part of these.

This should surprise no one. There is a vast accumulation of historical evidence, as we have shown, for the intensity and duration of same sex partnerships, against all the odds of institutional denial and legal oppression (for example, see Donoghue 1993; Haggerty 1999). What is new is the coming out of same sex relationships, and the claim to rights and full recognition which is a part of this. This is reflected in our own research: the large number of people we interviewed were in couple relationships; and most had been in a relationship at one stage or another. Some felt very strongly that to be part of a couple was the most important experience they could enjoy. Others, both women and men, felt it was not particularly important to be in a one-to-one relationship, and some maintained two or more serious committed relationships simultaneously. Some preferred to be single, as long as they had friendships. Some of our interviewees believed that it was easier for women to form committed relationships than men, and in general, the women were more likely to favour exclusive and monogamous relationships than the men. In practice, however, as we demonstrate in this chapter and in Chapter 6, women and men alike are alive to the difficulties of maintaining sexually exclusive relationships. For the vast majority, the friendship ethic offers a framework to survive and grow, either through the vicissitudes of couple relationships, or in the absence of one-to-one involvements. However, at the same time, there is a widespread recognition that partnership relationships offer unique opportunities, as well as challenges, for the exploration of love, sex and commitment, balancing the affirmation of one's individuality with strong mutual involvement. For Dan (M44), 'being in a relationship helps to affirm one as a person and we all need that'. And Dee (F06) says, 'I love the continuity. ... I like the sex. I like doing some things jointly. ... A sense that you are loveable.' These are the authentic voices of people in same sex relationships.

Such comments as Dan's and Dee's are a sign of the greater self-confidence and development of the non-heterosexual world, which is itself opening up new possibilities in one-to-one commitments. Early sociological accounts of same sex couples found patterns which suggested the difficulty of breaking away from heterosexual models of intimate relationships alongside the incipience of new patterns. Plummer (1978), for example, describes a three-fold typology of relationships among gay men: the homosexual marriage, the boyfriend relationship, and the gay partnership. The first model in essence replicated the traditional marriage model, with an explicit division of labour between the breadwinner/sexually active partner, and the housekeeper/sexually passive partner. Similarly, Tanner (1978), using a small sample, detects three types among lesbians: a traditional complementary style; a flexible, nurturing, caretaker style; and a negotiated egalitarian style (see also Oerton 1997). Only in the third type in each instance can we see the emergence of the democratic egalitarian partnership model which today, we believe, is the dominant one.

Within the egalitarian model, however, there exists a range of possible patterns. Several studies in the US have attempted to investigate what could be called the 'natural careers' of lesbian and gay couples. Harry and DeVall (1978) come to the same conclusion as us, suggesting the absence of predictable patterns because of the lack of institutional expectations. Other research, however, has attempted typologies, which tend to compare same sex couples with the heterosexual norm. Laner (1977) divides homosexual couples into 'parallel' and 'interactional' types, the former suggesting independent lives, while the latter share a single world. Bell and Weinberg (1978) divide male partnerships into 'open couples' and 'closed couples', based mainly on attitudes to sexual fidelity, while Silverstein (1981) offers a closely related division of 'excitement seekers' and 'home builders'. McWhirter and Mattison (1984), in their study of 156 male couples, present the most extensive typology, with a six-stage model of relationship careers, from 'blending' and 'nesting' to 'releasing' and 'renewing'. This latter work, in fact, comes perilously close to suggesting a new normative life-cycle for gay relationships, which is not a million miles from the heterosexual one.

While there is no doubt that varying patterns of relationships exist, we argue that no single model can capture their complexity and fluidity. We especially reject any automatic stages in non-heterosexual relationships, though obviously each relationship will evolve in complex ways over time. A democratic egalitarian norm suggests diversity of life choices within a common framework of values that has developed over time in the non-heterosexual world. Our interviewees starkly counterpoint these to ongoing heterosexual patterns: there are frequent observations that while some 'changes' may be occurring in the way in which heterosexual relationships operate, they continue to be structured by set patterns, expectations, and assumptions, which differ from non-heterosexual experience. As David, aged 24, and currently in a non-cohabiting relationship, says:

> I think there's a lot less structure in gay relationships, in that heterosexual relationships follow a pattern. ... Whereas [in] a gay relationship, I don't think there's the same kind of 'career structure', as it were ... there's a lot less 'you do this here, this here and this here'. (M12)

Rather than concentrate on models and distinct patterns, we prefer instead to explore values, patterns of negotiation, and forms of commitment. We tend to agree with Blumstein and Schwartz (1983) that the most enduring non-heterosexual relationships are those – like enduring heterosexual ones – which are most committed in a variety of ways, but in the end this is a tautology. The critical point is that each of the forms of commitment has to be negotiated afresh, and though these negotiations may follow relatively well-defined pathways, the end result is not predetermined. Commitment based on mutual trust is seen as the key to sustaining a relationship (cf. Weeks 1995), and this is not dependent on any institutional backing. As Mo (F43) puts it, 'why do I need a licence to commit myself to somebody? The very idea is really quite abhorrent.' Dan makes the same point when referring to the Quaker celebration of his partnership:

> we were very insistent when we had our meeting of thankfulness, that this was not a form of marriage and it was not creating a relationship or commitment because the commitment had been there for nine years. (M44)

The will and wish to go on is the most vital component. For Sue,

> It's very fluid – and like we were saying about being monogamous or not – we're neither. There's no point in making a commitment to something that you don't know you can be committed to. And, there's a lot of changes in the boundaries of our relationship, and I'd much rather keep it as something fluid [rather] than commit to one thing and not be able to keep that commitment. (F15)

This sense of the fluidity of relationships is clearly shaped by the lack of a sanctioned institutional framework for intimate relationships in the non-heterosexual world, but is also seen as an opportunity for creativity and choice that is still largely denied to the heterosexual world. The freely chosen, equal relationship is the ideal.

The strong emphasis on 'the relationship' has, of course, a wider echo in the heterosexual world, and is related to the social and cultural transformations which society as a whole is experiencing. In a culture characterised by growing individualisation and the breakdown of tradition, the couple relationship is increasingly regarded as the focus of hopes and aspiration, the context in which personal meanings are made and sustained (Beck and Beck-Gernsheim 1995; Weeks 1995). Some commentators have seen this strong emphasis on intimate interpersonal relationships, as opposed to family relationships, as a key change in our time.

As noted earlier, in practice most of the heterosexual majority continue to have a sense of involvement with family and kin, and other complex social interactions. What we are discussing here are tendencies to prioritise the dyad over the family as the prime focus of intimacy and emotional commitment.

Blumstein and Schwartz (1983) have suggested that in many ways by the 1980s the couple relationship had become more important than the family as the focus of emotional involvement – and significantly they discuss lesbian and gay coupledom as being on a par with other sorts of couple relationships, subtly eliding difference, and normalising the non-heterosexual relationship. Other social critics have observed a similar tendency. As Jamieson suggests: 'The historic shift from "the family" to the "good relationship" as *the* site of intimacy is the story of a growing emphasis on the couple relationship' (1998: 136).

This intimate relationship is, however, the focus of both hope and insecurity. Beck and Beck-Gernsheim (1995: 24) have argued that the more equal men and women become, the shakier the foundations of the family (marriage, parenthood, sexuality) appear. The individualisation process that underlies this has a contradictory impact:

> while men and women are *released* from traditional norms and can search for a 'life of their own', they are *driven* into seeking happiness in a close relationship because other social bonds seem too tenuous or unreliable.
>
> (Beck and Beck-Gernsheim 1995: 24)

That puts an enormous burden on relationships: people want to make them work, strive to make a go of it, but are often equally prepared to cut their losses when things go wrong, and try all over again. From this point of view, there is little difference between heterosexual and same sex relationships. We are in a world where people have to make things up as they go along, with all the opportunities, but also hazards and dangers, that this implies. Giddens (1992) describes the resulting patterns as the precursor of a new emotional democracy, and as indicated in Chapter 1, we can find some evidence to confirm his arguments in our interviews. Sympathetic commentators, like Giddens (1992), have indeed argued that same sex couples are in the vanguard of these changes, pointing the way forward to their less advanced heterosexual brothers and sisters.

There is considerable controversy, however, about the extent to which these arguments can be applied to heterosexual life. The context for Giddens' work is very much interpersonal relationships in the private domain. Although he does refer to socio-economic factors that may constrain people's ability to participate in the transformation of their intimate lives, it is only in passing. Other authors have commented that Giddens' theorisation lacks any thorough empirical basis (Holland *et al* 1998; Jamieson 1998). While Jamieson concludes that Giddens does examine male resistance to change, she describes his thesis as being so optimistic as to constitute only a 'vision of an incipient alternative world' (Jamieson 1998: 57; see also Jamieson 1999). Consequently, for many heterosexual women, their ability to make choices in favour of living a relationship based on full equality, intimacy and transparency is limited to the extent that their male partners resist it (see Duncombe and Marsden 1993).

Our own view is that while there may be common underlying patterns reshaping heterosexual and non-heterosexual possibilities, the differences between non-heterosexual and heterosexual relationships are at the moment, perhaps, more significant than the similarities. Whatever the insecurities of heterosexual life, there remain strongly gendered patterns of behaviour and normative assumptions which are perceived to be largely absent among same sex couples. And despite the passionate espousal of same sex coupledom in much of the literature emanating from the lesbian and gay world, especially from the United States, which suggests the emergence of a desire for the same recognition as heterosexual relationships (Sullivan 1995 is a representative example), none of the participants in our research wished to establish a new norm of couple commitment that created new divisions within the non-heterosexual world, dividing the 'good gays' – the monogamous couple – from the 'bad' – the single, the 'promiscuous'. People are too aware of the hazards of intimate relationships, and the contingencies that beset even the most committed partnerships. Above all, there is a widespread awareness of the power of the heterosexual assumption, from which individuals consciously want to distance themselves.

The general attitude is one of principled pragmatism, with individuals prepared to work at making a go of one-to-one relationships, trying to combine a sense of individual autonomy with strong reciprocity, not least because many non-heterosexuals strongly believe they have greater opportunities than most heterosexuals for succeeding in building genuinely egalitarian and democratic relationships.

In the remainder of this chapter, we attempt to put flesh on these perceptions, by examining in turn the egalitarian ideal, the play of power in relationships, ideas of intimacy, and forms of commitment and affirmation in same sex relationships.

The egalitarian ideal

The dominant belief in the non-heterosexual world is that same sex partnerships offer unique possibilities for the construction of egalitarian relationships. A democratised, flexible model of couple relationships has become the ideal. The reality, inevitably, is more complex: non-heterosexuals strive to achieve equality in terms of intimacy, sexual relations and the division of labour in the household against all the inequalities that continue to structure our societies. Creativity and choice may be the leitmotifs of relationships, but there are very real limits to choice. The key issue, we nevertheless argue, is the commitment to striving for an equal relationship, which is the prime characteristic of non-heterosexual ways of being.

The most significant factor for us is that many non-heterosexual women and men have consciously attempted to shape their relationships in opposition to assumed heterosexual models. A number of women, particularly, see their lesbianism in itself as a conscious alternative to subordination to men. As Mollie, a lesbian in her early fifties, says:

[women are] much more, sort of, helpless, weak – I think that's one of the things heterosexuality does to women. And I feel I've got stronger and stronger [since coming out as a lesbian]. And, of course, some of that could be just getting older and more experienced. But I think some of it is to do with being a lesbian. (F30)

Many gay men feel the same, however. The majority of the people we interviewed feel that heterosexual relationships are inherently unequal because of the predefined gendered roles of women and men. Many believe that this makes it very difficult for heterosexual women to negotiate equal relationships with men, even if those men are also interested in equality (cf. Van Every 1995). Same sex relationships are seen as essentially different in this respect. Many believe that because there is no preordained script which they must follow, the possibilities for egalitarian relationships between women are endless. As Jackie strongly asserts:

You've no power, there's no stereotyped power about the man and the woman and, you know, who's on top, and all this crap! You know … it's the most loving relationship I have ever been in [with Sam]. The most equal one. And very, very gentle and caring. I have never, ever, ever had that [before] from anyone and I've never been able to express that with anyone. (F05)

The possibilities for communication, closeness and intimacy are opened up because two people (or indeed more than two, as in the examples of Mollie, quoted above, and Melanie, quoted below) join together and are able to communicate with each other from a similar stand-point and a similar set of life experiences. The assumption, among men as well as women, is that 'it's much easier to have equal relations if you're the same sex' (Liam, M31), because this equalises the terms of the intimate involvement. Or as Marilyn (F33) argues, 'the understanding between two women is bound to be on a completely different wavelength'. Equal standing means that issues, for example, around the division of labour in the household, are seen to be a matter for discussion and agreement, not a priori assumption. This is because, in Luke's words (M04), of 'being able to negotiate, being on an equal level to be able to negotiate in the first place'. Melanie (F29) concurs with this: 'Everything has to be discussed, everything is negotiable' (cf. Tanner 1978; Blumstein and Schwartz 1983; McWhirter and Mattison 1984; Dunne 1997). This is true not only of one-to-one relationships, but also of the complex multiple, and occasionally bisexual, relationships that some of our interviewees have.

Negotiation is possible, our interviewees suggest, because of a common understanding of the basic issues that are involved. Charles, aged 30, lives with friends while having a long distance relationship with his partner. He observes that:

so much is somehow assumed in heterosexual relationships, whereas in gay relationships it has to be made somehow more explicit. … You can't slide through recognised patterns of relationships. You've got to make a more conscious decision about what you want from each other … same sex couples are much more obliged to be explicit about – or scrutinise what they want from a relationship – what they're expecting – [they] think about it. (M25)

There are three interrelated themes that emerge from our interviewees' accounts of 'looking out' at heterosexual relationships. These relate to concepts of freedom and choice, the 'irrelevance' of dominant models of relationships for same sex relationships, and the extent to which non-heterosexuals must be both explicit and reflexive with regard to their relationships. All three can be summed up in terms of the necessity of negotiating relationships in a world of unprecedented flux. Implicit in the above comments by Charles is the belief that informs many of our interviewees' accounts of 'being different': that same sex relationships involve personal fashioning in a way that heterosexual forms do not. Here, Miriam's (F44) observations clearly illustrate this point: 'it is also about being creative and being pioneering, about not wanting to be defined … not wanting to conform in terms of what family needs to look like'. We maintain that this emphasis on self-invention and agency is very powerful in the non-heterosexual world. It is very potent in one-to-one relationships: because of the lack of institutional supports and cultural guidelines, members of same sex couples believe they are free to fashion their own modes of relating to each other (Harry and DeVall 1978; Mendola 1980; McWhirter and Mattison 1984; Johnson 1990; see also Peplau, Venigas and Miller Campbell 1996; Weeks, Donovan and Heaphy 1996). As Blasius (1994) notes, it is not only that non-heterosexual couples are 'free' in this regard, but they may, in many senses, be obliged to be so:

lesbians and gay men must create a self out of (or despite) the heterosexual self that is culturally given to them. … They must invent ways of relating to each other because there are no ready-made cultural or historical models or formulas for erotic same-sex relationships, as there are for different-sex erotic relationships.

(Blasius 1994: 191)

Among our interviewees, this 'freedom' was articulated widely in terms of the opening up of choices (see also Weston 1991; Giddens 1992; Dunne 1997). Rachel observes:

I think straight relationships are unbearably boring, in terms of – there's just so many rules about how they do things and how they don't do things and why they do things and when they do it, … I mean, I like the freedom that you have with lesbian relationships. I think that's a big difference. (F02)

The potential offered by same sex relationships is framed most widely in terms of the extent to which the 'irrelevance' of heterosexual models of relationships allows for the possibility of moving beyond gendered roles. In this sense, the lack of cultural or historical models of same sex relationships may be experienced as being a negative factor with potentially positive effects. Jenny argues that:

> In a way, not having had any role models, any of us, as we grew up – in certain ways that's still very damaging, I think, for lesbians and gay men – but in certain ways it at least means we haven't had so much to throw out. Whereas I do think that heterosexual friends who are trying to create more equal relationships are having to be very conscious about it all the time. (F21)

Luke also sees positive elements in non-heterosexual patterns:

> I think they're different because they're more equal than heterosexual relationships. I think they're more equal because there is less of a male/female role. … that's what makes them different. (M04)

It is clear that the creation and maintenance of 'more equal' relationships necessitates a considerable amount of emotional labour, the application of conscious human effort to caring and supporting the other partner (cf. Hochschild 1983, 1989). Such labour, primarily spoken about in terms of the need for discussion and negotiation, is, however, overwhelmingly compared favourably to the labour that is perceived to be involved in challenging the assumptions and set patterns that inform heterosexual relationships. As Mollie says:

> I think [in] my heterosexual relationships and my bisexual relationships with men I had bigger expectations. I expected them to do more work in the relationship. If things went wrong, I would have felt guilty and thought it was me, but I would have expected them to do something about it. (F30)

Lesbian relations, by contrast, are more open to challenging both material and emotional inequalities. Melanie, involved in relationships with two women, believes that,

> with lesbian relationships – well, the lesbian relationships I've had – there are no assumptions about how you will relate, what you will do, who does what. … In relationships with straight men, certain things seem to be assumed and then you have to fight to get something else. That has been my experience. (F29)

Jenny confirms this perception:

> I'm aware that heterosexual friends who are feminists have to work much harder at creating equal relationships than we do, because they're fighting the rest of the world. (F21)

In this regard, gay men express similar feelings about their relationships. However, it is notable that while many male interviewees talk of the potential that same sex relationships offer in going beyond gendered roles, such potential does not, in the main, refer to the *structural* differences between men and women, nor does it address questions of unequal labour. Rather, the emphasis is placed on the pressure to conform to hegemonic notions of masculinity (Connell 1987, 1995). Their responses are often framed in terms of the extent that homosexuality and same sex relationships provide ways of imagining being men that are free from notions of conventional masculinity (cf. Nardi 1999). Heterosexual men are seen as unemotional and uncommunicative, which has an inhibiting role on the shaping of heterosexual relationships (cf. Duncombe and Marsden 1993). As William, who is 40, suggests:

> I'm not at all sure how heterosexual men of my age get emotional support. I think a lot of them don't. That's a tragedy for them … I mean, to be a heterosexual former public schoolboy … can you imagine how they cope with life? I just don't think they know who they are or who anybody else is, ever. I don't think they get beyond a certain level of knowledge of people. (M03)

Will, on the other hand, expresses recurrent ideals of honesty and openness that are held up in contrast to the experience of heterosexual men:

> I think partners in a gay relationship are much more honest and open about what they feel for each other; what they want from a relationship; I think they're much more honest about expressing feelings of like or dislike – and there's much more [of a] forum for discussion. (M23)

In these accounts, equality is located in reciprocal emotional relationships. Malika sums up the general perception of the differences between heterosexual and non-heterosexual one-to-one relationships:

> for me, they're based on trying to find some equality between two people. They're based on freedom … on not owning a person and not dictating to the person what they can and can't do. … [In heterosexual relationships] there is a role that is ascribed to the man and the woman. I don't mean roles as in housework and breadwinner – I mean roles as in game playing, manipulation, being passive, being victim-like – whatever. (F03)

Values such as equality, honesty, openness, a rejection of game playing and manipulation, suggest that our interviewees are committed to a high degree of self-reflection with regard to their relationships. As we have already argued, increasing individualisation and the undermining of traditional forms of life in contemporary society force people to be more reflexive about their actions (Giddens 1991; Beck 2000). Among non-heterosexuals this general tendency is reinforced by more specific political and cultural influences, even among those who would vehemently deny that they were in any way 'political'. In many of the accounts by women about the operation of heterosexual relationships, what is evident is the influence of feminist analyses of power (cf. Dunne 1997). From women's stories, it is clear that feminist discourses – what Benjamin and Sullivan (1996: 229) term 'the feminist value system' – are often employed as a personal resource in making sense of power in interpersonal relationships. This is also the case for some of the men we interviewed, as they are consciously engaged in a re-evaluation of what it means to be a man. But more pervasive, if often implicit, are the values embodied in the normative ideal of a lesbian and gay community (see Chapter 4). These values highlight the significance of equality in relationships, whether of friendship or partnerships. The actual living of the values is, of course, another matter.

Living with power

The egalitarian relationship might be the ideal, but almost all our interviewees identified factors that had the *potential* to cause inequality. This is particularly evident in the emphasis placed on the negotiation of domestic, emotional and sexual lives. Non-heterosexuals have a realistic perception of the actuality of their everyday lives. While the percentages vary dramatically across studies, some early North American work on same sex relationships has suggested that around only 60 per cent of lesbians (Peplau and Cochran, cited in Peplau, Venigas and Miller Campbell 1996) and of gay men (Harry and DeVall 1978) describe their relationships as being 'equal'. This is echoed in our own findings: most of our interviewees felt that their relationships were equal 'in the main', but none of them presented their relationships as a 'power-free' zone. As Rachel put it:

> the way I think about power is that it's one of those things that we all have. It's part of us and it's kind of like everything else. I don't think it's a big scary thing – it's something that you live with and you have to deal with. (F02)

Because of differential power, egalitarian relations do not automatically develop. They require constant work in the face of inequalities of income, the hazards of daily commitment, conflicts over personal space, the time-consuming pressures of emotional labour, and the various differences and imbalances which mark everyday life.

Heterosexuality as a social institution can be described as predicated on the attraction of opposites and the eroticisation of difference, in which different attributes, roles and behaviour are regarded as intrinsic to one gender rather than another (Dunne 1999). These differences are hierarchically ordered, and give rise to unequal opportunities, which historically have been associated with different domestic roles. They have proved resilient, despite massive social changes. At an empirical level, a large body of work has focused on the intimate and domestic lives of men and women, and suggests that gender relations, particularly within the home, continue to be marked and structured by inequalities with regard to labour and status (see Chapter 4; for discussions of change in this context, see Van Every 1995; Benjamin and Sullivan 1996). Gender difference, as a historical and social phenomenon, is constantly produced and reproduced in the division between the domestic sphere and work, the private and the public. It is difficult to escape dichotomous ways of being. As Dunne (1999, see also 1997) argues:

> Engagement with the everyday tasks and objects of the home is not simply about getting necessary work done, it is about engaging in the production of gender. ... The domestic division of labour (one needs to add here – between women and men) is about linking the *musts* of work to be done with the *shoulds* of gender ideals.
>
> (Dunne 1999: 69)

Thus, gender performance is mediated through sexual difference and the heterosexual assumption embodied in our institutions. As we indicated in the previous section, our interviewees believe they have unique possibilities for escaping from gendered assumptions, and for opening up new freedoms to explore ways of doing things. But as Oerton (1997) points out, if gender is a social construction which is only contingently linked to bodily differences, then it is perfectly possible for same sex relationships themselves to be reproduced in gendered terms.

This is not, however, how our interviewees perceive their own ways of living. In considering their own relationships, the idea that couples might organise their own domestic lives in accordance with male-female (or butch-femme) roles, or that they might be perceived by others as doing so, is sometimes seen as shocking, and almost always refuted by our interviewees. In the few cases where people themselves suggest that their household division of labour could appear to match such roles, the notion of choice is strongly emphasised. Jenny comments:

> I occasionally look and think 'My God, we're a 1950s butch-femme couple', [with regard to] who is doing what around the house. ... I'm reasonably comfortable with that, so it's okay. ... In some ways it feels less of a problem in a lesbian relationship than it would in a heterosexual relationship, where one would be working harder at getting rid of gendered roles. ... As I've got older, I've got easier about the fact that actually I do like cooking and I really don't like hammering nails into fences. ... I'm less bothered, because the fact that two adults of the same gender choose to do different things within the house doesn't give kids a message that says 'men are only supposed to do this one' or 'women are only supposed to do that one'. (F21)

Yip (1997: 36–7), in his study of gay Christian relationships, observes two patterns: the first is the 'equality pattern', where every household task is shared; the second is the 'specialization pattern', where partners take on specific tasks that suit their individual aptitudes. The point for Jenny, however, is that the latter is just as 'equal' as the first: both are products of negotiation between equals.

Negotiations can be complicated, however. For example, Dan is retired and lives with his male partner who is over twenty years younger than him. Dan highlights the fact that tensions around domestic labour may arise when one or both partners are not in paid employment:

> we very rarely get angry with each other. He still complains [that] I don't do enough housework. … We had a discussion the other day … he was busy and he couldn't clean the bathroom for a fortnight, and because he hadn't done it he thought that I should have done it. [I said] 'right, we'll sit down and make a list of the jobs that need doing, and write a list of who is going to do what, and then we're not going to have these misunderstandings' … because in a way I feel that … this is my retirement. [It's] when I should have leisure and the time to do things and what not … well, I feel as if I don't really benefit very much from being retired … and he's got a very exacting job. (M44)

Clearly, factors such as employment status (and age) can cause conflict in terms of expectations regarding domestic work. While Dan stressed the negotiated nature of the relationship when discussing household labour, it is clear from his comments that such dilemmas also necessitate ongoing reassessment. The following examples similarly highlight the extent to which power relations within same sex relationships are not static and stable, and can lead to a painful awareness of perceived inequalities. Mo, who is temporarily unemployed and lives with a partner who is in paid employment, observes:

> until I'm working and earning the same amount of money that she is, it can never be equal, in certain ways, and yet it can be in other ways. But I think as individuals we probably make it difficult to be equal because … even if she was perfectly fine … even if we had a joint bank account, which we don't at the present time, and I could take any of her money whenever I wanted it, I wouldn't feel equal. Because I wouldn't feel that I was making an equal contribution. So, I would make myself feel unequal. (F43)

And here, Mo discusses how her unemployed status puts a degree of stress on her couple relationship, expressed as limiting her choice about how she spends her 'leisure time':

> I used to find it more of a problem. But now I don't find it as much of a problem, because instead of staying at home and doing the housework while she's at work, I think to myself, 'fuck it, you can do it'. Because what you get for going out to work is that you get to go to picnics, you get to go to Super Bowl – you get to do this, you get to do that. I get to stay at home and do the housework, No way Jose. What I get to do is to stay at home and do nothing

while you're working hard at work. ... So, I kind of reassure myself with that at the moment. (F43)

Mo is sure that this is resolvable, especially when she gets a job, but for the moment she realises that it makes the relationship less equal than she would wish.

Beyond the division of labour and differences regarding economic resources, other stories, about power, inequality, and equality, also highlight the complexity of 'flows of power'. Consider the following extract from a couple interview, between Arthur (M38) and Sean (M37):

Arthur: Well, I would say that I think we're both equally [powerful] – but knowing Sean would say no. [to Sean] Go on ...

Sean: From my point of view, [it's] quite deep, or quite involved ... the fact that Arthur's older and black. He didn't have much formal education, but that's just how he was brought up in [his country]. The fact that I'm younger and white and got a degree – but I had the opportunity to do that. I mean, externally that would be viewed in a certain way. I think that it gets internalised and almost reversed. ... It's difficult finding the right terminology for all these things, but because of our social backgrounds and how we'd be perceived, I'm the one who would be seen as socially, if you want to use the word, 'powerful', ... it would be true externally, but within the relationship, in a sense, that's maybe been turned around, for different reasons. ... I would say – I don't like to speak on [Arthur's] behalf – but Arthur would see those perceptions, but [he] would try to overcome them by not ... giving me any space to exert [my] perceived status. And ... I would acquiesce to that, comply with that, try and deal with it in some way – negotiate it. So I would say ... for a long time we went through ups and downs and sticky patches and had a lot of difficulty. I think that was at the bottom of it. It took a long time to kind of fathom it out and work it out.

The tentativeness and hesitations in Sean's comments, above, illustrate the delicacy of negotiating power differences, especially where, as in this instance, educational disadvantage and racial difference intermingle. Peplau, Venigas and Miller Campbell (1996: 255–6) note that much of the work on same sex relationships identifies the fact that greater 'relationship defining power' can accrue to the partner who has the greater personal resources. While this has usually been framed in terms of financial resources and education, we suggest that a broader focus is more appropriate. Such a focus can allow us to take into account cultural, economic and social resources. Racial inequality is obviously one situation where all three aspects may be relevant. Our interviews also suggest, however, that another important potential source of differential 'relationship defining power', which has tended to be overlooked, is unequal access to *social* capital (see Wan 1995; Weeks 1996; and Chapter 4, this volume). Such capital relates to the extent to which individuals can access local or community knowledge and supports. In terms of being non-heterosexual, social capital can relate to questions of 'outness' and the ability to access the community supports. In this way we can understand comments such as the following, from Peter, who feels that his strong network of lesbian and gay friends gives him an advantage over his partner:

> There are a lot of things that potentially make it very imbalanced in terms of power because I'm more experienced in gay life and more comfortable in it than he is. I'm much more secure in my sort of – friendship networks than he is. I have a lot of people to talk with about my relationship with David, and he doesn't have those people. (M11)

This example shows that there can be important differences within a couple relationship. The problem can be compounded where both members of a couple feel cut off from social support, for example by living in the country, or in an urban area that is broadly unfriendly to sexual minorities, or when one or the other partner is overwhelmed by the pressure of events. In this scenario, the couple must usually rely on their own resources, with unpredictable results – and physical conflict is one possible outcome.

Amid the stories of equality and respect there are stories of violence and abuse, usually, but not always, with ex-same sex partners. It is only comparatively recently that violent and abusive same sex relationships have been written about (e.g., Kelly 1988; Taylor and Chandler 1995). A common reason given for the relative silence on these issues has been the difficulty, for lesbians at least, of challenging the image of same sex relationships as power-free – and therefore abuse-free – zones. Pat explains:

> I didn't talk to anybody about it and it was horrendous because … it was just like screaming matches and getting pushed about, and usually it was after she'd been drinking. … But … I didn't talk to anybody about it. I mean, how can you? You know, it's that thing about, when you're in a relationship with a woman it's supposed to be better than with a heterosexual man and here you are in this situation where it's awful. It's not meant to be like that, but what do you do about it? And I don't know [if] I was even in that frame of mind that I could have thought clearly about it. But … I certainly didn't tell anyone about it. (F36)

In this case, the community norms that support equality instead work to silence the abuse. Marilyn frankly recounts the temptations towards abuse, describing the 'once or twice' she has come to blows with her partner, usually when they have both had a little too much to drink:

> It's been a mutual thing, really. Well, when I say mutual, it's usually started with me going 'Bang!', and so Aletia goes 'You don't. Bang!' back. And it's usually something that we can get over. I think it's more any disturbance to

the children we're more concerned about. ... [but] I can be very impatient, and it's something that I've got to learn to do something about. ... It's usually loosened up by too much alcohol. It wouldn't happen normally. And, you know, in everyday circumstances it's not something that I'm happy with. ... I think I'm getting to grips with it now, but ... And it's stress related and things like that, but it's not, it's not nice. (F33)

Such accounts as these illustrate the limits of negotiation. This is particularly emphasised in situations where there is a lack of reciprocity and mutual commitment to the relationship, or when the grounds on which the commitment is based are radically altered, or when the sheer frustrations of everyday life get the better of people. There is a strong sense of shame in Marilyn's account, even as she rationalises her own behaviour. The fact remains, however, that violence occurred.

On the other hand, the prevalent egalitarian values support reflexivity, and a willingness to problematise abusive behaviour. Generally, our interviewees show an acute sensitivity to power imbalances, and a firm commitment to attempting to counter them in order to achieve the egalitarian ideal. Overwhelmingly, the emphasis is on the possibilities offered by negotiation for 'working out' tensions and conflicts. Indeed, it appears that the *more* our interviewees identify potential power imbalances in their relationship, the more the necessity to talk through and negotiate is emphasised. This resonates with the findings in Finch and Mason's (1993) work, where less discussion is equated with a more traditional division of labour and allocation of caring. In the absence of a pregiven gendered division of domestic, emotional and sexual labour, our interviewees believe that they can work towards a new kind of intimate equality.

Intimacy and love

Intimacy has become an ideal in modern cultures, and such commentators as Giddens (1992) have argued that it is at the heart of the transformations of personal life, the focus of the growth of an emotional democracy. Jamieson (1998), who has undertaken the most comprehensive review of the idea and ideal, writes:

What is meant by intimacy is often a very specific sort of knowing, loving and 'being close' to another person. ... The emphasis is on mutual disclosure, constantly revealing your inner thoughts and feelings to each other. It is an intimacy of the self rather than an intimacy of the body, although the completeness of intimacy of the self may be enhanced by bodily intimacy. Mutually shared intimacy of this type requires a relationship in which people participate as equals.

(Jamieson 1998: 1)

Jamieson's general conclusion is in fact that full disclosing intimacy has not become a reality for most people because of the persistence of inequality, and at best remains an ideal that people strive after (see also Jamieson 1999). However, like other commentators, she does leave open the possibility that it is more likely to be achieved by same sex couples.

Our interviewees believe that they have the possibility of creating intimate relationships, because of their commitment to the egalitarian ideal. Interpretations of intimacy are expressed in many ways. For Lilly (F47), it is 'emotional closeness ... sharing'; Craig (M14) considers the most important thing is 'being able to expose yourself as you are and being accepted for that'; and for Niamh (F34), intimacy is about 'talking, seeing a different aspect of myself ... it's in your most intimate relationship, where you're most vulnerable, that you see most of yourself'. Emotional involvement, love, is generally seen as the defining aspect of a relationship, which involves trust, respect for each other, a sense of mutual responsibility, care, and, as Paul (M21) says, 'knowledge – knowing what is going on' (cf. Weeks 1995).

Belief in the possibilities of full intimacy is in part belied by the realities of interpersonal conflict, as we suggest above. But the absence of significant structural inequalities and the prevalence of the friendship ethic provide some of the necessary conditions for greater intimacy. Previous attempts to address the equality of same sex male relationships suggest that they can be best understood as structured around 'best-friend' models of relating (Harry and DeVall 1978; Harry 1984; Peplau 1981; and Kehoe 1988). Peplau, Venigas and Miller Campbell (1996) suggest that,

> A friendship script typically fosters equality in relationships. In contrast to marriage, the norms of friendship assume that partners are relatively equal in status and power. Friends also tend to be similar in interests, resources, and skills. Available evidence suggests that most American lesbians and gay men have a relationship that most closely approximates best friendship.
>
> (Peplau, Venigas and Miller Campbell 1996: 403)

While the friendship model is not universally employed to explain same sex forms of relating, there is broad agreement, as we saw in Chapter 3, that friendship plays a large role in the structuring of these relationships. Indeed, Blumstein and Schwartz (1983), in their study of same sex and heterosexual couples, have argued that lesbians and gay men appear to combine the need for friendship and romantic love in one person to a greater extent than heterosexuals. From our own research, it is clear that for many lesbians and gay men friendship is central to the operation of 'successful' couple relationships. Here, for example, Lilly discusses her long-term, but now deceased, partner:

> I'm back again on my friendship kick, I'm afraid, I think that underpinned everything. ... I'm stuck in the groove on that ... I think that ... was the sort of rock, the underpinning, whatever you want to call it. (F47)

The term 'intimate strangers' has been used to refer to the different emotional goals that husbands and wives may have in traditional couple relationships (Mansfield and Collard 1988). Our own interviews with men as well as women tend to confirm that a more accurate term to refer to non-heterosexual relations is the one used by Dunne (1997): 'intimate friendships'. We would argue that the egalitarian ideals of same sex relationships dissolve some of the boundaries between friendships and sexual/emotional commitments, making possible forms of intimacy that are difficult to attain among most heterosexual couples.

Sexual attraction is the most obvious factor that draws individuals together in the first place, and provides the basic dynamic (see Chapter 6). But, as Jamieson (1998) suggests, sex is not in the end the only or decisive factor in making for intimacy, and many of our interviewees agree. When asked if his relationship was primarily sexual, David replied:

> I would say it's very much more a friendship ... we don't have a tempest-uous relationship at all. I think we have a very stable relationship. Sex is obviously part of it, but ... I wouldn't say our relationship was based on sex. (M12)

Frankie, a lesbian, similarly put sex in its place:

> [Intimacy] is about closeness really. And there are different degrees of [intimacy]. It's about trust ... friendship, right through to sexuality. It's about being close and trusting. (F41)

Thus, the vagaries of sexual desire are not necessarily negative: they can provide opportunities for exploring other aspects of intimacy. Malika believes that

> [In her present relationship] it's fine not to feel sexual, not to want sex at particular points in time. I think when we were starting our relationship it was quite difficult for me, because I'd come from not having relationships ... only having relationships with men. So, my experiences and my frame-work in that I'd been operating in were the heterosexual one, which was you had to give men sex all the time. If you didn't give them sex then they would leave you or they would stop loving you, or whatever. (F03)

Intimacies often survive the waning of sexual interest. A number of partner-ships are asexual, but are seen as being no less real and enduring than sexual relationships. Dan, now in his seventies, provides a good example of this. He considers his relationship with Simon to be the most important one in his life. While it is no longer a sexual relationship, it remains central to both of them. As Dan says: 'We're not lovers any more and we have separate sex lives, but he's the most important person in the world to me.' And he goes on to explain the relationship:

It's the most important relationship in my life and I'm sure it's the most important relationship in his life and – it's just central … we have now pooled everything. The house is in our joint names and we're tenants in common… . If one of us dies, the house is automatically the other's so family can't grab a portion. And we have a building society [account] which is a single signature account, so again, if one of us dies the other one automatically gets what's in the account. So, I mean, we've merged everything now. (M44)

Although Dan's relationship with Simon has not been without problems, he feels that they successfully continue to negotiate a relationship that works well for both of them. Over the years, they have worked out issues relating to their changing sexual desires and requirements, and unequal financial resources, to form a relationship based on a strong emotional commitment. As Dan comments: 'We're [still] both learning … I mean, he depends very much on me and my being there, but then I depend on him being there for me.' In this respect, this has been a particularly special relationship for Dan:

every relationship is unique. … Well, I've never before had a partner that I don't have sex with. That was something I never conceived would happen. If someone had said to me [that] the most important person in your life, your partner, will be somebody you don't have sex with, I would have said, 'who are you kidding?' … That's the major difference. But there's this total sense of commitment, and financial commitment, which I have never entered into with anyone else … but he's far more aware of what's going on in the relationship and so am I, of course … there just hasn't been the same sort of commitment with other people. (M44)

Dan's and Simon's story illustrates the importance in non-heterosexual lives of the idea of *emotional* fidelity. Among gay male couples particularly, fidelity is frequently seen in terms of emotional commitment and not sexual behaviour (McWhirter and Mattison 1984: 252; Marshall 1995: 227). For many couples, male as well as female, sexual and emotional fidelity are inextricably linked. For others, however, they can be kept separate, so long as there is an underlying sense of commitment and trust, and an adherence to the agreed rules. The importance of negotiating explicit 'ground rules' for establishing and maintaining 'open' relationships – and for protecting the primary bond – is widely emphasised in the literature on the subject (McWhirter and Mattison 1984; Marcus 1992; Davies *et al.* 1993; Marshall 1995). Our own interviews confirm this. For example Luke (M04) says: 'William could sleep with somebody, and have sex with them, and I wouldn't feel that was being unfaithful. I would feel he would be unfaithful if he never told me about it.'

Monogamy is frequently seen by men and women as something that needs both negotiation and redefinition in the changing circumstances of a relationship (see also Chapter 6 for further discussion on this). Giddens (1992) notes that one of the central differences between lesbians and heterosexual women in their approach towards non-monogamy is that, with the former, actual or intended non-monogamy is far more likely to be revealed to each other. One reason for this is the higher level of communication between same sex partners – a view confirmed by many of the people who we interviewed (see also Dunne 1997), though it has to be said that we also came across evidence of non-disclosure. When interviewed together, couples may present a front of being fully open to each other, but conversations with individuals alone may reveal a more complex picture. This parallels evidence from some writers on heterosexual relationships that 'even private testimonies given in research interviews are themselves publicly-scripted' (Burgoyne and Clark, cited in Duncombe and Marsden 1996: 150). Duncombe and Marsden (1993, 1996) note that a key influence in heterosexual couples' stories may be the desire to conform to the model of the happy companionate relationship. They state:

> A key part of emotion work where the couple relationship is old or shaky may be the couple's management of their image to outsiders – including interviewers – so as to present a picture of companionate love.
>
> (Duncombe and Marsden 1993: 237)

We can cite similar examples from our own research: some couples publicly present a common story of their monogamy, but one-to-one interviews reveal a more complex account – of sex outside the partnership, for example, which relies on the belief that both 'know' about the act, but never speak of it. We also came across flexible definitions of monogamy: several couples, for instance, described their relationship as monogamous but admitted to engaging in threesomes. As long as both partners are involved, it appears, it is not seen as breaching their mutual commitment (see Chapter 6).

Perhaps a difference lies in the fact that in many non-heterosexual relationships, monogamy or non-monogamy becomes a referent, not for the relationship itself but as a criterion of trust between partners (cf. Giddens 1992). Sue's (F15) and Julie's (F14) story about monogamy illustrates this narrative of trust and commitment:

Sue: We don't sleep with anyone else unless it feels right and we talk to the other person first. So, we haven't excluded non-monogamy and we haven't decided on monogamy. It was just we decided to have not slept with other people very much since we've got together.

Julie: And when we have, we've done it together.

Sue: Yes, that's been very mutual, we've both wanted it, and it was special. ... I've seen too many people saying 'we have a monogamous relationship' who are off screwing someone behind their partner's back.

Here, talking, checking with each other, and negotiating for mutual satisfaction – both emotionally and sexually – has resulted in Sue and Julie shifting the boundaries to do with monogamy, and allowed the inclusion of a third party in selected sexual encounters. The crucial factor, therefore, is not so much whether a relationship is monogamous or non-monogamous, but the basis of trust which has been negotiated. As Yip (1997: 101) remarks, it is not sexual non-exclusivity *per se* that causes tension, but the violation of previously agreed ground rules (for more on this, see Chapter 6).

The agreement of ground rules may be an essential factor in all relationships, but it should also be seen as a highly pragmatic practice. We can see plentiful examples of the working through of intimate involvements, and the building of commitment and trust, but a superficial reading of the stories of partnerships suggests that passionate love is not to the fore. Are we seeing the emergence of a new type of narrative, one in which romance is downplayed in favour of intimate friendship?

We would argue that this depends on what is meant by the term 'love'. Although narratives of life-long romantic love may well be less common than they were, there are strong arguments to suggest that concepts of love are becoming more, rather than less, salient in the late modern world. Beck and Beck-Gernsheim (1995: 49) refer to the importance of 'person-related stability' in the contemporary world, for which, in the absence of other fixed points, love becomes all the more significant: 'The more other reference points have slipped away, the more we direct our craving to give our lives meaning and security to those we love' (Beck and Beck-Gernsheim 1995: 50). If this is true, then one would expect non-heterosexuals, who have considerably fewer fixed reference points than their heterosexual peers, to put even greater emphasis on love – and there is strong evidence for this. Indeed, Lewin (1998: Chapter 6) argues that for many lesbians and gays, in the absence of legal recognition for couple relation-ships, love has become the authenticising element of a relationship, and the justification for campaigns for same sex marriage (see also Weston 1991: 149).

As we observed in Chapter 3, British non-heterosexuals seem to be less fervent in their use of the language of love than their American counterparts, and there is a distinct lack of the language of eternal romantic love in our stories. However, love, as some recent studies demonstrate, is not an essential quality that exists eternally outside the bounds of history: it is something which changes its forms and meanings over time (Weeks 1995). In its broadest sense, it encompasses a variety of emotions, which can be characterised in terms of the intermingling of feelings of mutual care, responsibility, respect and knowledge – mutual recognition between equal subjects, and an awareness of the necessity, yet delicacy, of reciprocal relationships. In this respect, love is certainly a strong element in non-heterosexual narratives.

These narratives are in many ways similar to what Giddens (1992) describes as 'confluent love'. While particularly apt for discussion of our narratives, this notion has been developed in an attempt to conceptualise broader transforma-tions in patterns of intimacy that cut across the homosexual–heterosexual dichotomy. Giddens remarks that:

Confluent love is active, contingent love, and therefore jars with the 'forever, 'one-and-only' qualities of the romantic love complex ... Romantic love has long had an egalitarian strain ... *De facto*, however, romantic love is skewed in terms of power. For women dreams of romantic love have all too often led to grim domestic subjection. Confluent love presumes equality in emotional give and take, the more so the more any particular love tie approximates closely to the prototype of the pure relationship. Love here only develops to the degree to which intimacy does, to the degree to which each partner is prepared to reveal concerns and needs to the other and to be vulnerable to that other.

(Giddens 1992: 61–2)

This clearly suggests that the potential for love is in large part dependent on the building of intimacy, commitment and trust – and that can be hard work. It can lead to a sense of contingency in couple relationships, a sense of the delicacy and uncertainty of permanent commitment. This is echoed in our interviews. For example, Amy (F27) comments that, 'on a very unpolitical level, I can't imagine meeting someone and promising to spend the rest of my life with them. ... That, to me is an unrealistic kind of thing. It's a strange concept.'

Many couples behave as if a relationship might last for ever, they work at making it work. However, on a pragmatic level they also recognise that it might not work. Greg (M17) and Mark (M18), for example, are realistic about things: 'we said at the beginning that we'd work at it and see what happened, or something along those lines. ... But we weren't going to make plans or a lifelong commitment.' Dee (F06) makes the following point about her relationship:

We've never, ever said, you know, ''till death us do part'. But we do plan long term – while the relationship is going well, we will be planning long term. Because you can't keep planning short term and expect long-term things to sort themselves out.

For many non-heterosexual couples this involves a rejection of the mutual dependency or symbiosis which is seen as a common trait among heterosexual couples. Amy, who is in a relationship, nevertheless rejects what she clearly believes would be an over-dependence on one person:

ideally, who I'd like to look after me [if Amy were ill] wouldn't be anyone who I had a [one-to-one] relationship with ... because I think the thing about power is really important in my relationships. So, if you're dependent on someone for your physical or mental, or whatever, well-being, and there's a dependency there ... it's obviously going to have a massive influence on your relationship, whether it's a friendship or a sexual relationship. (F27)

The ideal expressed here is one of love and commitment in accord with an egalitarian belief. Within that framework, the goal is the achievement of a relationship which avoids the gradual erosion of equality through one partner becoming over-reliant on the other.

However, this is not the whole story. Bauman (1993: 98) has argued that there are two characteristic strategies for dealing with the perceived flux of modern relationships: what he calls 'fixing' and 'floating'. Fixing takes place when the potential openness of 'confluent love' is set firmly in place by the demands of duty. The best example is of couples who stay together 'for the sake of the children'. This does occur, but is less likely among non-heterosexual couples. Floating occurs when the labour of constant negotiation on the terms of a relationship leads to people cutting their losses and starting all over again. This is often the case in non-heterosexual relationships. As Miriam observes:

> a lot of lesbians and gay men split up more often than heterosexuals because they're not necessarily conventionally married, and they don't have to go through all the hassle, so it is easier to split up, I think, in some cases. (F44)

Splitting up or 'letting go' is not about casually throwing away a relationship; it is to do with recognising the reality of the situation for both partners. There is no doubt that the emphasis on independence within same sex relationships might make it easier for members to leave (cf. Weston 1991; Dunne 1997). But as Juliet observes, the situation is often more complicated than one assumes:

> it seems to me as if relationships between lesbians and gay men are ... I was going to say less long-standing than heterosexual relationships, but I don't actually think that that is the truth. What probably is the stereotypical judgement is that lesbians and gay men have short-term relationships ... I think that they're just more acknowledging of when relationships have run their course. I also think that it has a certain amount to do with the way that lesbians and gay men socialise, which means that the possibility of finding new partners is more possible for more people than it perhaps is for some heterosexuals. (F01)

A final break is not, however, the only outcome of the end of an affair. Passionate sexual affairs can transmute into life-long, if non-sexual, partnerships, as the example above of Dan and Simon shows. Even when the couple relationship is declared over, close friendships may endure, not only among women, where the literature suggests it is common, but also among men (see Chapter 3). Many others, on the other hand, work through the vicissitudes of their relationship, trying to 'make a go of it', remaking their relationships on a day by day basis. As Tom (M15) says, 'just the very fact of carrying on living together is a sort of ... daily renewal of commitment'. (M15). In other words, neither floating nor fixing, but continuously confronting the challenge of relationships, 'working through' the ups and downs.

Affirming commitment

In this chapter, we have tried to show the various ways and the variety of circumstances in which same sex partners assume mutual responsibilities and make commitments. Although these are perhaps not that fundamentally different from emerging heterosexual patterns, there is one basic difference: a lack of cultural legitimation. The variety of ways of signalling heterosexual commitment, from the private affirmation of friendship and love to the legal and sacramental bonds of marriage, are generally accompanied by some sort of public recognition. In general, non-heterosexuals lack such a formal imprimatur, and more specifically, they are excluded from the ritual approval represented by marriage.

In the wake of the campaign for partnership rights and same sex marriages, there has been a considerable debate about the significance of the public recognition of non-heterosexual relationships. Eskridge (1997: 278), for example, from a communitarian viewpoint, has strongly argued that there is a risk in seeing our most significant human relationships as nothing more than a 'market place of intimacies'. He argues that stable partnerships are necessary for a stable sense of self, and in a culture which emphasises status, to deny the recognition of the formal status of marriage to lesbian and gay couples is to deny them full citizenship. Conservative gay commentators, such as Sullivan (1995, 1997), argue that the recognition of same sex marriage is a fundamental requirement of equal status. Heterosexual marriage has, of course, itself become less an essential status transition and more a public affirmation of commitment (Morgan 1985), and many non-heterosexual people now feel the need to make such a statement of commitment. This need not mean the abandonment of a sense of individual autonomy, Nussbaum (1997: 333) has argued, but would strengthen same sex relationships.

At the time of writing, formal partnership rights, in various forms, are in place in several countries, including Denmark, Sweden, Norway, Iceland, Greenland, the Netherlands and France, with related shifts in policy under debate in several other western countries. Legislation was introduced in Germany in early 2000 to register same sex partnerships. It received popular support in the opinion polls, but sharp hostility from conservative political parties (*The Economist*, 29 July 2000: 45). In 2000, Vermont was the first US state to pass a law which recognised same sex 'civil unions' (Whitworth 2000: 21), despite fierce opposition and the prospect of reference to the US Supreme Court. Other US states, such as California, Rhode Island, West Virgina, as well as Hawaii (which pioneered the idea of same sex marriages), have been following a similar path. Each country is clearly moving in line with its own specific traditions and legal processes. For example, the Scandinavian countries were heavily influenced by their social democratic traditions of justice and equity; the US by sustained minority rights campaigns and a commitment to the legal process. In Britain, the shifts appear to be more pragmatic than programmatic, in line with the traditions of common law which moves by the accumulation of precedent rather than the laying down of fundamental principle. For example, in a landmark judgment in 1999, the House of Lords ruled that with regard to tenancy rights, a homosexual couple could be seen as members of the same family (Burrell 1999: 1; O'Hanlon 1999: 7). Hailed as a legal breakthrough, which in many ways it is, it still remains unclear, however, what the wider significance will be.

Such movements on the public front reflect a growing activism in the non-heterosexual communities across the West for formal recognition of same sex partnerships. The arguments for this vary. In Britain, the (openly gay) economist and broadcaster Evan Davis has argued for same sex marriages precisely on the grounds that 'quite simply, marriage helps foster stable relationships and stable relationships are socially advantageous – as well as fulfilling to the individuals involved' (Davis and Phillips 1999: 16). Others, like the American lesbian writer Ellen Lewin (1998: xix), have come round to believing that 'the ritual dimensions of [same sex] marriage have the ability to transform identity and to shape identity' – presumably for the better.

Our own evidence suggests that formal recognition of same sex partnerships arouses mixed feelings, and attitudes are often shaped by pragmatic considerations. For some of our interviewees, legal partnership rights or same sex marriage are attractive (see Chapter 8). Among non-heterosexuals, especially those who are involved in parenting, there is an acute awareness of the potential problems which can arise at times of illness and death, where the 'rights' of same sex partners to adopt or care for a child are easily contested. Yet despite these hazards, there is an ambivalence about formalising such relationships in legal partnerships or same sex marriages, should they be available. For many, the real challenge is of ensuring legal rights and protection, without surrendering what is seen as the real core of non-heterosexual partnerships – the ability to maintain a more democratic relationship, and the possibility of creating something different. Juliet makes this point:

> I couldn't say that, for instance, I would never want to celebrate my relationship with someone. And that might go for a relationship with someone who's not a sexual partner. But, you know, we have to create those things for ourselves. They don't exist currently [for non-heterosexuals]. (F01)

For Juliet, and others like her, a new legal framework might be necessary, but it is not sufficient. If commitments represent responsibilities which are accepted, with all their implied and explicit consequences, those which are personally negotiated are likely to feel as much, and perhaps even more powerful, as those that are imposed or recognised from outside (Finch and Mason 1993). Privately made commitments are no less forceful than publicly made ones. They carry ethical values that are built into personal narratives. Recognition of, and respect for privately made commitments are the most crucial goals for the participants in our research. As Greg (M14) says: 'People need markers in life, don't they? To remind them of things that have happened, and the way things are' – and these need to be acknowledged by others.

In his self-help book *The Two of Us*, Uhrig (1984) suggests that there are four things that many lesbians and gay men look for in relationships: affirmation, celebration, symbolisation, and something that goes beyond traditional ways of doing things. In practice, Driggs and Finn (1991) argue, this often takes place through two processes: the creation of couple traditions, and the creation of couple rituals as symbolic ways of affirming bonds and deepening attachments. Our own research suggests that these two processes are usually merged: rituals become part of the traditions of a relationship, though this is not without problems. Partners seek ways of confirming their involvement, but they are often reluctant to do anything that seems too 'heterosexual'. Many find ways of celebrating with irony, or play with traditional models, balancing feelings of ambivalence with an underlying note of seriousness. These have intense meaning for the individuals concerned, but they also provide opportunities for wider recognition. Anniversaries can be particularly important – celebrations of first meeting, first sex, when partners moved in together or made a commitment (cf. Johnson 1990; Marcus 1992). Greg (M18) and Mark (M17) illustrate this:

Greg: We have two [anniversaries]. The first night we met, or the weekend you moved in, which was a bank holiday.
Mark: The weekend I moved in is usually celebrated, isn't it?
Greg: Yes, that's usually the one we …
Mark: You usually turn up with a huge bunch of flowers – and tell me not to! And then you come through the …
Greg: If you can't tell me the date of our anniversary, then …!
Mark: You tell me not to, you shit!

Partners may also celebrate St Valentine's Day, with flowers or gifts. Others, however, are made of sterner stuff: Jill (F22) is 'very anti-Valentine's day because I've always thought it was heterosexual'. For some, anything can be an excuse for celebration, as Marilyn (F33) says, 'anything we can think of, we celebrate'; for Luke (M04), it's 'birthdays, Christmas, New Year, St Patrick's night, and the Eurovision Song Contest night'.

The chosen focus for celebration is less important, perhaps, than the fact that many people feel the need for a symbolic cementing of the relationship. Mo (F43) changed her name by deed poll to that of her partner: 'I think it's a strong sign of commitment to someone', she comments. Some people exchange rings, like Rob (M06) and Scott (M07): 'We bought ourselves rings … because that was our way of saying "this is our commitment" '. For others, however, like Coral (F13), such symbolism arouses faint horror: 'Exchange of rings … it's just something I've never believed in. … I just don't think I would need to go through an exchange of rings, I just don't believe in it.' Or there is playful rejection, as in the case of Sue (F15) and Julie (F14):

Sue: We're completely against marriage …
Julie: I gave you your nose ring …

Sue: I gave you an eyebrow piercing. It had nothing to do with the relationship. But, you know, it's the nearest we've got.

Private rituals, such as Julie's and Sue's, act as symbols of what has been gained,
but they can also indicate what has been lost if the person has been rejected by
his or her family of origin. Celebrations with partners and friends, therefore, can
affirm a new sense of belonging. Birthdays may be particularly important,
especially if there are painful memories of rejection, as Malika suggests:

> especially birthdays, because I think that a lot of my friends are people who
> don't have close relationships with their families and who don't see their
> families. So when birthdays come round it's really important. (F03)

Traditional 'family' feast days and holidays can be a particular trial for many
partners, creating feelings of tension to do with the sense of obligation to one's
family of origin and to one's current relationship commitments (cf. Tanner
1978). As Sam remembers:

> we [her partner and their daughter] celebrated Christmas together as a
> family. ... That was quite difficult. Well, I found it a bit difficult because my
> mum and dad saw it as a rejection of them ... after Christmas she did
> actually say ... 'Yes, you've got your family now'. (F04)

Non-heterosexual celebrations, however, such as Mardi Gras or Pride, the
annual parades and carnivals which commemorate the start of the gay liberation
movement, offer alternative foci for 'family' celebration, as Jackie (F05) recalls:
'I'd never seen Sam so animated as she was there. ... I thought she was going to
take all her clothes off.'
    Recognition of these rites from friends are of the utmost importance, espe-
cially if relations with one's family of origin are difficult or non-existent. But
responses from families of origin remain vital in confirming recognition of the
reality of the relationship. For Rob (M06) and Scott (M07), the breakthrough
came when their respective parents acknowledged their relationship:

Rob: Our anniversary is important.
Scott: Our anniversary, it's important for us, and we get a card from my mum
and dad. ... We always did off your mum and dad. We do now off my
mum and dad. Well, we have now for the past four years.

Both these forms of external recognition can bind: one in opposition to a hostile
world, the other as a recognition that this non-traditional relationship is seen by
the family of origin as a living, creative force.
    But if there is widespread acceptance that partnership rites are important, the
question of formal commitment ceremonies arouses much greater controversy,
evoking as it does similarities to marriage. Darryl (M19), for instance, would 'like

to do some kind of marital type ceremony, but I don't want it to be legal'. For others, like Jenny who is contemplating a Quaker celebration of commitment, they offer the forum for an important public statement:

> Partly, I think, it's political. Partly, I think, it's about visibility and about saying publicly that our relationships are – some of us might say better – but are certainly no less worthy of celebration and public acknowledgement than heterosexual relationships. (F21)

For Dan, also a Quaker, the celebration is an important way of affirming his commitment to his partner:

> we had a Quaker meeting to celebrate our relationship, not to get married, not to create the relationship, but to celebrate nine years ... [I]t was a Thanksgiving. A 'meeting for thankfulness'. ... What we were doing is giving thanks to God for what we had. ... It was a celebration, it wasn't even a recommitment, but after the event, I realised it was a watershed for me. I was totally committed to him after that. (M44)

The problem for those who are non-religious is finding the right balance between playfulness and seriousness. For Warren, who went through a wedding ceremony with his partner, the combination of the two was part of the pleasure:

> I suppose what was really important for me was getting the balance right between it being a pastiche (which is what it was, clearly) and it being deadly serious. And ... that was what I was most happy about, that we got that right. People weren't quite sure – you know, 'Are you just taking the piss?' 'Is this unbearably serious?' 'What's this about?' ... That balance was quite difficult to find. Fortunately, the people with us were great, and it was a huge send-up but also extraordinarily moving ... I think that was [the] most important thing for me, that we could, you know, be taking the form of something but sending it up, and being incredibly serious about it. ... It was kind of making a commitment to be true to each other, but also to be reasonable about our differences. (M34).

The growth of a self-help literature (for example, Driggs and Finn 1991; Uhrig 1984) suggests the developing importance for many non-heterosexuals of finding ways of publicly, as well as privately, affirming their commitment, without necessarily following traditional heterosexual models. In the 1980s, in their study of gay male couples, McWhirter and Mattison (1984) commented on the absence of set rules and of ways of formalising relationships. Today, in the twenty-first century, it is clear that this situation is rapidly changing. Partnership rites help bind individuals together – and signal the distance that has been travelled in the recognition of partnership rights.

6 Sexual pleasures

The value of sex

Sex, Michel Foucault (1979) famously stated in *The History of Sexuality*, has become 'the truth of our being'. Over the past two hundred years or so, questions of who or what we are have been answered by accounts of our object choices and forms of sexual practice. To describe people as homosexual has been to place them in a hierarchy of value: what they do is what they are, and we know that for long periods the sexual acts have resulted in the execration of the sexualised being. Not surprisingly, our erotic practices have played a significant role in our self-understandings and personal and social identities (cf. Prieur 1990).

Foucault himself deplored the tendency to fix a person by what he or she does in relation to the erotic. For him, as we saw in Chapter 3, releasing the potentiality for friendship and creative relationships – 'practices of the self', 'practices of freedom' (Halperin 1995) – was as important as the 'liberation' of sexuality. In the previous chapters, we have shown that non-heterosexuals in their everyday life are living precisely these injunctions. But we cannot, of course, divorce 'homo*sexuality*' from the erotic. Sexuality plays a central role in the lives of non-heterosexuals, as it does for everyone else.

Erotic encounters have a multiplicity of meanings. While they can be an important source of pleasure, they are also a key means of connecting with others. In coming out, non-heterosexuals bring questions of sexuality and the erotic to the forefront of their lives in very particular ways. In this chapter, we explore the diverse and complex meanings that individuals attach to the erotic, and the forms of negotiation which take place around sexual practice itself. Non-heterosexual understandings and practices are influenced by the meanings attached to sexuality in the wider society, but they are also shaped by local cultures critical of dominant (hetero-)sexual values. At issue in the lives of 'queer folk' are different ways of thinking and doing the erotic. But equally at stake are ethical ways of being that problematise the traditional doing of sexuality *and* gender.

There are, of course, broad differences in the value that particular individuals attach to their bodies and to sexualised interactions with others. The erotic can mean many things to many people. In secular societies, however, the separation of sexuality from traditionally 'repressive' meanings, has opened up opportunities for sex to be enjoyed for its 'own' sake. For late modern individuals generally, the body, and the pleasures it can afford, has become increasingly important as a focus for self-fulfilment (Giddens 1992; Shilling 1993). In contemporary western society, sexuality has become 'a focus for considerable personal emotional investment' (Mellor and Shilling 1993: 422). Consider Dan's account, who began to live his sexual 'adolescence' when he came out as gay in later life:

> in the three years before he [his partner] met me, I had lived my adolescence. I'd never had so much sex in my life and I now know what 'nothing succeeds like success' really means. And I got more and more confident. I had a terrific time. I really felt like I was an attractive man and I could get lots of sex with lots of people and it did my ego an enormous amount of good. (M44)

Dan indicates here some of the rewards to be gained from sexual and erotic encounters: they can be simply about having a good time; they can provide a sense of being valued by others; they can provide a sense of self-value. At an obvious level, sex can be 'about' pleasure and the enjoyment of the sensuousness of the body. As Annie puts it:

> it just feels good. It's such a powerful ... positive [feeling] ... it feels like it's really good for you – it's really good for your health, you know, your physical and mental health. It's really positive. (F40)

In the West, sexuality has long been viewed as an all-powerful, engulfing force (Foucault 1979; Mort 1987; Weeks 1991). However, what is significant about Annie's comment is the way in which this powerfulness is articulated. Far from a destructive and threatening sexuality that must be controlled and harnessed to protect moral and physical well-being, Annie presents an account of the 'positive' power of sex: for physical and psychological health. In contrast to more traditional incitements to deny and repress sexual desires, various forms of knowledge at the beginning of the twenty-first century are as likely to suggest the beneficial potentials of fully developing 'healthy' sexual lives (Coward 1989). At the same time, sexuality, divorced from reproductive imperatives, can have a significant role to play as a medium of self-realisation (Giddens 1992: 164). Pat, for instance, expresses it in these terms:

> there's something about having sex and feeling attractive. Or feeling more or less attractive when you're not having sex, I think. Or not feeling as fulfilled or a sexual being ... if you're not having sex, there's something missing. (F36)

Eroticised interactions can offer the opportunity for a sense of connectedness with others. Desiring others, and being desired, can provide a sense of alertness to one's own physicality, and the physicality of others. The possibility of physical (and emotional) intimacy is also potentially offered, as Niamh comments:

> I like feeling desire and I like being desired … it's often very intimate be-cause it's such a vulnerability thing … because everyone thinks they're completely crap in one way or another sexually. Either they don't like their bodies, or they just feel inept or they feel, you know – something – so it's a very exposing kind of thing in that way. … I like sex with another person. You know, being a sexual being myself, I like that. (F34)

In societies where the bodies of only a few individuals match the images of desirability that are sold to them, sexual interactions have the potential to make individuals feel vulnerable. But, as Niamh suggests, there are rewards to be gained from exposing the 'real self'. These can include confirmation of the degree to which individuals *are* the possessors of 'attractive' and 'desired' bodies. In turn, this can play an important role in shoring up a sense of confidence, self-esteem and feeling of self-worth (Mellor and Shilling 1993). But eroticised or sexual interactions do not have to consist of what is traditionally understood as sexual intercourse. In continuing her account of the value of sexualised interaction, Niamh makes this point clear:

> when I was not in a relationship for four and a half years, I was celibate in the sense that I wasn't having sex with anybody else. And it wasn't a big deal, actually. So, yes, it is important to me – but not in the sense of *having* sex all the time. But I love sexual attraction, I love sexual desire – mine and other people's. (F34)

A complex set of issues arise here. The first concerns making a distinction between sexualised and eroticised interactions and the notion of 'having' sex. While the former can include activities like flirting, the latter is used mostly to indicate what is commonly thought of as 'making love'. Second, in contrast to Pat (F36), quoted earlier, Niamh suggests the possibility of operating and feeling complete without actually engaging in sexual activities with others. Sexual activity is not everything. Third, this account also highlights that the value given to sex varies over the course of an individual's life. The complexity of the various relationships between sex and how individuals see themselves is brought into sharp focus at times of bodily crises which threaten to desexualise the individual (in his or her own eyes or in the eyes of others). Dan describes such a situation:

> Since they fried me guts [for cancer treatment], I can't ejaculate – because they fried me viscera and that's, you know, I think for a gay man that is very important. I mean, if you're with another guy, normally he wants you to

come, he wants you to have an erection – and I can't have that. It's a great grief to me. ... I think sex is very important. ... To have sex is part of being a man, being a human being, and I need sex. (M44)

In this account, certain tensions which individuals might attempt to contain around sex are articulated. For Dan, the inability to engage in what is considered 'full sex' (ejaculation) is presented as a sense of 'great grief'. Further, the account indicates that Dan's inability to have an erection potentially compromises his desirability as a sexual partner. Yet, on the other hand, sex is also presented as the route through which affirmation of gayness, manhood, and even 'humanity' are gained. Thus, for Dan, sexual encounters have both the potential to undermine his confidence and to shore up his sense of self. In this regard, they can be both a very desirable experience *and* a risky endeavour.

As Dan indicates, sex and sexuality have a significant role to play in our self-understandings – particularly for non-heterosexuals who have historically been defined by their sexuality and sexual preferences (Foucault 1979; Weeks 1989, 1991). Traditionally, talk of sensitisation to homosexual 'feelings' has focused on desire for particular physical or sexual relationships with others of the same sex. It is hardly surprising, then, that among many lesbians and gay men sexual activity is a crucial way of affirming one's non-heterosexuality. As Phillip says:

Well, as a gay man, sex is going to be important for me – even if it's mastur-batory – because I think if I were just suddenly to become asexual, would I still be a gay man, you know – I wonder what I would be. (M27)

Here identity and sexual practice are interlocked. For some people, however, it is not quite as simple: sexual desire doesn't always fit easily into neat categories. A bisexual identity, for example, requires more complex choices. Sarah makes this clear:

I went through a period of some months when my relationship with my female partner was very platonic and the only sexual relationship I was having was with my male partner. And I really felt that the bisexual, the gay side of me that I recognise and acknowledge and accept, was just not being allowed to express itself. And I didn't find it very helpful. So I just negotiated the fact that I would from time to time have sexual relationships ... with another woman. (F23)

These accounts underline that there is a strong link between engaging in same sex erotic activity and *being* lesbian, gay or bisexual. However, it is also clear that engaging in sexual activity is not necessary to either the formation or mainte-nance of non-heterosexual identity. As David recounts:

[up to the age of] 21, [I had] still not met anybody or told anybody par-ticularly. At that stage I had a core of friends of about five people that I'd told I was gay, and, you know, they were all – 'Well, how do you know?' But I'd not had sex with anybody or anything at all – any contact with anybody. (M12)

As with other participants in our research, David had developed, and made public, his non-heterosexual identity prior to any sexual encounter with someone of the same sex. This is presented as problematic for those around him (particularly heterosexual friends), but David himself doesn't view it in those terms. Narratives about coming out, such as David's, indicate that homosexual self-understanding is not necessarily dependent on homosexual (sexual) activity (see Troiden 1993). They are not one and the same thing. While some personal narratives suggest that engagement in same sex sexual activity can precipitate the formation of a homosexual identity, it is also the case that claiming a gay identity can precede gay sexual activity practice (see also Hall Carpenter Archives 1989a, 1989b). This indicates that there are differences in the ways that individuals come to know themselves as 'homosexual'. It also indicates that non-heterosexuality can be about 'more' than sex itself. For some individuals, the idea that sexual activities are *the* defining element of non-heterosexual experience is a remnant of heterosexist 'ideology'. As Miriam (F44) firmly says: 'I think otherwise we're colluding with people's interpretation of what defines us – which is sexual activities.'

This highlights the value in distinguishing between homosexual desires, practices and identities (Weeks 1985, 1986), though many people fail to make this distinction. An example is provided by Jayne, here recounting her attempt to explain to her mother that her identity is not reducible to sex:

I said, 'Mum, so far as I'm concerned, lesbianism isn't about having sex – lesbianism is about where you put your emotional energy and whether your emotional attachment is to women or men.' ... I suppose that's to do with my sense of identity, that I know I would still feel like a lesbian if I wasn't having sex. (F07)

For Jayne, identifying as lesbian is more about emotional connections than erotic practices. While the category 'lesbian' is most commonly understood and talked about as a 'sexual identity', what it represents for Jayne is emotional commitment to others. Sex plays a significant part in Jayne's life and relationship, but in terms of identifying as a lesbian, it 'has its place'. A similar point arises in the account of Matthew, a 'closeted' gay man who has struggled with the issue of sexual identity for much of his adult life. In his story, same sex erotic encounters are located as an aspect of 'something bigger':

Sometimes when I've had an orgasm I think ... 'is that what this is all about?' You know? Is it about me ... shooting – is this what all the angst, all this trauma is about. And I don't think it is. I think it's an aspect. It feels my identity is much more than, you know, wanting to have sex with another guy. … It feels quite hard to explain this, but it feels like there are loads of dimensions to choosing to say, 'I'm this person', rather than just the sexual bit. (M28)

In identifying as lesbian, gay, bisexual or queer, individuals bring the issue of sexuality to the forefront of their everyday lives (since to do so is to publicly claim to be the possessor of a problematic or marginalised identity). But there is more at stake than sex itself (Davies 1992; Troiden 1993). As several writers have argued, what *is* at issue are broader ways of being in the world (Blasius 1994; Weeks 1995; Bech 1997; Heaphy 1999). Among non-heterosexuals themselves, the importance of sex to personal and social identity varies widely. Like Matthew above, however, the predominant tendency is to view sexual practice as an important aspect, but not *the* defining aspect of 'who I am'. What emerges from a consideration of the diversity of accounts is a sense of the messy and complex relationships between sexual identities and sexual practices (Dowsett 1996). This is a point that is illustrated particularly well by individuals who have *sexual* relationships with members of the 'opposite' sex, but who identify as strictly lesbian or gay (see French 1992). While the tendency until recently has been to characterise such relationships as phases in the development of authentic (lesbian or gay) identity (see Bozett 1981a), such understandings cannot account for narratives such as Miriam's, who identifies as a lesbian but continues to have sexual relations with men:

> When I came back to London I decided that if I wanted to be sexual with men then it was permissible – that I would allow myself … But I was very, very clear … It didn't make me bisexual. And it didn't make me heterosexual – I was just a lesbian having sex with some men, when I wanted. It didn't change … the innateness of my identity and my being – which is as a lesbian. And people might say I'm confused, but in my eyes the confusion is about lesbians [who have sex with men] who feel that they now have to identify as either heterosexual or bisexual. (F44)

Certain men can identify as gay but recognise their relationship with a female partner as the primary ongoing relationship. Craig, for instance, identifies as a gay man but has lived with his female partner for over twenty years:

> We recognised that there was an issue with my sexual orientation but we thought we'd get married. Because I knew that I had a feeling for her. So we got married. We didn't know whether anything would work or not. … We still have a sexual relationship. She knows I have problems with it. But I have made a commitment to her which we reaffirmed. (M14)

Understanding sexual identity as a simple reflection of particular sexual practices or the gender of sexual partners is problematic. Neither Miriam's nor Craig's account of their 'heterosexual' relationships provide evidence of a 'counterfeit' (Bozett 1981b) identity. Miriam presents herself firmly as a lesbian who has decided to continue to have sexual encounters with men as she chooses, while Craig is clear that he is a gay man who has chosen to reaffirm his relationship with his wife and work at maintaining a sexual relationship with her (see also French 1992: 94–8). These accounts are in line with broader stories of the complexity of sexual relationships and sexual identity that have emerged through debates on 'queer' identities (see Bristow and Wilson 1993). Similarly, the much debated category of 'men who have sex with men' that was developed in the context of HIV prevention (Deverell and Prout 1995; Gatter 1999: 95), indicates that there are also a number of men and women who have sexual relationships with members of their own sex, but hold strongly to their heterosexual identities. While the tendency in the past has been to view this in terms of an individual's inability to 'come out', there is an increasing sense of the various possibilities that are open to individuals. In the end, while sex and the erotic may be pivotal aspects around which narratives of non-heterosexual identity tend to be built, these identities are not reducible to particular types of erotic interactions or sexual practices.

Doing gender?

An important way in which sexuality has been linked to identity is through its historical ties with gender. It is in regard to the 'appropriate' relationship between gender and sexuality that non-heterosexual men and women have traditionally been viewed as problematic (Weeks 1985, 1989, 1991). Gendered assumptions that exist in the broader society have also played a major role in constructing commonsense understandings of what the lives of non-heterosexual women and men are like. As we argued in Chapter 3, these have often translated into positions that construct lesbians as asexual beings and gay men as the possessors of ferocious sexual appetites (Cruikshank 1992).

While gendered assumptions structure heterosexual understandings about non-heterosexual sexualities, they can also impact on the private stories, self-perceptions and expectations of non-heterosexuals themselves. Popular notions of what constitutes 'sex' have been highly influenced by heterosexual (male) understandings. 'Real sex' is broadly understood to be penis-vagina penetrative intercourse (Jackson 1995: 21) – something that men 'do' to women: the implication being that for lesbians the absence of the penis must imply inauthentic (or no) sex. Richardson (1992) suggests that as a consequence, women lack access to a language which can be used to describe, discuss and negotiate sex. She argues that although there are numerous terms to describe sex from male perspectives, there are far less to describe sex from female perspectives, and even fewer from the perspective of sex between women.

It is not only assumptions about qualitative differences that inform our perceptions of women and men's sexuality, but also quantitative notions of what constitutes 'enough' sex. In a critique of Blumstein and Schwartz's (1983) study of lesbian, gay and heterosexual couples, in which lesbians were identified as having the least frequent sex, Frye (1991) has challenged the validity of a comparative focus. She suggests that what heterosexuals might do more than once a month takes on average eight minutes to do:

> what we [lesbians] do that, on average, we do considerably less frequently, takes, on average, considerably more than eight minutes to do. It takes about thirty minutes at least. Sometimes maybe an hour.
>
> (Frye 1991: 2)

Blumstein and Schwartz (1983) also suggest that lesbians are more likely to value non-genital physical contact than other couples. They are likely to see this as an end in itself rather than foreplay. Indeed, many lesbians do identify non-genital physical intimacy as a form of sexualised intimacy (see Johnson's (1990) study of long-term lesbian relationships, where physical contact was rated as being highly important – whether or not genital sex still occurred). Bisexual women can also struggle with the lack of a language and limited behaviours available under the accepted lexicon of 'sexual' when describing their relationships with men. As Joan explains:

> It also depends on what you mean by sexually involved, because with one of the men there's not any kind of – genital contact, I suppose you could say – but it is, I would say, it still was sexual contact because it's not just physical affection – it goes further than that. So it's a bit sort of complicated, really – it's not that clear-cut. ... It's not what most people would think of as having sex, I think. (F32)

Assumptions about the non-penetrative nature of lesbian sexual relationships have led to their characterisation as 'cuddly' rather than 'sexy'. This dovetails with the dominant representation of 'political lesbianism' as being physically comforting but non- (or anti-)sexual. Another factor that has contributed to the perception of lesbianism as a desexualised form of existence is the popularisation of the notion that Joanne Loulan (in Stein 1993) has referred to as 'lesbian bed death'. This refers to the situation where the sexual nature of a couple relationship discontinues but the relationship itself carries on. It is a 'condition' that can supposedly set in after the 'honeymoon' period is over (from two months to two years). The extent to which this is an accurate description of lesbian experience is not verifiable, and is arguably less important than the degree to which the understandings and expectations of lesbians themselves have been influenced by the notion.

The image of the desexualised lesbian can be conjured up by women themselves when commenting on lesbian culture, through references to lesbian bed death; the almost 'innate' disinterest in sex for its own sake; the 'inability' to engage in casual sex; and the 'inability' to separate sex and emotion. Jill, for example, refers to the lack of sex in her twelve-year relationship as typical:

it's just something that happens. I think that when you've been together with people – well, it happens to lots of lesbians who've been together for a long time. We're certainly not alone. (F22)

Most external accounts of the desexualised lesbian, however, can be in stark contrast to the accounts that lesbians provide of their *own* active sexual lives. With regard to lesbian bed death, Amy (F27) refers with surprise to the ongoing sex that exists in her relationship because 'we've been together for a year and a half [so] you would have thought it would be completely over by now'. Yet, most women cannot imagine continuing in a relationship of any length of time that was devoid of a significant erotic element – indeed, Jill was the only woman in our research who was in a relationship that was no longer sexual. Several women, however, can imagine (or have experienced) periods of time without sex due to reasons of moving house, heavy pressures of work, childbirth, and so on. There is some evidence that the frequency of sexual contact in lesbian relationships does decrease over time (Johnson 1990). For the majority, however, sexual intimacy (and sexual satisfaction) continues to be important to the quality and permanence of the relationships. The majority of older lesbians appear to remain sexually active (see Kehoe 1988; also Raphael and Robinson 1984). Virginia (F48), for example, who is 61 and has been in a relationship for thirty-four years with someone thirteen years her senior, remarks that sex 'still has its place very definitely'. Women's masturbation is afforded significant importance in the literature, and in the lives of women we interviewed. Further, many women have engaged in casual sex (defined variously as a one-night stand or a two- or three-week affair). This was not the reserve of the younger women we talked to, who might be viewed as more influenced by the dominant pro-sex culture. Jenny, a lesbian in her forties, talks about enjoying casual sex in her early twenties, and bemoans the lack of support for casual sex among the lesbian community in which she lived:

> there have been times in the past when I have rued the fact that, at certain points at least, the lesbian community was almost anti that sort of thing and … [sometimes] I envied the men's community because there were times when really what I wanted was something fairly light-hearted and sexual and enjoyable and not to have to make a deep commitment in the middle of it. I don't know if that's changed these days or not. I'm not really on, you know – on the scene. (F21)

Recent writing on the subject has tended to compare and contrast non-heterosexual women's sexuality with that of non-heterosexual males. In critiques of the myths that surround female and lesbian sexuality, dominant understandings of gay male sexual cultures have been employed to advocate the development of pro-sex lesbian sexualities: female cruising has been advocated and public female sex campaigned for; lesbian sex clubs with go-go girls and lap dancers have been viewed as a positive development; and some people have advocated the broadening of lesbian sexual repertoires to include sex with men as a strategy for subverting heterosexuality. Also, the ever-growing visibility of bisexuality and queer has alerted both lesbian and gay communities to the possibilities of sexual relationships between women and men that are not 'heterosexual' (George 1993). For some these shifts would represent a freeing of lesbian sexual desire. Others have suggested that non-heterosexual women have (misguidedly) compared themselves with a mythical notion of gay men's sexuality and found themselves lacking (see Richardson 1992).

As we have seen, lesbians' accounts of their *own* sexual lives are often in tension with their accounts of lesbian sexual cultures generally. The latter are, to a significant degree, based on received wisdom about 'what lesbians are like' – but also about gay men's sexual lives. An illustration of this lies in the pervasive myth that non-heterosexual women are less sexually active – or interested in sex – than their male counterparts. As Melanie puts it:

> I get the impression that gay male relationships are *more* likely to be just [about] sex – pure sex – and [are more] short-lived than lesbian relationships. Lesbians are, on the whole, looking for something a little bit more than pure sex. (F29)

A fairly common view among lesbians is that gay men have a much greater capacity to engage in casual anonymous sex. Lesbians, on the other hand, are thought to require an emotional connection before they can engage in sex. This does not mean that these received beliefs are not also critically interrogated. However, while women might tend to refer to the myth, contradict it, and question its validity, the temptation is to conclude by favouring the veracity of the myth. For example, Niamh comments on the differences between gay and lesbian relationships:

> Do lesbians have less sex? I don't think they do, actually. But I think that they're often not pre-eminently sexual. And again, it's so irritating because some of the clichés are *bloody* true – it's that gay men's relationships may organise themselves more around sex. (F34)

The understandings of these women are framed in terms of witnessing gay relationships, but are also based on the notion that gay men are likely to carry the gender stereotyping of all men. As Melanie comments:

> My feeling is that because of the society we live in – nothing biological, but because of the society we live in – men tend to put more emphasis on sexual things and less emphasis on talking and communication. And therefore a lot of gay male relationships might be much more reliant on sexual physical sex than [are] lesbian relationships. (F29)

Gay men, in contrast, are more reluctant to speculate on the importance of sex for lesbians, and the role of sex in lesbian relationships. Among gay men, the most usual account was similar to the one that Frank provides below, which acknowledges the existence of 'myths' about lesbians and sex, but also suggests that these could well *be* myths:

> the myth that you were brought up with, you know, that lesbians might take more time to get to know each other before they hop into bed. These days, maybe that's totally wrong – maybe they hop into bed on the first day. I don't know. (M36)

However, a few gay men did suggest that whereas many gay men might be more concerned with the 'physical side' of sex, lesbians might want more than sex. Such accounts reproduced the commonsense understandings about lesbians *and* gay men, as Sean shows:

> I guess the biggest general difference, superficially, seems to be that gay men are much more into going out looking for sex. And that's more like the physical, sexual side of things ... I guess gay men would go out looking for men for sex, whereas lesbians might go looking for a partner to relate to in other ways as well as sex. (M37)

This view of gay men's sexual lives is commonly presented in broader local knowledges. While writers, like Cruikshank (1992: 168) for example, are critical of the stereotype of gay men which portrays them as promiscuous and obsessed by sex, they tend to concur with these commonsense understandings in discussing the differences between gay and lesbian sexualities. The reality of gay male lives and sexual practices is, however, more complex than these narratives would suggest.

As the research of Project SIGMA (Socio-sexual Investigations into Gay Men and AIDS) (Davies *et al.* 1993) suggests, to discuss gay male sexuality in this fashion undermines the huge diversity of sexual experience which exists among gay men (see also Dowsett 1996). Project SIGMA has provided some of the most detailed information on gay men's sexual lives through research developed in response to AIDS and HIV. The research is based on the largest ongoing study in Britain of men who engage in same sex sexual activity (see Davies *et al.* 1993). In terms of casual sex, note that numbers of sexual partners in one cohort of their study ranged from 0 to 1,000 (Davies *et al.* 1993: 152). The number of sexual partners varies according to relationship status, and whether those who are in relationships are monogamous or not. Our interviews suggest that many gay men seem to fit the stereotype. Simon told us:

> I enjoy having sex with new people and at times that seems to be a very important thing for me, and I try to get it in ... various ways. So I go cot-

taging, I go cruising, around. ... And I go to clubs. I seem to be looking for it much of the time and spend a lot of time doing it. (M05)

Davies *et al.* (1993: 151) note that 'the easy availability of sex without commitment is one of the most notable features of the gay scene'. This is an aspect of gay culture that has received criticism from both outside and within the gay community. Patton (cited in Davies *et al.* 1993: 152) suggests that the advent of AIDS in particular allowed for 'morally offensive judgements' that were based on a valorisation of heterosexual norms. The gay man's reputation for sex in public sex environments (see Davies *et al.* 1993: 153; Keogh, Holland and Weatherburn 1998) or 'erotic oases' (Henriksson 1995) – clubs, pubs, backrooms, saunas, cottages, cruising grounds, and so on – has often caused moral outrage from some heterosexuals, and unease among some gay men themselves. As Davies *et al.* (1993) suggest, there is not a single 'type' of gay man who engages in casual or public sex. Rather, there are likely to be a variety of motivating factors at play – and the desire for these forms of sexual lives is likely to vary over the life of the individual. Even for many of those most devoted to casual encounters, there is more than 'just' sex at stake, as Charles explains:

I mean, it's very difficult to say what an *average* amount of casual sex is for a gay man, but ... I do sleep around a fair amount, but I'm also quite ... I have to really fancy someone. So that keeps the number down I would have thought. (M25)

A weaker story about gay men, but (perhaps surprisingly) a more frequent one in our research, is that of the undesirability of casual sex and the 'necessity' for an emotional or intimate connection. David, for instance, highlights his desire for intimacy:

I could have sex frequently if I wanted to, but I don't. And along those lines, that's why I'm not somebody that would ... go cottaging – particularly because sex for me is not a physical thing. So, you know, a lot of people say that they would go to a cottage at least once a day. ... I mean, I would get very little release out of that because ... I think I have to feel intimate with somebody before I enjoy it. (M12)

Many gay men emphasise the undesirability of casual sex *for them* – and the link between sex and emotion. Phillip makes the comment that

there are long periods when I've been on my own, when I've been celibate, and I haven't even had sex. And that's largely because when, in earlier times ... I had one-night stands and things, I've actually felt quite unfulfilled by them, and ... woken up the next day and thought, 'Oh God! What will we talk about now? What was all that about?' ... And I actually think I would prefer to do without that – I'd just as soon have a wank – have a masturbatory life at home, you know, rather than engage with people – [rather] than the next morning, think, 'well, I've not actually got much fulfilment out of that'. (M27)

At an abstract level at least, the majority of men we interviewed could separate 'sex' from 'love'. But interestingly, this is easier to put into practice for those who are in committed emotional relationships, like Peter:

> Well sex for me, it can either be recreational or it can be loving. And some-times I have recreational sex with David, and sometimes I have loving sex with David, and I only have recreational sex with other men. And it's – that's the difference really. (M11)

This again raises the question of the relationship between sex and love, which was briefly touched on in Chapter 5. As Alan says:

> [I think that] sex is an important part of love sometimes. I mean, I do think that separating sex and love is, well – for me – quite difficult (although not impossible I have to say). I don't know – I mean, either I've been socialised or I'm just hopelessly romantic, but I've always had difficulty with totally unemotional sex – I mean, it's just who I am really. (M39)

For Alan, as with a significant number of the men and women we interviewed, separating sex from *some* form of close emotional connection is in practice a difficult thing to do. For many people, engaging in sexual encounters with others is part of a quest for sexual *and* emotional fulfilment. Indeed, while it is clear that some gay men may find it relatively easy to separate sex from emotional attachments, other accounts by men suggest that sexual encounters are often pursued as a route to more long-term, committed, emotional relationships. Particularly for some men who are not in a couple relationship, casual sexual relationships can offer the potential for meeting the 'right' person. However, as Phillip's earlier comments indicate, they can also lead to disappointment: while casual contacts may provide a temporary sense of physical intimacy, they often fail to provide the emotional goods that are being sought. In response, individuals are likely to adopt one of two approaches: first, they continue to engage in casual encounters in the hope that they might eventually come into contact with someone who is willing to build something 'bigger' (and to suffer what one individual described as the very depressing consequences); or, second, they avoid casual sexual encounters, and seek out other ways of meeting a committed (both sexually and emotionally) partner.

In the end, what these accounts reveal about the quantity of sexual partners is probably less important than the insights they afford for the implications of increased sexual choices. There is some evidence to suggest that the separation of sex from reproduction, and the value increasingly afforded it as a form of pleasure, has meant that both heterosexuals and non-heterosexuals are faced with new choices with regard to sexual relationships (see Giddens 1992).

However, the *particular* opportunities that arise for non-heterosexuals must also be understood as resulting from the separation of sex from dominant heterosexual meanings. This allows for experimentation with a multiplicity of possible ways of being. It can also necessitate personal interrogations of 'what works best for me'. In organising and managing their sexual lives, non-heterosexuals have little option but to be both reflective and reflexive. As Tom (M15) puts it, 'I constantly sort of review as to why are you constantly wanting to have sex, or ask myself "was that really worth it?" '. In so doing, individuals are not only engaging on a critical level with their own desires and practices, but also with a set of gendered assumptions of what they 'should' want.

Undoing gender?

The relationship between 'doing' sex and 'doing' (or undoing) gender is posed sharply in attitudes to specific sexual practices. For gay men these are usually debated in terms of the practice of anal sex, and for lesbians through the 'sex wars' that began in the mid-1980s. In this section, we examine each controversy in turn.

Despite the historical demonisation of 'sodomy' as an unnatural act, and the consequential tendency of early homophile writers to downplay its significance (Weeks 1977), there is no doubt of the symbolic significance of anal sex to many gay men, and the challenge it poses to received ideas of 'active' masculinity and 'passive' femininity. As Dan (M44) says, 'I was active before I discovered the delights of being fucked.' Such delights are by no means universally agreed upon. The findings of Project Sigma (Davies *et al.* 1993: 131) has shown that anal intercourse is not necessarily central to the sexual lives of the majority of gay men (for 46.6 per cent it is primary, central, very or quite important; for 34.5 per cent it is coincidental, secondary or of minor importance; for 18.9 per cent it is of no importance or has negative qualities). Even for those gay men who do not engage in anal sex, however, it is likely to remain a practice of significant meaning. As Connell *et al.* note:

> Anal intercourse ... is a practice that has had major historical significance in the social construction of men's homosexuality. It was specifically targeted by religious and criminal sanctions against 'the abominable crime of buggery' and has remained central to hostile stereotypes of homosexual men. Accordingly it became a major issue in attempts at law reform and in the Gay Liberation movement's claims for sexual freedom ... It is a practice which carries a heavy load of social meaning. For gay men it is likely to symbolise oppression and freedom even for those who do not find it a significant part of sexual pleasure.
>
> (Connell *et al.*, cited in King 1993: 158)

As the writers suggest in this quotation, anal intercourse has a diversity of conflicting meanings. It can signify identity, pleasure, orgasm, pain, closeness, health, love and intimacy, trust and relaxation, power, dominance and control (Davies *et al.* 1993: 130–7). Of course, as Jackson (1995: 21) and others have pointed out, penetrative sexual acts are generally afforded highly gendered meanings in our societies. Likewise, Davies *et al.* suggest that the stigma attached to anal sex, and male fears of being penetrated, have much to do with gender:

> It seems to us more likely that the fear of being receptive stems from the danger to the regard one is held in by other men … or the regard one holds oneself in. Being receptive is associated with being not 'wholly masculine', or in being identified as a woman in some way. … One way of dealing with this is to reject the implicit values of a patriarchal culture.
>
> (Davies *et al.* 1993: 129)

In negotiating the 'doing' of anal sex, gay men can be involved in negotiating the gendered meanings attached to penetration. However, it is also possible to challenge these hegemonic values. Even in heterosexual sex, as Jackson (1995: 21) points out, there is no absolute reason why the conjunction of a penis and a vagina has to be thought of as penetration, or as a process in which only one of those organs is active. She argues that the coercive equation of sex = coitus = something men *do* to women, is not an inevitable consequence of an anatomical female relating to an anatomical male, but the product of the social relations under which those bodies meet. For gay men, a particular opportunity to subvert the dominant gender meanings afforded by penetration can arise through a disruption of the active–passive dichotomy. As Dan states:

> sex with a guy who wants both and you want both, he'll screw you and you can screw him, can be *fantastic*. I always say, what's the point of being gay if you can't have it both ways? (M44)

The 'improper' doing of sex offers some potential for the undoing of gender (Blasius 1994; Nardi 1999), and this has been true of women as well as men. The so-called 'lesbian sex wars' (Healey 1996) is a key arena where the formation of lesbian sexual values and the meanings of femininity have been at stake. In the 1970s, a dominant feminist construction of lesbianism was as a 'political' form of existence – divorced from sex, desire, attraction and behaviour (Smyth 1992; Wilton 1996). This was articulated in different ways, but it emphasised particularly the emotional attachments and commitments – rather than the sexual activity – that exist between women (e.g., Faderman 1981; Jeffreys 1990); the male-defined and -focused (and therefore oppressive) nature of heterosexual sex; and the male meanings that infused particular sexual practices between women (for example, flirting, initiating sex, vaginal or anal penetration).

The broad implication of these positions was the necessity of analysing and politicising sex in an endeavour to challenge and reject male influence and power inequalities. This position often implied that sex was not necessary to lesbian identity. While political lesbianism was sometimes held up as the ideal practice of all feminists (Richardson 1992), some critics have argued that the strategy of de-emphasising sex in favour of an identity politics was aimed at sanitising lesbianism for the benefit of heterosexual feminists (e.g., Wilson 1983). In the 1980s, however, there were a series of strong responses to what was perceived as a lesbian feminism that was anti-sex (see Smyth 1992). The catalysts for these were the emergence of lesbian sadomasochism (S&M), the anti-pornography movement, which precipitated debates about censorship and lesbian pornography, the re-emergence of lesbian butch-femme, and the resulting debates about power and inequalities in lesbian sexual relationships.

In Britain, these debates were highly influenced by those in the United States, and such writers as Joan Nestle (1987), Pat Califia (1988), Joanne Loulan (1987) and Andrea Dworkin (1987), as well as the magazine *On Our Backs*. The so-called 'battles' that took place in Britain were initially focused on whether lesbian/gay and women's bookshops should sell S&M literature and lesbian porn (for example, *Quim*, the first British lesbian sex magazine; see Wilton 1996). There were ongoing conflicts in London, England about the rights of S&M dykes to use the Lesbian and Gay Centre, and also disputes about their inclusion on Lesbian Strength marches. An ongoing area of debate concerned the appropriate response to the anti-pornography movement (Smyth 1992; Healey 1996).

An underlying feature of these debates is the broad consensus that a key 'success' of the 'wars' was that sex was put back into lesbianism (see Richardson 1992). Together with the emergence of queer, and the increasing strength of a politicised bisexual movement, this has created a context in which the notions of the sex-positive lesbian, and 'radical' queer women, have emerged as visible presences in the ever-increasing literature on non-heterosexual women's lives. Visibility is also enhanced through the burgeoning lesbian sex industry, which includes literature (see Cartledge and Ryan 1983; Snitow, Stansell and Thompson 1983; Barrington 1991; Rednour 1995), sex clubs, films and videos, art and theatre (Kiss and Tell 1994). It is, of course, difficult to measure the impact of these developments on the everyday lives of non-heterosexual women. While Stein (1993) argues that the impact has been limited, Richardson (1992) has speculated that a narrowly defined sexual 'norm' is being created where so-called 'vanilla' sex is seen as almost 'abnormal' – as the dominant discourse in the new industry concerns practices that involve S&M, penetration, dildos and sex toys. She states that 'what we are witnessing, in the absence of a diversity of cultural representations of lesbian sex, is a redefinition of what lesbian sex is' (Richardson 1992: 198).

Yet, significantly, these are debates that are far from over, and are still in the process of being worked out – not least at local and community levels (see, for example, Farquhar 2000). Sue (F15), for example, talks about the 'judgement' she has faced in coming out as an S&M dyke (see Chapter 3). Coral, on the other hand, cannot understand S&M lesbians:

> [There was] someone I did go out with for a very short period, [and] we sort of talked about it and I said if I was going to get off on S&M then I would have got off on it when I was a kid with my mum beating the shit out of me. I'm sorry, I can't – you know, I can't find pleasure in pain. (F13)

It's unlikely that these debates will ever be fully resolved. They are, however, core areas where the question of 'how we want to be' as sexual beings (and as women and lesbians) are being considered. They can be understood as negotiations of meaning that have a crucial part to play in both collective and individual attempts to work out the role and value of sex. While it *is* difficult to measure the relationship between these broader discourses and individual practices, the former should not be understood merely as talk, that can be neatly separated from 'the doing' of sex. Rather, they are discourses that influence, and are influenced by, negotiations of sex at the level of practice. Sexual acts in themselves carry no intrinsic meaning. Meanings depend on the specific contexts in which sexuality is practised: it's not so much what you do, but how you do it (see Weeks 1995). Ultimately, the significance of sexual activities depends on the values that frame them.

Ethics of relating

Questions of values and ethics emerge strongly in the everyday negotiation of sexual relationships. In Chapter 5, we saw the importance of these negotiations in couple relationships. However, they can be as important in a range of other sexual interactions, from the casual to the multi-partnered relationships. In the following quotation, Peter touches on this theme as he outlines the dilemmas he encountered in making a choice to commit to one of two partners. He frames this in terms of sexual and emotional satisfaction:

> I had this whole 'what's going on here' thing? I'm having great sex with Frank but I don't think there's much of a relationship here. I'm not having great sex with David but [there's] great potential for a relationship. ... I talked to both of them ... But gradually, within the space of weeks rather than months, it was pretty clear that I was much more emotionally involved with David than I was with Frank. (M11)

For those who are in an ongoing couple relationship, the most common narrative about sex is that it is a complement to the emotional bond between partners. Dee (F06) and Jane (F07) discuss this situation:

Dee: Yes, it's important [i.e., sex]. But I wouldn't say it's *the* most important thing.

Jane: And I think it's very male, I suppose, to measure sex by the quantity rather than the quality of it – and [rather than considering] the trust and what it means to the relationship, and the quality of the emotional bond that you have without having to have sex to uphold that [bond]. And all those things are important, and the quality of being able to talk about it.

In relationships where sex is a crucial indicator of the 'specialness' of the relationship, or is conceptualised as *the* form of expression for the emotional bond, its discontinuation can mark a serious crisis for the relationship. In such situations, the decline of sex can be a marker of the inevitable decline of the relationship. As Charles narrates:

> he didn't want to stop seeing me, but he didn't want to have sex with me and I didn't want to necessarily see him if it wasn't going to be that kind of relationship. ... I wrote him a really angry letter – he'd never received one like that before from me. And I think it had quite shocked him ... I think he was more frightened than angry. And [he] realised that ... we had to negotiate around this somehow. But at the same time, I was seeing this as fairly untenable because you can't say to someone, 'I don't care if you don't want to have sex with me – you've got to have sex with me ...'. (M25)

As Charles indicates, individuals within relationships do not necessarily attach the same value to their sexual interactions, and there is not *necessarily* a consensus about the relationship between sex and commitment. For Charles, a relationship without sex would radically alter the nature of the commitment – to the degree that he would not consider this arrangement to be a 'relationship' as such. But we are also provided with a sense of his partner's belief that the abstraction of sex would not necessarily undermine the commitment to the relationship. This quotation indicates two ethical imperatives that tend to be at work in same sex relationships. First, it points to a belief in the necessity of attempting to negotiate two opposing beliefs or values. The impulse is to attempt to 'work things out' (McWhirter and Mattison 1984; Peplau, Venigas and Miller Campbell 1996). However, as Charles suggests, the impulse is also to recognise that the sexual relationship (and commitment it might indicate) must be freely entered into, and not be based on a sense of obligation or 'force'. This resonates with Blasius' (1994) account of equality in same sex erotic relationships. These, he suggests, are based on *reciprocal* giving and receiving of pleasure, and the power of one partner to shape the actions of the other is limited by the freedom of individuals to leave the relationship.

The question of sexual fidelity, as we saw in the last chapter, raises these issues most sharply. There is no general agreement as to the extent to which non-heterosexual relationships are non-monogamous. Johnson (1990), however, notes that while the majority of lesbian couples she studied were monogamous at that present time, they had previously had phases of negotiated non-monogamy or had non-negotiated affairs followed by a renewed commitment to monogamy. McWhirter and Mattison (1984) suggest that gay male couple relationships are often based on a *conscious rejection* of dominant heterosexual values and practices around monogamy (see also Harry 1984), and this is echoed in our own findings, outlined in detail in Chapter 5.

Nearly all of our research participants had considered the question of monogamy, and rarely could the monogamous or non-monogamous nature of relationships be assumed. Even where monogamy is described as a 'natural' trait of the individuals involved, it remains an issue which requires discussion, and making sense of in the particular circumstances of the relationship in question. This brings us to the broader issue about the relationship between sex, love and commitment. Blumstein and Schwartz (1983: 195) suggest that as gay male relationships mature, they rely less on sex as a focus for commitment. Sex with others, they note, often balances the decline of sexual activity within the primary relationship. They also suggest, as we have done in Chapter 5, that in such relationships, sexual non-monogamy may be balanced by strong emotional monogamy. While our own research suggests that there is likely to be some basis for these claims, we would argue that for both gay men and lesbians alike it is not necessarily the decline of sex in their primary relationships that is the major influencing factor in non-monogamy. Rather, the principle of 'co-independence' that structures the operation of same sex relationships, the break from heterosexual assumptions, and the *abstract* possibilities of separating sex from emotional ties, mean that non-monogamy is always (at the abstract or the practical level) a possibility for non-heterosexual relationships. In Amy's (F27) view, monogamy is 'something we negotiate all the time – the rules … we had a discussion about it and decided that we were basically monogamous but with holidays from it rather than non-monogamous'.

Even in cases where there is a reluctance to fix absolute rules, there is a tendency to form contingent ones which guide the operation of the various possible relationships. Depending on the situation, these are worked through and re-worked. As Amy's comments indicate, tension can occur over quite contra-dictory impulses: between not *wanting* the partner to have sexual relationships with others, and not believing in monogamy 'for its own sake'. The following question arises: for whose (or what) sake is monogamy required? This is often framed in terms of giving the relationship, trust and commitment, time to develop or to grow. As Paul says about his new relationship:

> I wouldn't make a general rule. He and I at the moment do [have a sexually exclusive relationship]. But we've already discussed that that could and may change without it being fatal to the relationship. Generally speaking, I wouldn't make a rule, because I've experienced both kinds of arrangement. (M21)

Once trust has been satisfactorily established in a relationship, many people feel they can then 'take the risk' and engage with others. While it might make considerable 'common sense' that couples change *from* monogamy to non-monogamy, there are also cases – although fewer – where couples attempt to shift from non-monogamy to monogamy. This is not necessarily influenced by issues of emotional exclusivity; as Charles suggests, rather, pragmatic reasons might be at play:

> We discussed [monogamy], the possibility. I mean, it wasn't something we'd ever set out to design our relationship around, but basically it came up when we wanted to have safe sex – I mean, unsafe sex – unprotected sex together. … So we decided [that] maybe we should be monogamous for a while. The decision lasted for about five days … but what we did do was … we said, okay, we'll have unsafe sex together but we have to be completely careful with other people and completely honest with each other. (M25)

If negotiation is a key theme in accounts of sexual (non-)monogamy, trust is the key notion that permits and guides the operation of open sexual relationships. Regardless of the reasons for adoption of non-monogamy, a leap of faith must be made in terms of each partner's integrity. Whereas the nature of the couple bond, the value afforded sex and the shifting nature of love and desire can be accommodated and negotiated, breach of trust can seriously threaten the relationship. Here, Peter offers this view:

> So, if you have casual sex and you're not honest with the person that is your main sexual partner, say you haven't told them you're having casual sex, it threatens it [your relationship] then. But I don't think it does otherwise. I think if you negotiate your sexual life as well as the rest of your life, then it doesn't threaten it. (M11)

For some this is not a risk that they are ready or willing to take. As Julie notes:

> *that's* where the betrayal comes in, because you've made a commitment to one thing and you're not doing it. So, rather than set rules in stone that you may break, and then feel betrayed over – I'd rather not set them in stone and just sort of take it a day at a time. (F14)

For those who desire both sexual exclusiveness in the relationship *and* the opportunity for sexual encounters with others, negotiation of monogamy requires significant creativity. This is also where the multiple or ambiguous meanings that 'monogamy' can have in everyday practice emerge. Rob (M06) and Scott (M07), for instance, initially defined their relationship as monogamous. However, while discussing their relationship in more detail, a different picture of their sexual life emerged – one which involved occasional sex with others. The complexity of the different meanings of the term 'monogamy' was addressed implicitly by the account given of various encounters with third parties, but also explicitly by the couple themselves:

Rob: I would still define us as monogamous ... but, we're not in the true sense of the word, are we?

Scott: If monogamy is having sex with each other ...

Rob: I define monogamy as ...

Scott: It's ... well, I define 'open' as me going off tonight and having sex with a man and coming back and talking about it. I define that as 'open'. Monogamy is ... it's just us and, if a third party is brought into us, then I would still define that as monogamy.

Rob and Scott view having sexual relationships with others as a couple as a successful means of negotiating the tensions that can occur between openness and insecurity. Giddens (1992) has argued that both lesbians and gay men place in question the traditional integration of marriage and monogamy by reworking monogamy as a matter for negotiation in the context of commitment and trust. But we want to emphasise here that it is not non-monogamy itself that is *the* key aspect of the non-heterosexual ethic of relating. Rather, it is the emphasis on trust (and honesty) as the basis for commitment that makes this a possibility – together with the impulse towards explicit negotiation. As essential components of the 'friendship ethic' (see Chapter 3) that underlies same sex relationships, these make the achievement of the various sexual and emotional 'needs' at play (the individual's, the partner's, the couple's) a very real possibility. Viewed from this perspective, it is not surprising that sexual relationships can be articulated as being 'about' friendship in various ways (see Nardi 1992b). Frank (M36) recalls that he 'spent quite a number of years on my own or with sort of casual relationships, and sex friends; friends ... affectionate friends and one-night stands and all sorts of things'. Similarly, Dan says there are 'sensual friendships':

> I've had sexual friendships that have been really good. I've had really good sex with somebody and I like them as a friend but I don't want them to come and live with me and I don't want to live with him – it's friendship and it can be very good friendship. (M44)

By combining friendship with sexual relationships, non-heterosexuals – like Frank and Dan – are suggesting that significantly new forms of intimacy are possible. In bringing sex and friendship together, traditional boundaries relating to 'appropriate' ways of knowing the other are blurred, and dominant heterosexual ideologies of the (monogamous) couple as *the* location of sex and love are challenged. Niamh explains that:

> There's probably not that many people who I love that at some level I'm not attracted to ... I think they're often related but I don't think that they're related in the sense that if I had sex with somebody I would automatically love them. Or if I fancy somebody I love them, but I think often if I love somebody, I may have ... desire for them. (F34)

Erotics and ethical practice

Outside of the determining contexts of heterosexuality, individuals find ways of 'doing' sex and sexual relationships differently – a task that requires significant working out and creativity. A clear testament to the creativity of non-heterosexuals has been the shaping of new sexual selves as a consequence of the crisis of AIDS. It is hard to escape the impact that HIV and AIDS has had on the sexual lives of non-heterosexuals over the past twenty years. In the West, the epidemic has had the greatest impact on gay men and has (apparently) affected lesbians the least. However, this does not mean that there is not a story about HIV and the sexual lives of lesbians to be told (see Farquhar 1999). While the numbers of lesbians living with HIV is relatively low, many have been deeply touched by its existence. While some women suggest that HIV has had little relevance for their personal sexual lives, this is a conclusion that has been reached after consideration and knowledge of the risks. As Melanie, a 52-year-old lesbian, explains:

> I suppose it feels like it's not terribly relevant because … I feel that most lesbian practices aren't high-risk anyway, or those that I indulge in aren't risky … it doesn't feel like I'm terribly at risk and it doesn't feel like any of the people that I care for closely are very at risk. (F29)

A significant (and perhaps surprising) number of lesbians have tested for HIV – and demonstrate considerable awareness of the issue of safer sex (cf. Gorna 1996). Most have reflected on and made an assessment of the riskiness of their own sexual behaviour. For some women this has led to decisions about the level of risk with which they are prepared to live. Jenny, for instance, outlines the decisions she has made on the basis of her knowledge of safer sex.

> At the moment I have monogamous sex. … I know that lesbian to lesbian transmission is possible, I also know that lesbian to lesbian transmission is pretty low down on the list of possibilities, so I do have a bit of a tendency to define lesbian sex as 'safe sex'. … if I weren't in a monogamous situation, I think I still probably wouldn't worry, unless it were somebody I knew had either been a drug user or had a number of heterosexual relationships. No, if you're talking about things like dental dams or rubber gloves or whatever – no. (F21)

HIV has encouraged a degree of self-reflection and public discussion about sexual behaviour that is probably unique in sexual history (Weeks 1993). As Amy indicates, the reality of HIV has presented many individuals with an opportunity to explore their sexual selves:

> Certainly that's how it happened for me [in my home town] – people starting to talk about sex because [they] had to start talking about sexual practices – because there was so little known about lesbians and HIV. And that was quite a good thing, that people started talking about it. And I think through talking

> about it with sexual partners and with other people you can actually enjoy it
> a lot more than it just being something you do when you go to bed. (F27)

Particularly among gay men, AIDS has facilitated the development of historically different sexual selves and sexual practices. This is clearest with regard to the issue of safer sex. As King (1993) and others have noted, safer sex has now, in some senses, been established as a gay community norm. This can be understood in terms of the ways in which community support has been crucial in enabling gay men to develop and maintain 'new' ways of being sexual. Early community publications, such as Callen and Berowitz's *How to Have Sex in an Epidemic: One Approach* (partly reprinted in Callen 1988: 164–5), were important resources 'from within', which took the position that it is possible to avoid the transmission of HIV and maintain an active and enjoyable sexual life.

At times of crisis, the tendency for individuals and groups in late modern worlds is to 'reskill' (Giddens 1991). As Heaphy (2001) suggests, through accessing and developing 'new' information, reskilling endeavours are aimed at managing risk through regaining a sense of control. Reskilling in the context of AIDS has offered significant opportunities to non-heterosexual individuals and communities. It has allowed for the *generation* of important (emotional, material and social) resources, and for significant agency in the formation of new sexual selves. For most of the gay male participants in our research, HIV has necessitated a significant 'reskilling' in the form of efforts to become familiar with both safer sex information and AIDS/HIV knowledge in a broader sense. For many of those who were sexually active prior to the advent of HIV and AIDS, this reskilling has in turn led to a 'rethinking' of their sexual lives, particularly with regard to the practice of safer sex. Consider the following extract from an interview with Phillip:

> we're ... you know, happily engaging in safer sex. And it's fine. I think we
> feel – well, I feel, certainly [that it's okay] – and I think he would probably
> say he feels okay about that and fulfilled enough with that, and it feels com-
> fortable enough. And even if we ... both went and tested, and say we were
> both negative, I can't imagine getting in to any sort of grave risks with sex
> now. I can't imagine that happening because it just feels [like] it's a part of
> my life to practise safer sex now. (M27)

Here, Phillip is suggesting that safer sex has become an almost 'naturalised' form of sexual practice for many gay men – and has become central to who they are as sexual beings. David agrees:

> we don't have unsafe sex now – I think it's habitual in that ... when you're
> used to having safe sex and you enjoy it, then there's no need to stop having
> safe sex – so it's not as though I would never trust him [his partner]. ...
> Firstly, I would always trust Peter in that sense anyway – I think he would
> always say something if he had [had unsafe sex]. And I mean, the thing is

we both know now we're negative, so – as sure as we can be. Yet we still have safe sex now, whereas it could be quite easy for us not to have it at this point in time, but we choose not to – so I don't think that it's ever likely to get to that stage. (M12)

It is, however, worth making the distinction between unsafe sex and unprotected sex. As a few of our research participants who were in committed couple-type relationships suggest, these are not necessarily one and the same thing. Alex comments that:

we fuck without rubbers. We started fucking with rubbers for … oh, a good few months, a *good* few months, we used them. And we … talked about what we thought our statuses were and I'd tested slightly before … well, I hadn't fucked without a rubber with anyone since well before my last negative test and neither had Warren. It just seemed like, you know, in the scheme of things a fairly good basis to go ahead and decide not to use them – which is what we did. … It was a convenience thing … it was more it didn't seem much point in carrying on using them. But since then, coming in each other [has] made a bit of a difference. (M26)

Following on from the work of, for example, Prieur (1990), Davies *et al.* (1993) and Henriksson (1995), we would suggest that in such contexts the temptation to characterise 'unprotected' sex as an irrational act is of limited value. Rather, it may be more productive to understand such acts in terms of rational processes of decision-making, leading to negotiated safer sex. There can also be other less 'rational' motivating factors that encourage unprotected (but 'safer') sex – such as emotions related to love, commitment and trust. Charles explains:

Ultimately, I think what we were both talking about was a sense of trust between us and the fact that here was something special between us that we wouldn't do with other people … both of us, have a fair amount of sex with other men, anyway, somehow it makes the sex between us more special as well. (M25)

As Henriksson (1995) notes, in the context of unprotected anal sex, the giving and receiving of semen can have symbolic meaning for some gay men, and can signify an agreed border between 'casual' and 'real' relations. In the stories told in our research, unprotected anal sex was reserved for the central relationship, and was often presented as both an indicator and an expression of trust. For some in non-monogamous relationships, like Charles, the emotional decision to practise unprotected sex came about as a result of explicit negotiations with the central partner, and is presented as a marker of the 'specialness' of the primary relationship. But, ultimately, it is the ethic of trust that demarcates the possibility that 'unprotected' sex can be safer sex. This is clear in Alex's response to the question as to whether he would always have protected sex outside of the relationship:

> Yes. And so would he … I find it unthinkable that either of us would [have unprotected sex with others]. And I find it unthinkable that either of us would and then not tell the other if we did. (M26)

Along with the ethic of trust that can allow this leap of faith, the issue of safer sex also highlights another ethic at play among non-heterosexuals. Initially, safer sex knowledges were developed and 'invented' as a result of concerns for both individual and collective care and safety (Weeks 1995). Weeks writes:

> Safer sex became a means of negotiating sex and love, of building a respect for self and others, in a climate of risk and fear. From this point of view safer sex was a way of recovering the erotic, not a defensive reaction to it, based on minimization, if not complete elimination, of risk, in relationships of mutual trust and responsibility.
>
> (Weeks 1995: 181)

In a similar way, Watney (1994: 31) argues that what was at stake in establishing safer sex as a community norm was an ethics which affirmed sexual desire 'in all its forms with an active, practical commitment to mutual care and responsibility'. The issue of safer sex, then, highlights that the notions of 'self concern' and 'care for others' are not mutually exclusive. Rather, it is the combination of the two that has allowed non-heterosexual sexual practices to be *ethical* practices.

But non-heterosexual community responses to AIDS also demonstrate the extent to which meanings attached to sexuality and sexual activity can be understood to be collectively and socially constructed. They indicate that far from being intensely private events, sexual encounters can be the meeting place of both individual and collective concerns. They also shed light on the changeability of sexuality and sexual practice. The sexual lives of non-heterosexuals confirm that sexuality is not a natural given, unchanging or unchangeable throughout a personal life-history. It is best seen as a potentiality, which is shaped by a host of cultural possibilities and relationship choices. Sexuality is a focus for creativity. Few examples are so clear of the possibility of reinventing and transforming the sexual self and sexual practices – and that this can be both an individual and a collective project.

7 Parenting

The 'gayby' boom

Few issues spark such passionate reaction and debate as 'parenting'. As attitudes towards the family shift, the question of the responsibilities of adults towards children becomes increasingly the focus of social concern and moral anxiety. Poor parenting is seen as a major factor in the ills that beset late modern societies. It is blamed for almost everything – from rampant drug abuse to poor achievement in school (see, for example, Etzioni 1995; Morgan 1995) – and is seen as being a decisive factor in social breakdown and exclusion. In various ways, governments throughout the major industrial countries seek to bolster parenthood: chasing errant fathers, providing help-lines for harassed mothers, attempting to reduce the number of teenage pregnancies, condemning or trying to find means of supporting single parents, introducing lessons on marriage and parenting into the school curriculum – the list is potentially endless (for a characteristic set of proposals, see Ministerial Group on the Family 1998). It is scarcely surprising, therefore, that questions of non-heterosexual parenting have aroused especial passions. The ordinary challenges of parenting are compounded by unresolved questions about social attitudes to different sexualities.

For a morally conservative commentator such as Melanie Phillips, the issue of parenting rights and responsibilities is the decisive justification for heterosexual marriage, and a major reason for opposing moves towards recognition of same sex marriage. In an article, 'Debate: Gay Marriage', she writes: 'Because men are naturally promiscuous, two men will stick together as naturally as the two north poles of a magnet. It is not marriage which domesticates men – it is women' (Davis and Phillips 1999: 17). Thus it seems that without marriage the stability needed for good parenting by men will not be there. Although she does not discuss whether two women together provide the right conditions for successful parenting, one must assume that, like their male counterparts, they do not. Crucial to her position is the belief that women tame men in marriage, while the presence of a male parent in a parenting duo provides by extension the appropriate gender balance that children need (see Phillips 1999). By this definition, then, lesbian and gay parents cannot provide the stability and fidelity that marriage guarantees, and if same sex marriage were accepted, it would ultimately undermine the heterosexual union itself, to the detriment of children.

This is a more sophisticated version of widespread opposition to the very idea of recognising the legitimacy of non-heterosexual parenting rights. The arguments are familiar and well rehearsed (see Tasker and Golombok 1991). Non-heterosexuals, it is argued, lack the stable relationships that heterosexual marriage guarantees. They lack the necessary balance of male and female role models. They threaten the sexual development and identities of the children. Children are in danger of becoming little more than commodities, and their interests subordinated to the selfish desires of adults. These have become commonplace responses to the attempts by non-heterosexuals to achieve proper recognition of rights to legal parenthood. Despite growing toleration of sexual difference among adults, non-heterosexual parenting continues to arouse acute anxiety.

This pattern is followed in even the more liberal jurisdictions, such as the Scandinavian countries, where same sex partnerships can be registered in law and given rights and responsibilities similar to marriage relationships. In general, lesbians and gay men are specifically excluded from the possibility of adopting (Bech 1992; Griffin and Mulholland 1997) – though, since 1998, Denmark has allowed those who are in registered partnerships to adopt their partner's children. As the French socialist government in 1998 and 1999 found when it first attempted to pass a law giving greater legal recognition to non-marital relationships, whether homosexual or heterosexual, parenting and adoption rights tend to be a major sticking point for the conservative opposition (for a survey of attitudes, see International Lesbian and Gay Association [ILGA] 1999a and b). Parenting has become the touchstone issue for attitudes towards non-heterosexual relationships, the yardstick by which social acceptance may be judged.

In Britain, nowhere has the dominant attitude towards non-heterosexual relationships and children been articulated more clearly than in Section 28 of the 1988 Local Government Act (Weeks 1991), which outlawed the promotion of homosexuality in schools and created the concept of the pretended family relationship. This symbolised a widespread belief that young people were peculiarly susceptible to proselytising by adult homosexuals, which by implication made parenting by them peculiarly dangerous. During the 1980s and 1990s, there were various attempts to specifically exclude lesbians and gay men as potential adopting and/or fostering parents. Department of Health guidelines in the 1990s, for example, made reference to how the 'chosen way of life of some adults may mean that they would not be able to provide a suitable environment for the care and nurture of a child' (quoted in Hicks and McDermott 1998: 234), and this has been used to exclude some non-heterosexuals as potential adopters. These barriers to same sex parenting have been more or less successfully challenged (Donovan 1997; and see below). It remains the case, however, that only married heterosexual couples can adopt jointly, so although non-heterosexuals have been accepted as adopting parents, they can do so only as single parents, even if they are in a relationship and intend to parent jointly.

The assumption underpinning Section 28 that children were at risk from open lesbians or gay men was, as we suggested in Chapter 1, a catalyst for the mobilisation of non-heterosexuals nationwide to campaign and debate the issue of family, especially the place of children in non-traditional relationships. Behind this was a growing involvement by many non-heterosexuals, both men and women, who had practical experience of being a parent. Despite the legal pitfalls, increasing numbers of non-heterosexuals are opting for parenthood, whether through attempts to foster, adopt or procreate. There have always been mothers and fathers who were lesbian or gay, but until recently the vast majority had conceived in heterosexual liaisons (Hanscombe and Forster 1982; Bozett 1987; Pies 1988). The notion that parenting can be chosen by openly non-heterosexual people is relatively recent, and marks a radical change in the relationship between non-heterosexuals and child care. It wasn't until the 1970s that there was any real urgency among lesbians to claim the right to motherhood *as* lesbians. Previously, many feminists had in fact been hostile to motherhood as it was considered to be a crucial element in female oppression (Clausen 1987; Lewin 1993). Since the 1970s, however, there has been a growing movement among lesbians to choose to openly conceive as lesbians, and to create distinctly lesbian families (Pollack and Vaughn 1987; Weston 1993). Indeed, many commentators now refer to an emerging lesbian baby boom (e.g., Lewin 1993; Benkov 1994; Nardi 1999) – in fact, a 'gayby' boom that is increasingly influencing gay men as well.

While it has always been possible for women whose emotional affinities and sexual desires were primarily directed towards other women to be mothers, it has been very difficult to be a mother *and* openly lesbian. In Britain, Hanscombe and Forster's (1982) pioneering study was one of the first to acknowledge this long historical reality, and to address the concerns of lesbians as mothers (for the US, see Lewin 1993). There were inevitable dilemmas about surviving within the heterosexual family. If a marriage broke up, there were endless custody problems if the mother was known to be a lesbian. These problems were compounded by a lack of understanding, or an invisibility, in the lesbian community itself. And, when they did get involved, many lesbian mothers often felt excluded from the leisure and political activities of their community due to lack of organised and individual child care (Romans 1992). Other mothers faced, and still face, difficulties when their male children were excluded from women- or lesbian-only events (Lorde 1987; Bowen 1990).

Many gay men, of course, have become fathers through heterosexual relationships, but in many ways the idea of a gay father is even more controversial than that of a lesbian mother – not least because of the deeply embedded myth associating male homosexuality with the 'corruption' of the young. Yet there is strong evidence, as we indicated at the beginning of the book, that many openly gay men are involved in parenting, and wish to be even more involved (see Dunne 2000). In addition to the generalised hostility, three major issues regularly come to the fore in discussions of gay male parenting: the somewhat negative responses of gay men who are not parents; the concerns of gay fathers with their own parenting; and the issue of how to come out to children (Miller 1978; Harris and Turner 1986; Bozett 1987). Each of these points is indicative of the ambivalent attitudes that continue to prevail with regard to gay fatherhood, both within the non-heterosexual communities and in wider society.

In this chapter, we want to explore the changing meanings of non-heterosexual parenting, and place these within a broader cultural context as already discussed in this book. In particular, we shall examine the ways in which non-heterosexuals come to parenting, and the ways that parental relationships are and can be negotiated. We argue that some of the perceptions about the possibilities for parenting that are available to non-heterosexuals are reflected in the types of parenting stories they tell. Where and when people come out, and what kinds of community resources they have had access to, are crucially important for their narratives. We explore some of the factors that, when combined, have both opened up possibilities and presented obstacles for non-heterosexual parenting. In so doing, we also intend to document the ways in which non-heterosexuals develop parenting practices that establish the authenticity of their families and parenting relationships. Parenting matters a great deal – and it is increasingly central to many narratives of non-heterosexual relationships.

Parenting stories

It is worth noting here that for a number of our interviewees the two concepts of 'family' and 'parenting' are co-extensive: involvement in parenting means being a 'real family'. This signals a significant shift in language and priorities in the non-heterosexual world as parenting becomes a more common situation (cf. Ali 1996; Nardi 1999). While, as we have seen, the use of the trope of friends as family is widespread, this broadly signifies peer relationships. The presence of children in a non-heterosexual relationship, whether a one-to-one partnership or a more complex arrangement of friends who are carers and co-parents, inevitably changes the balance and priorities. In Chapter 5, we argued that while there is a strong emphasis on the idea of negotiated relationships rather than concepts of duty or obligation among non-heterosexuals, dependants, and especially children, provide the major exceptions to this. Regardless of the complexities of relationships, and the hazards and contingencies of their natural careers, a commitment to children is seen as absolute. For many people, this is what being a 'family' is all about. Parenting necessarily involves the acquisition of new skills and the development of new everyday practices to care for young dependants. This can radically transform the meaning of being non-heterosexual in contemporary society.

We can identify three main types of stories that non-heterosexuals tell about parenting: stories of impossibilities, stories of opportunities, and stories of choice. Each one is shaped by a host of individual circumstances and social possibilities. Depending on where and when non-heterosexuals come out, there will be dominant societal constructions of homosexuality, which have a shaping and constraining effect on non-heterosexuals' understanding of their relationship to parenting, and their access to the different methods available to become parents. One of the important factors that can influence people's stories is their access to community knowledges, which can supply both an alternative (more positive) construction of non-heterosexualities and the resources to support non-heterosexual parenting. The ability of individuals to 'reskill' in community knowledges (see Chapter 4) is affected by their socio-economic resources, their gender and ethnic positioning, whether or not they are disabled, their geographical location, and other variables that open and foreclose possibilities.

Naseem's story offers a graphic example of what is at stake, the balance of forces at play, the choices available, and the compromises that must sometimes follow. Naseem (F37) is a black lesbian who lives in an arranged marriage (to a man of Indian origin) with her disabled daughter. Due to the immigration laws, Naseem thought that her husband would not be able to enter Britain. But a letter campaign, participated in by Naseem, secured his entry several years after their marriage had taken place in India. Naseem is very close to her family of origin, and has made the decision that her and her daughter's safety is best secured by continuing to live as a married woman in the Asian community. At the same time, however, Naseem has negotiated a degree of independence in her life which allows her to pursue friendships and support from other black lesbians, although these friendships and her sexuality are kept as separate and secret from her community as possible. In planning for her daughter's future, Naseem has asked her closest friends, a black lesbian couple, Rachel (F02) and Malika (F03) (see Chapter 2), to be her daughter's guardians, and they have agreed. Naseem has been able to carve out a space in her life where she can be open, and receive support about her identity as a lesbian and as a parent. She has gained access to community knowledges about the possibilities of living as a non-heterosexual. However, her story illustrates how access to community knowledge may not make the reality of living as an openly non-heterosexual a possibility if other factors are understood as more compelling for survival.

Naseem has created certain possibilities, albeit not always in circumstances of her own free choice. Her narrative is balanced on the cusp of change, and her life story tells of severe limitations on personal choice. But it also shows new openings: it looks backward and forward at the same time. In her story, we can see latently the three dominant stories identified at the beginning of this section: of impossibilities, of opportunities, and of choice.

Stories of impossibilities

In the not too distant past, the opportunities to parent that are now available for many non-heterosexuals simply did not exist. People tell stories of impossibilities, shaped by their particular histories, and a more intrusive and difficult moral climate. Through these stories, we learn that many women and, more particularly, men have never believed that they can become parents as overt non-heterosexuals. Aubrey (M42) exemplifies these stories, as someone who came out prior to the 1970s, when both the dominant construction of, and community knowledges about, non-heterosexuality coincided in their understanding of non-heterosexuals as isolated individuals living in a twilight sub-culture outside family and dominant society. In answer to a question about whether he had ever considered having children, Aubrey, who is 72 years old, says: 'Well, it's only been recently that … such an idea had parlance. Nobody would say that in the old days. … It's brand new. It's only about twenty or twenty-five years old.'

When Aubrey was younger, and newly coming out, the dominant story about non-heterosexuality was shaped by the need either to hide your homosexuality by passing as heterosexual, or to reject that sham, and therefore live a life on the margins of society. The latter option in turn shaped a life which made parenting difficult, not least as Bozett (1987: 10) has observed, 'because their parental obligations … conflict with certain characteristics of the gay world'.

Even as little as thirty years ago, parenting was rarely a viable option if you were overtly homosexual, especially since the possibilities for becoming a parent were limited to engaging in heterosexual sex and/or getting married. However, despite the risks, some homosexuals took this route to parenting (Hanscombe and Forster 1982; Dunne 2000). Craig (M14), for example, knew he was gay before his marriage. He now has three children and still lives with his wife. He explains: 'the kids are very important to me. That was another reason I wanted to get married. And my wife knows this – I had a great longing to have children.' Like Naseem, but with more resources as a white man, Craig made a conscious decision to live, in effect, in two worlds.

Craig has a wife who is prepared to accept the situation, but that does not mean that it is free of potential pitfalls and dilemmas (cf. Miller 1978, 1986). Gay fathers have to negotiate the expectations of the straight world, the taken-for-granted assumptions about what a father is and does. And, as Bozett suggests (1987), he must also face the assumptions of the gay world. But above all, there are the tensions with his children's assumptions and anxieties (Miller 1979; Bozett 1980; Schulenberg 1985). Yet not having the opportunity to parent also has its effects. Many, especially older male, non-heterosexuals, who have felt that parenting children was never an option, express a sense of loss in their lives. Bob (M43), who is 61 and gay, is typical when he says, 'I've regretted that very much'. This is perhaps more understandable for an older generation, but there are also many younger non-heterosexuals – again mainly men – who have been or still are influenced by the dominant story that, as the brother of one lesbian told her, 'once you become gay, you give up the right to have children' (Pat, F36). David vividly illustrates this feeling:

> it was sort of thinking, 'Oh God, I'm never going to have children', when I first became aware of the situation I was in. … you know, [my thoughts were,] I can have everything else, I can live with somebody, but I'm never going to have children. And I did worry about that. (M12)

David says that in retrospect he thinks he was only worried about not having children because his parents wanted grandchildren. Now he feels that he can choose not to have children, although he is happy to be involved with his friends' children.

Among our interviewees, non-heterosexual men, like David, were inevitably more aware than women that their sexuality might preclude active parenting of children. While an increasing number of non-heterosexual men are opting for fatherhood (see, for example, Martin 1993; Benkov 1994; Drucker 1998; Hicks and McDermott 1998; Dunne 2000), the dominant construction of gay men presenting a risk to children has still to be successfully countered. Most of the challenges to this dominant view have taken place in North America. In Britain, and by comparison with lesbian parenting, gay male parenting still remains relatively hidden, and public stories about individual attempts to achieve parenthood often meet with feelings of shock and warnings about children's safety (e.g., Sebag-Montefiore 1997; Hicks and McDermott 1998). As John says:

> I could not conceive of having children now. But ... I don't think it's an option anyway, in this country [Britain]. I think it's an option for women, for lesbians, and good luck to them. ... it would be nice if men could have children in this country. And it should be discussed more openly. But I think with AIDS as well, ... it would be extremely difficult for two men. And I think that any gay couple, or single gay man for that matter, that chooses to bring up a child, ... bloody good luck to them ... they should do it. In spite of all the prejudices, in spite of the horror that people would express at it. (M16)

Inevitably, gay men see their lives in comparison to their heterosexual friends. Liam, for instance, makes this point:

> I think that [same sex and heterosexual] relationships can be the same up until a certain age, but because women have a biological clock it starts to change. And I'm finding that with a lot of my peers ... by the time people are getting to their late twenties they're thinking more about settling down [with] a suitable boy, or a suitable girl, ... with which to have babies. (M31)

Children, or the lack of them, mean that life paths between heterosexuals and non-heterosexuals frequently diverge relatively early in the life-cycle, and this is experienced by many gay men as a decisive break. The stories of impossibilities are significant here because they shed light on the choices made by some non-heterosexuals to get married or engage in heterosexual relationships in order to have children. They also illustrate the sorts of expectations some non-heterosexuals – especially men – have about their lives.

Stories of opportunities

In today's society, however, new stories of opportunities for parenting are prolifer-ating. In these stories, we can identify several shifts in the construction of possibilities for non-heterosexual parenting: the dominant construction of homosexuality is challenged; general understandings about sexuality are changing; and the possibilities for living outside the traditional family are increasing. As a result, society has seen a rise in the number of openly non-heterosexual people who have, for example, left their heterosexual relationships and marriages, come out, and yet claimed the right to continue their parenting relationships.

This in part reflects, and in part is an explanation for, the fundamental shift in non-heterosexual communities away from a focus on issues of identity towards ones of intimacy, which is one of the central themes of this book. To a significant extent, this shift has been about the recognition that once the question of identity is in the main resolved through greater openness and the shaping of a supportive environment, other issues which underline continuing prejudice and discrimination will inevitably come to the fore. Parenting issues have starkly revealed the force of discrimination, and have become the focus of campaigns for equal rights for non-heterosexuals.

Since the 1970s, a great deal of work has been done, at both an individual and a collective level, to campaign for the rights of lesbian mothers to retain custody of their children following separation from a heterosexual relationship (see, for example, Hanscombe and Forster 1982; Rights of Women Lesbian Custody Group 1986; Benkov 1994; Drucker 1998). Running parallel to this have been efforts to secure visitation rights for gay fathers on the break-up of marriage. Both women and men have been subject to similar judgements about their unsuitability as parents if they are openly lesbian or gay (e.g., Benkov 1994). One result of these various struggles has been the initiation of research into claims made in the courts that lesbian mothers are not fit to parent because of their sexuality. As well, sympathetic literature about married gay men has been published (e.g., Buntzly 1993). The majority of this research finds that non-heterosexual parents compare favourably with their heterosexual counterparts (see, for example, Lewin 1984, 1993; Bozett 1987; Tasker and Golombok 1997). It also overwhelmingly reveals that children of non-heterosexual parents are no more, or no less, likely to be homosexual than the offspring of heterosexual parents, but they appear to be more sophisticated in their sexual attitudes, and more tolerant in accepting sexual difference. This research, combined with avid media attention and the increased visibility of lesbian mothers and gay fathers in general, has in turn been incorporated into community knowledges, providing new possibilities for non-heterosexual parenting, as well as offering warnings of what might be faced by challenging the heterosexual assumption.

This has resulted in the gradual recognition by the courts that lesbian moth-ers and gay fathers are more than capable of providing good parenting for their children. In contrast to the 1970s, it is now far less likely for a parent's sexuality *per se* to be a reason to refuse 'care and control' (the new term for custody) in contested cases (Radford 1991). Jane has felt the benefits of the change in attitude: when her husband challenged her care and control of their son, she not only knew how to find a sympathetic solicitor, but she also won her case. She explains:

> I rang up Rights of Women in London, and they've got a list of supportive lawyers ... [Her husband] tried very hard [to make an issue of her lesbian-ism] ... I think there were all these lies in [his] statement, because he was ferreting around for something that he could use. But no, every single time it was 'so?', 'and?' ... (F16)

Jane's experience illustrates how the established community networks have shaped responses to government and legal attempts to limit the possibilities of non-heterosexuals to parent, or to undermine those who are parenting. And in turn these accumulated knowledges have been strengthened by the experience of resistance.

Resistance has been facilitated by the development of support and campaign groups (such as the Lesbian and Gay Foster and Adoptive Parents Network, the Rights of Women Custody Group, the Stonewall Parenting Group, and Pink Parents), who have successfully been able to use the research, case law and legal loopholes in order to support individual parents. For example, there are some signs, as Jane's story suggests, that the courts are less likely to use a mother's sexuality as the reason to prevent her having custody of her children (Donovan 1997). In addition, some adopting and self-inseminating couples have success-fully used the Children Act 1989 to get legal recognition of the non-legal/biological parent through a joint residence order (e.g., Harne and Rights of Women 1997; Hicks and McDermott 1998).

These stories of opportunities reflect the growing confidence of non-heterosexuals in asserting their competence as parents, and the validity of their continuing as parents after coming out. Increasingly, however, and more controversially, a major factor affecting the growing trend of non-heterosexuals to become parents is the development of new reproductive technologies. Presenting society with the realisation that conception can be achieved without the need for heterosexual sex, this must stand as one of the key moments in the history of possibilities for non-heterosexual parenting. As such, they radically alter the opportunities for creating intimate lives that include children.

Stories of choice

These new possibilities constitute the third set of stories: stories of choice. They present perhaps the most radical challenge to traditional family life because here opportunity and risk are at their starkest. The two technologies that offer the most realistic chances to non-heterosexuals for biological parenting are insemination and surrogacy. The first primarily affects women, either through donor insemination in medically controlled clinics (Donovan 1992), or through self-insemination, which is organised informally. Surrogacy has become an issue that affects gay men, though it obviously also involves women. Both issues arouse fierce controversy. Since the 1970s, both donor insemination and lesbian self-insemination have become increasingly popular among lesbians, with gay men often acting as donors – although the existence of the HIV virus initially made it more difficult for gay men to be informally involved in self-insemination (see Weston 1992), a difficulty that has been largely overcome through widespread HIV testing. Surrogacy is a more recent possibility, and is surrounded by particular debate because it involves gay men claiming direct parenting responsibility, usually after having paid a woman to carry a baby conceived with the man's sperm; and because more generally it raises complex legal, social and ethical concerns, and has led to an outcry in the media (see Reynolds 1999: 9). As we saw at the beginning of this book, some gay men have been able to organise this successfully (see Martin 1993; Hicks and McDermott 1998; Dunne 2000), but surrogacy tends to be expensive and lacks the community-based support of self-insemination.

Community knowledges about self-insemination, and to a lesser extent surrogacy, have provided a vista of opportunities for non-heterosexual parenting for men (as known and/or involved donors/fathers) and women that previously would have been unimaginable. Aided by the media, the issue of non-heterosexual parenting has resulted in an explosion of literature and television programmes: for example, handbooks offering legal and technical advice, as well as providing suggestions about how parenting can be organised both pre- and post-natally (e.g., Pies 1988; Martin 1993; Saffron 1994); explorations (and celebrations) of the many and varied ways that non-heterosexuals have become parents and do parenting (e.g., Benkov 1994; Drucker 1998); anthologies of essays and experiential stories from potential or actual non-heterosexual parents (Pollack and Vaughn 1987; Arnup 1995) and children (Saffron 1996); and television documentaries, for example, *Pink Parenting*, (Aylewell, for Timewatch, BBC1, 1998) and *Child of Mine* (Thynne for Channel 4, 1996).

The challenges presented by the new reproductive technologies in Britain – especially donor insemination – have, to an extent, been regulated by the Human Fertilisation and Embryology Act 1990. This requires a doctor to take account of a child's need for a father before giving a woman access to a licensed fertility service (see Donovan 1992). However, the fact that insemination can be organised informally is posing significant challenges to this legislation. Collective self-help activities have rapidly spread the word – through local community activity such as parenting workshops and support groups which share personal experiences, and through increasing numbers of self-help handbooks that offer reskilling about creating families (e.g., Pies 1988; Martin 1993; Saffron 1994). For the first time, women and men, as non-heterosexuals, can choose to become biological parents without having heterosexual sex. Although this awareness is most apparent among the women in our sample, there is also a growing number of men who tell this story of choice. In what is an increasingly common story, Matt (M10) says, 'I'd feel my life was a failure if I didn't have children.'

Of course, the possibility of insemination is not always a solution for those wishing to be parents. Women have to be fertile, and donors of sperm have to be found, either through social networks or via fertility clinics, which require a range of resources. The preferred circumstances in which to inseminate may take some time to negotiate (for example, Donovan 2000). Frequently, the desired imagined family has to be re-negotiated in order to resolve any practical difficulties. Nevertheless, the result of using either donor insemination or self-insemination has meant almost endless permutations of family and parenting relationships, and structures which are being experimented with by many non-heterosexuals (see below).

For those who do not want, or are unable, to use medical means, adoption and fostering have also become more available as possibilities for parenting. This remains easier, as noted above, for single people than for gay or lesbian couples. Jenny began fostering three children in the early 1980s, and did so as a single parent (she already had one 'home-grown child'). She explains:

> I think a couple of the social workers suspected [that she was a lesbian], but it was to both our advantages not to mention it. If they didn't bring it up, then they didn't have to try and decide whether they needed to do anything about it. (F21)

Since the mid-1980s, the issue of fostering and adoption by openly non-heterosexual people has gained a much greater public profile (Hicks and McDermott 1998). Decisions to accept non-heterosexual people as parents are dependent on the individual policies of adoption/foster agencies and the attitudes of individual social workers. And in part because of a shortage of suitable carers, openly lesbian or gay potential adopters or fosterers are being taken on. These local variations in the treatment of potential non-heterosexual parents can become part of local community knowledges and affect under-standings of the options available. For example, Amy, who recently moved to a city in the north of England, says:

> I mean, all the time that I lived [in my old city], the only way I'd thought of doing it was through self-insemination because that seemed the only possi-bility [there]. Now I've moved [to a new city], there's quite a lot of lesbians and gay men who have fostered or adopted … and it makes me think, 'Oh, that's another whole area I hadn't thought about'. And I actually like the idea. (F27)

Regardless of how non-heterosexuals come to be involved in parenting, almost all have to reskill in terms of thinking about and 'doing' family. As discussed earlier, breaking away from the traditional heterosexual nuclear family remains a fraught topic (see also Silva and Smart 1999b). Beck and Beck-

Gernsheim (1995) argue that contemporary modern society is characterised by fundamental changes in interpersonal relationships, and those changes can be understood as opening up possibilities or presenting risks to those involved. The view from the margins can change from day to day: being on the outside can be simultaneously liberatory and risky. Liberatory because of the opportunities that arise for reformulating family and parenting relationships in the absence of traditional assumptions – often gendered – about the roles, responsibilities and relationships enacted in family life. Risky because families of choice that include children fundamentally challenge the heterosexual assumption about the centrality of marriage. The nature of the challenge can be articulated slightly differently depending on whether the parents are non-heterosexual women or men. Lesbian families have typically been constructed as risky for children (and society) because of the assumed lack of a father figure. Gay male parents have been understood as risky to children because of a pervasive (if tendentious) association made between gay male sexuality and paedophilia. Whatever the reasons, however, there is a perceived threat to the conventional order of things, which continues to restrict the possibilities. At the same time, it has provided a spur to redefining the necessary practice of parenting.

Parenting practices

Being 'a good parent' does not come naturally; it is a skill that is acquired. Following our discussion of family practices in Chapter 2, we will use here the concept of 'parenting practices' to describe the planning and reflexivity involved in being a parent, and the defining and doing of parental relationships. All parents are engaged in a continual dialogue about their parenting – with themselves, other parents, their children, and anyone else they think might need to be included. We maintain that this ongoing process of self-monitoring and reflection shapes parenting practices, and is essential to the active defining and doing of family.

Living outside traditional family life requires a continual vigilance on two fronts. First, there are the risks presented by the heterosexual assumption, which can lead to a constant sense of being disapproved of, and at worst can mean losing one's children (e.g., Drucker 1998; Hicks and McDermott 1998). Second, non-heterosexual parents are doing parenting 'on the hoof', without obvious guidelines. This is especially the case when children result from insemination. Many of the traditional assumptions about parenting do not and/or need not apply. While this can allow people the freedom to experiment in parental and family life, and can be experienced as liberatory, it can also be experienced as a daunting task that requires careful and constant thought. The required reflexivity helps constitute family practices. In her study of lesbian parenting couples, Dunne (1998) concludes that the planning and preparation they engaged in prior to parenting was the reflexive project *par excellence*. Most of the parenting couples that she interviewed tell stories of choice in relation to parenting. People engaged in rehearsals for decisions that might be made in the future also tell stories of choice, and this is reflected in the narratives we have gathered. For example, several gay men have already considered how they might respond to a request from lesbians to donate sperm. Peter explains his response to one such request:

> I've been asked and I'd be happy to do it, but I haven't done it. … I wouldn't want to be a known donor to a child where I knew the mother and knew that the child was my genetic child, because I don't quite know how I would react to seeing – I've got somewhere going in the back (tick, tick, tick) of my head … And because I don't know how I'm going to react to it, I don't think it's a good idea for me to do it … because of carrying around some baggage somewhere about genetic fatherhood. But anonymous dona-tion – absolutely no problem whatsoever. I haven't got a 'my sperm is my lifeblood' kind of thing. (M11)

Peter has had the opportunity to reflect on his feelings about donating sperm because of the local community knowledges. He knows lesbians who have inseminated and has been asked to donate sperm, so he has had the opportunity to engage with the issues, identify the risks to himself and rehearse his response.

Anthony, however, has actually taken the plunge. Now 33, he is single, and has fathered a child with two lesbians. Anthony sees the child at least once a month, and has plans to move closer to the city where they live so he can be more involved. He describes himself as the 'father' but not a 'co-parent'. The conception itself was the result of a lengthy period of negotiation:

> When I was working at the school, a woman came to do some work, and I was working with her for about two weeks. She was a lesbian and talked about friends that she had who were keen on having a child … [They] wanted to have a gay man to donate sperm, but who was [also] keen to have some relationship with the child, and the child would know that this was the father. And I said, 'Well, I'd be quite interested in doing that'. And then I went up to stay with her and met these two women, and I got to know them for about a year … a year and a half. And we talked about things like child care and what we thought about raising children, and what our involve-ments would be respectively. And once we got to know and really trust each other, we started inseminating – that took about six months, and bingo, basically. (M33)

Things don't always run as smoothly as Anthony's story, however. Other more challenging situations, which require careful reflection and discussion, can occur if the social location of the parents is different and results in them having different approaches to parenting. This is clear from Phillip's story of his chosen family, which includes his partner Alan, and Alan's 13-year-old nephew Lewis. Lewis lives with Alan, and has done so since the beginning of Alan's and Phillip's relationship. Alan and Phillip do not live together, and in the last fourteen months, Phillip has started having Lewis to stay over at his house for two nights a week. For Phillip, race and ethnicity are significant factors to take into consideration since Alan and Lewis are black and he is white:

> we do have lots of discussions about race and our differences as a black man and as a white man. And issues, I mean, are particularly important, about Lewis as a young black man growing up with a significant white relationship and coming into a white home. And Alan feels okay about that, because he's really into giving Lewis as many opportunities to explore as many different facets of living as he possibly can. I probably suppose I feel a bit less comfortable about that and I just think, well, you know, am I kind of loading influences on Lewis that maybe I oughtn't to? And [the issue of Lewis] coming into this sort of white, fairly middle-class household, you know – although there are quite a few black images around my house now. (M27)

For Phillip, as with other parenting relationships, there is a continual review process whereby things get checked out and tried on for size so that different needs and issues can be recognised and tackled.

The lack of role models, information and expectations about how non-heterosexual parenting is done is often keenly felt. The availability of different knowledges in the form of literature aimed at non-heterosexual parents, therefore, can be invaluable in the reflexive process, and the increasing number of books on the subject reflects this demand, and, of course, helps generate it. They discuss the range of issues that now arise – from what to call biological or social parents, through the forms of social recognition of different parenting responsibilities, to what happens if agreed relationships break down (e.g., Pies 1988; Martin 1993; Saffron 1994). Pat exemplifies the importance of such self-help texts, as, here, she reflects on the decision-making process she went through with her partner and known donor (who co-parents with his partner) which led to the birth of their son David:

> I think we'd have been much clearer about what co-parenting actually meant [if they had had self-help texts]. We didn't really define it. We didn't really know, I don't think. But I also got a book, *Lesbian and Gay Parenting Handbook* by April Martin, and I wish I'd had it before. I'd tried to get it but couldn't … and then they … sent it to me. And it's very good about the things you really need to think about, sort of legal issues, and there's a whole load of things, but certainly about what co-parenting actually meant. I think we should have made it much clearer to each other. (F36)

It is obvious from what Pat says that the decisions made during the planning and preparation for becoming parents have to be continuously assessed and re-enacted throughout the actual parenting process. This can involve revisiting decisions and accommodating new circumstances and unpredictable emotional responses which arise in the course of family life.

The definition and doing of parenting among non-heterosexuals involves a re-evaluation of the work of parenting, and of the relationship between biological and social parenting. Smart (1999) argues that there has recently been a shift in the orthodoxy of what parents' responsibilities and children's needs are post divorce. Encapsulated in the Children Act 1989, this change concerns how the role and responsibilities of biological fatherhood are conceived as being equally as important as biological motherhood (see also Harne and the Rights of Women 1997; Martin 1993; and Saffron 1994 for discussions about how the effects of recent legislation have contributed to this socio-cultural shift that attempts to re-establish the significance of biological fathers in their children's lives). There has also been an emerging story among lesbians about using known donors when inseminating as a way of providing a 'biological', though not necessarily 'social', father for their children (Donovan 2000). The term 'parenting' is used precisely to make a distinction between biological parenting and parenting practices. We have seen this distinction in earlier stories, but Charles provides a further example. He is happy to donate sperm to a lesbian couple and be identified as the biological father, and have a degree of involvement in the upbringing of his child, but he is less happy with social parenting. His decision is partly based on the fact that he will not be living in the same country as the lesbian couple. He explains:

> the arrangement with them, if it succeeds, is that the child is theirs. They're the social parents, but they'll never lie to the child and I'll always be known as its biological father. And I will have access to it – to see it and spend time with it and be openly acknowledged as its father. But at the same time, Belinda and Maggie will be the social parents, and that's who it'll live with. (M25)

The discussions that Charles has had with Belinda and Maggie have resulted in negotiated roles and responsibilities that make clear both who the child is biologically related to and who will do the work of parenting.

This negotiation over parenting not only occurs in self-insemination families. In many non-heterosexual families with children there exists a large degree of flexibility about the extent to which, on the one hand, biological parents – usually men – and on the other hand, co-parents – especially women – undertake parenting roles and responsibilities. Usually, biological parents (in the main, this means fathers) are recognised as such, but most non-heterosexual parents implicitly assume that the work of parenting has no *necessary* connection with the role of a biological parent – especially the father. This flexibility in people's understanding of parenting means that some non-heterosexuals enact family caring with young lesbians or gay men alongside the young people's traditional families. Whilst respecting the traditional family relationships, non-heterosexuals believe they are providing aspects of parenting for the young that their own parents are not able to offer. Several gay men have informal fostering arrangements with young gay men who have had difficulties with their families of origin because of their sexuality. For example, George and his partner Harry have developed what they regard as a parental relationship with Kyle, who was 15 when he first met the couple. As George explains:

> we have what we call our gay son. … He rang the [local] gay phone line and I was his contact and helped him come out. I introduced him to Harry and we became very close. So [much so] that he calls us his 'gay dads' and sends Father's Day cards. And we know his parents very well, and we're very close to his parents. (M48)

George and Harry have no qualms about describing their relationship with Kyle as 'parental', even though Kyle's biological parents are on the scene, and the couple are on good terms with them. This illustrates the ways in which many non-heterosexuals are able to define parenting roles for themselves, and establish their own contribution to parenting young people, regardless of their biological relationship to them.

Traditional assumptions about family are challenged not only by disrupting the primacy of biological parenthood, but also by validating the role, status and responsibilities of co-parents. This is often problematic. A pre-existing single parent family that changes its structure to a two parent one can be difficult to negotiate in heterosexual lives. However, when the new parent is the same sex as the existing one, the possibilities – and limitations – can be of a different order, the implications of which may not be understood until they are lived. Miriam's (F44) story illustrates this.

Miriam lived with her partner Sacha until Sacha's death, which was about six months before we met Miriam. Sacha's son, Jason, was 5 when Sacha and Miriam met. Miriam moved in with Sacha and Jason, and eighteen months later became pregnant through self-insemination and had a son, Benjamin. Miriam is now the legal guardian of Jason, and the three live together as a family. The fact that Sacha already had a son was important to Miriam, as together they represented a family which Miriam could join, and have her own child within. However, she was initially cautious about developing her relationship with Jason, stating that 'I was very, very careful not to assume anything about my role with him.' Jason did begin to identify Miriam as a parent, but this was a gradual process, as Miriam explains:

> I think Sacha definitely wanted me to co-parent but … he [Jason] was 5 and I didn't even know what co-parenting would have looked like. I mean, we did co-parent in lots of ways, but she took ultimate responsibility for him – she sorted out child care … his schools and stuff – and I supported that. She talked to me endlessly about his education or about his health … so in that way, yes. However, I don't know, [if you mean] co-parent in the strict sense, if everything's shared like that – but everything wasn't shared. But I certainly took an active role … I took some responsibility. I mean, she always generally put him to bed and she read to him, and sometimes I did. So it wasn't equal, but yes, we were both parenting, definitely. But I think it

was [more] a process, [rather] than I went into that relationship deciding I was going to do that. The process enabled me to do it, but certainly not equally – particularly when Benjamin came along, because then all my time was taken up with parenting Benjamin. And the same [for] Sacha, [she] co-parented Benjamin, but she couldn't do it absolutely, because there was Jason. So I guess it's a little different to how other lesbians set it up – that I did come in after Jason was 5 years old. And, I guess, had Sacha lived, over the years it would have looked more like co-parenting. ... But I suppose I would have been primarily concerned with Benjamin and she with Jason. And I would be interested to hear if people can manage that differently – when you both have a biological child. (F44)

In this family, biological fatherhood plays no role in the parenting, yet in negotiating what co-parenting can mean, the biological relationship between each mother and son has a significance which has to be recognised and accommodated. Miriam identifies some of the activities that constitute parental practices – putting children to bed, reading to them, organising child care and their education – and describes how in the process of doing such tasks co-parental relationships might develop. And although her family practices opened up opportunities for developing co-parenting, she also describes how the dominant value attached to biological relationships limited her possibility for considering co-parenting and biological parenting as being of equal status.

Annie (F40) and Frankie (F41) are also involved in a co-parenting relationship, with Annie's daughter Lisa. In practice, however, the day-to-day work of parenting is not shared equally, and this leads to an ongoing monitoring and evaluation of what co-parenting can mean. We asked both women whether they felt like co-parents to Lisa:

Frankie: Yeah, I do. [long pause] Although I think Annie would say I'm not really ... not doing enough.
Annie: [laughing] What can I say? It's, well, it's not what my idea of a co-parent would be – and that's quite difficult really. ... I suppose my idea of a co-parent is someone who shares the responsibility fifty-fifty. Who shares the work fifty-fifty. And it doesn't really work out like that. ... I don't know ... because if you've been a parent to a child for years and then some-body else comes in – how much responsibility is Frankie prepared to take? But how much am I prepared to allow her to take? And just how does a person who's come in – especially if there's a father in the back-ground – how do they then deal with that triangle?

In the relative absence of established frameworks for defining co-parenting relationships, non-heterosexual families are negotiating family practices that are contingent on shifting circumstances. Annie says that, in her experience, the similar issue arising in heterosexual relationships is dealt with by the couple having another baby – a solution that she and Frankie have considered and rejected. It is difficult to compare a situation such as this with heterosexual equivalents because parenting is traditionally understood to be enacted by two parents, a mother and a father. Two women or two men who decide to parent together have few role models to assist them in the working out of how the gendered assumptions of parenting can be negotiated (see Dunne 1998, 2000). This can lead to tensions, with non-biological parents feeling insecure, and the expectations of biological parents failing to be realised.

Caring practices

At the centre of these complex relationships are the children and the ways in which their care is organised and their responsibilities and obligations secured. As Silva and Smart (1999b) argue, and as our interviewees strongly confirm, a focus on caring practices open up the debates about what constitutes family relationships. But this can be viewed from two different perspectives: parental intentions and practices, and the children's own understandings of their family life.

Of the non-heterosexual parents we interviewed, all believe their children have particular needs arising from the fact that they are in an unconventional family situation. Non-heterosexuals are acutely aware that the dominant culture fails to recognise the validity of their family and/or sexual relationships, and above all, they are concerned that their children should not be unduly penalised for a situation over which they have little control. We have already referred to one aspect of these caring practices: the belief of many women that a child should know the identity of his or her father, and that the mother should facilitate ongoing contact with the father until the child is old enough to take responsibility for the relationship. All the female non-heterosexuals who tell stories of opportunities, and have children from previous heterosexual relationships, intend that their children should know their biological fathers, and are generally involved in maintaining a relationship between them. This is accepted unquestioningly as a child's right, even if the father is 'difficult' or indifferent. As Jane explains:

> I still feel that he is their father and so I feel committed to make sure that I get them there [to see the father] – because I do the ferrying so far as that's concerned. And as much as I dislike him, there's no way I would take [that] away because I feel committed to them. It's not their fault that us two have split up, or that he's their father and I'm their mother and we don't get on. (F16)

Even if keeping up these paternal relationships creates tension, the risks for the children of not maintaining them are believed to outweigh any potential decision to cut the ties. It is ironic that lesbian families are often held up as one of the greatest challenges to the traditional family because of their apparent disregard for fathers, yet the evidence would suggest that in many lesbian families it is more likely that children are in touch with their fathers than in heterosexual single parent families (see Tasker and Golombok 1997). There is also evidence that gay fathers work to maintain relationships with their children. Only one gay man we interviewed lived with both his gay male partner and biological child – Greg (M17), with his partner Mark (M18), and daughter Becky (as outlined in Chapter 2, they do this part-time, acting as co-parents with their daughter's mothers). Other men who live with their young biological children live as gay men with their wives or ex-wives (cf. Dunne 2000). Several of these men told us that they remained in the marriage because of the children. As Matthew explains:

> I know for me what feels like a really difficult issue is the issue of my kids. I work with a lot of kids who have been separated from their fathers … and I don't want to be an absent father and I don't want to be an inaccessible father. At the same time, I've said to myself, 'I'm a gay man'. (M28)

The rest of the gay men in our sample who have biological children either have adult children who live independently, or else they live separately from the mother and have their children to visit regularly. But absence, as we have stressed, does not mean lack of care or responsibility.

Another way that non-heterosexuals adopt caring practices in relation to children is in how they manage issues to do with explicitness and their sexual identity, both within the family and in relation to the external world. Many non-heterosexuals understand that children do not necessarily share the same narrative of family as them. They are also sympathetic to the fact that their children have not 'chosen' their current family situation, and this requires them to address the way in which they negotiate self and family presentation in the 'outside' world. This means being particularly sensitive about those interactions that are located in the spaces defined as the children's – in schools and children's friendship networks especially.

In our experience, a difference in approach to accommodating children's perceptions of the family can be discerned depending on which type of parenting stories are told. Perhaps the recognition that their children have to make a transition from being brought up in a heterosexual family situation to living in a predominantly non-heterosexual world causes some parents to compensate for what they believe their children experience as loss – of status, friends, security, and possibly their father and family as it was before, in other words, their children's loss of 'normality'. Parents telling stories of opportunities are more likely to adopt practices that allow their children to take the lead in their own spaces about deciding where and when their parents' sexual or parental relationships will be known. For example, Jane describes an incident with her 7-year-old daughter:

> [she has told] most of her close friends … about me and Margaret [Jane's partner], you know, it's not been a problem. But there was a little lass in the line as we took them to school one morning – that she's had a few arguments with in the past and [she] can be quite lippy – and this little lass said,

'Who's that then?' So she said, 'That's mummy, my mummy.' And she said, 'No, that person with your mummy?' And she said, 'Oh, she's ... she's a friend of mine, a friend of mum's.' And it's like, you know, we chatted about it afterwards. She said, 'Mum, was that all right?' And I said, 'Well, it's fine, you know, we're quite happy to be whatever you explain us to be. Because you know your friends a lot better than we do. So you say what's comfortable and we'll go along with that.' (F16)

By contrast, many parents who tell stories of choice have children in the context of identifying as non-heterosexual, and often embark on having children as a joint project with non-heterosexual co-parents. This leads to a different perspective, as parents are open from the beginning about their sexuality and relationship in their social networks, and prepare them for the coming parenting project. In this case, their children's experiences may be filtered through a gradual realisation of difference rather than a sense of loss (see Lewin 1993; Tasker and Golombok 1997).

Hazards

Thus far we have focused on the possibilities of non-heterosexual parenting in situations where, in the main, the different members share a degree of consensus about the authenticity and validity of the chosen family pattern.. This is not always the case, of course, and can lead to serious rifts which damage the relationship. Non-heterosexual parents who tell stories of opportunities may be particularly susceptible to experiencing tensions around the recognition of their parenting relationships – especially if they are co-parenting – because of the presence of a father from a previous heterosexual relationship. For example, Frankie, who co-parents Lisa with her mother Annie, feels that Lisa's father undermines her relationship with the child:

it's when he's around, or even if she speaks to him. It's like I become slightly ostracised. ... I sense a lot of resentment around me being here – from her. ... He's not very supportive, financially or anything like that, yet he's ... in there ... it's an issue that's really around me, Lisa and her father. Annie's always going to be Lisa's mum, but ... I'm okay one minute, but another second I'm just not flavour of the month. ... Maybe when he's in the picture she doesn't know who to be loyal to. But, you know, her dad's her dad, so it feels like I'm going to be outed. (F40)

Lisa's father did not take part in the decision-making that created and defined this family, and his unpredictable presence disrupts and – in the eyes of their daughter – invalidates it by throwing Frankie's role into abeyance. When families of choice rely on strong validation from within, this sort of emotional conflict can be deeply disruptive.

Sam's story recounts what can happen when a parenting arrangement collapses, to the extent that one of the parents stops recognising, and challenges, the legitimacy of another parent. Sam is 42 and his child is 7, and although he is not the biological father, he has co-parented since his son's birth and is named on the birth certificate as the child's father. However, two years ago the mother decided that she no longer wanted Sam to continue his involvement in the child's upbringing. Sam says of his ordeal:

> we went through the whole ghastly business of the court and all the rest of it … trying to stop her taking him away (he didn't want to go), and then for me to secure my position for my right to have contact with him. Which means now she hates me – having been an honorary woman, I'm now a 'potential child abuser', and [it's] completely horrible. And I see [the son] every four weeks, daylight hours only, for one day, which is very hard for me and him. (M20)

Despite the accusations levelled against him, the judge found in Sam's favour and granted access because 'my name was on the birth certificate as the father and the agreement we had was quite definite, this was co-parenting. … The judge was lovely, he just said: "At the end of the day what I hear is a perfectly normal happy child and you both love him … you must keep contact".' As this suggests, the breakdown of non-traditional parenting arrangements can cause as many problems as the painful breakdown of a marital partnership – complicated by the ambivalent relationships between biological and social parenting, and the dangers in facing court battles around non-traditional family and parenting arrangements (Wolf 1984; Clausen 1987).

In some cases, non-heterosexual parents have to face their children's hostility and denial of their relationship. With regard to this situation, several of our interviewees talked about the non-negotiable limits they operate in trying to manage their children's responses. For example, once Jodie realised that her mother Jackie and Sam were in a relationship, she became concerned about her mother's sexuality. Jackie recalls that:

> [Jodie] asked, 'Are you a lesbian?' And I said, 'Well, I suppose I am really, yes.' And she said, 'Please don't be a lesbian. I don't want you to be'. And I said, 'Well, you know, okay then [laughs]. But I love Sam very much, and I love you very much too and, you know, you two are the most important people to me. And I love us all living together, and that's really nice.' And I left it like that, I think. (F05)

Similarly, Greg (M17) talks about how, in trying to accommodate his daughter Becky's needs, the bottom line is that she is not allowed to choose to live with only one parent, 'because either parent would be severely [unsettled] and we love her. As parents we actually look after each other's rights in that way.'

In trying to protect their children from an unsympathetic and sometimes hostile world, there are some who make choices about the extent to which they live openly as non-heterosexuals. But they also describe the limits they have in trying to address their children's adjustment to their parents' sexuality.

The needs of children

The ultimate question, of course, is how children who grow up in these non-traditional arrangements respond, and how it affects their subsequent lives. For an earlier generation, it was often a story of rejection of gay parents by their offspring (Schulenberg 1985; Bozett 1987). Dan was married in the mid-1940s and had two sons with his wife. They separated after twenty years, but did not divorce officially until the early 1980s. While he still sees his sons, who are in their forties, and is keen to have some contact with his grandchildren, the fact that they don't accept his sexuality makes him angry and disappointed:

> After I split up with my wife … it was quite a number of years until I got round to telling them [that he was gay]. … But they both said almost the same thing … almost the same words, it was weird. [They said] 'Oh, mother had dropped lots of hints but we didn't believe them.' But then they also said, 'Well, you can't stay with us and bring Simon [Dan's partner] because I'm not having that sort of thing going on under my roof.' I tried to bring my kids up to be, you know, liberal and tolerant, accepting of other people. (M44)

While Dan's sons are willing to see him, there remains a strong resistance to the acceptance of his partner, even though they have been together for over ten years. As Dan sadly comments: 'My son and his wife once came here and they were supposed to stay overnight but decided that they wouldn't and went. They made Simon feel very awkward and they don't accept our relationship.'

However, there is other evidence to suggest that children of gay fathers can and do accommodate to the changing realities (Miller 1979; Bozett 1980, 1987). Research indicates that being gay is fully compatible with effective parenting, while the father's sexual identity is of little importance in defining the overall parent–child relationship (Harris and Turner 1986; Bozett 1987; Bigner and Jacobson 1989). Similarly, there is overwhelming evidence that lesbian mothers and their children do as well as their heterosexual counterparts in all crucial areas of upbringing (Gibbs 1988; Falk 1989; Tasker and Golombok 1991; Patterson 1992). In fact, there is very little difference between children of non-heterosexual families and those of heterosexual families. Indeed, some commentators have argued that lesbian mothers should be doing more to free their offspring of traditional values (Pollack 1987; Polikoff 1987). In one regard, however, there is good evidence that the children of non-heterosexual parents are a little different: they tend to be more tolerant. In their study, Tasker and Golombok (1997) suggest that, though there was little difference between the proportion of young adults from lesbian and heterosexual single parent households who recorded at least one instance of same sex attraction, the offspring of lesbian families were more likely to have considered the possibility of developing same sex relationships. They conclude that the young adults from lesbian homes had a wider view of what constituted acceptable sexual behaviour. On this evidence, Dan's experience with his sons, above, is becoming less common.

The overwhelming message we received from the few children and young people available to us in our research was one of tolerance. The children whose stories we heard were conscious of the unconventional nature of their domestic lives, and, as we have seen, sometimes experienced anxiety about it. As children often do, they might have preferred things to be different at key points of their lives (cf. Tasker and Golombok 1997).

Children are active participants in the family of choice, and they do not always see things in the same way as their parents, co-parents or carers. As one teenage son of a complex domestic unit (each of the lesbian partners has two children from marriages) comments, 'I don't think I would say that we're one family ... I would say that it's a sort of co-operative union type thing, but it's not a family.' However, a 'co-operative union' is not a bad description for the complexities of many contemporary arrangements, where individual interests and mutual needs are intertwined, but where active parenting is the ultimate focus. In the end, what matters is the authenticity of the care and love that the children receive, and we have no reason to doubt that it is received, and reciprocated, in non-heterosexual families.

Stories about non-heterosexuals' parenting and caring practices constitute important challenges to traditional narratives of family life and the heterosexual assumption, as popular anxiety frequently reveals. Yet there is overwhelming evidence that parenting issues are being taken seriously by non-heterosexuals, and that the needs of children are seen as being the central concern. Non-heterosexual parents must always be aware of the general climate of opinion in which they care for their children. But there is a growing tendency to affirm positively both the right to parent, and the responsibilities that this entails. These are not 'pretended' families, but genuine experiments in finding creative new ways of responding well to old needs – to care for the young. Many non-heterosexuals are extremely proud of their families, their children and the choices and decisions they have made and continue to take to make them work. The children are also proud of them. Although these are often stories of struggle, they are also stories of love and commitment, and of self-belief in ways of being good parents.

8 Towards intimate citizenship

The unfinished revolution

Over the course of a generation, the possibilities for living openly non-heterosexual lives have been transformed. As outlined in this book, this transformation is the result of a dual process. First, there has been a radical change in attitudes within the non-heterosexual social community itself, which has resulted in a new-found self-confidence among the sexually marginalised and produced a sense of agency and creativity. This has subtly shifted the main focus of self-activity from asserting identity around sexuality to affirming a new relationship ethos. However, and second, this transformation of life chances is part of a wider change in intimate life which has given rise to the perceived 'crisis of the family', a reordering of the gender boundaries, and a more tolerant climate towards sexual difference. This dual process, as with all social change, has had uneven effects: the revolution is unfinished. For many middle-aged non-heterosexuals, the changes that have occurred during their lifetime are far beyond anything they could have imagined when they were younger. As Craig, 56, says:

> I think this is one of the things about my age – that, you know, there's been a lot of change within my lifetime. … When I was in my teens and early twenties it was illegal to have a sexual relationship with another man … nowadays, you know, it's acceptable. Certainly within the conurbations, you know, the large cities and so on … there's not as much policing of this sort of thing. So long as it's within the constraints that the police lay down … and I suppose that has to be better from what it was thirty years ago. (M14)

Yet, as Craig's phrasing and hesitations reveal, while he acknowledges that there have been genuine gains, it is clear that his life still feels circumscribed. Craig's comments are illustrative of the broader position in which all non-heterosexuals find themselves at the beginning of the twenty-first century. On the one hand, there is cautious optimism that non-heterosexuals will continue to build on the increasing self-confidence of recent decades, and establish a legitimacy for their intimate relationships and families of choice. On the other hand, there is also the knowledge that many non-heterosexuals continue to face the often hostile consequences of the lack of full recognition given to their lives. Thus a sense of real achievement is counterbalanced by continuing feelings of uncertainty – the effect of the persistence of the heterosexual assumption, and lives that must still perforce be lived from the margins. As Craig says, 'it's got a long way to go'. In this concluding chapter we explore the road ahead: the possibilities for change that exist in the everyday lives of non-heterosexuals, the ways in which individuals are engaged in practices of freedom that both challenge and potentially liberate them from the heterosexual assumption, and the idea of sexual or intimate citizenship, the realisation of which would imply the ultimate legitimisation of non-heterosexual ways of life.

The possibilities

Throughout this book we have argued that a growing toleration of non-heterosexuality has occurred against a backdrop of much broader socio-economic and cultural changes in western societies. Among the first manifestations of these changes were the liberal law reforms of the 1960s and 1970s and the new social movements which were committed to radical sexual change (Weeks 1977/1990). These were harbingers of the shifts in intimate life that were to take place over the following decades (Castells 1997), and which collectively have been characterised as a new phase in the history of modernity, known as 'reflexive modernity' (Beck 1992; Giddens 1991, 1994). One of the major features of this new period, highlighted by recent sociologists, is the apparent breakdown of traditional assumptions about individual life trajectories. Rather than people following what Beck and Beck-Gernsheim (1995) have called the 'standard biography', which includes heterosexual courtship, marriage and nuclear family life (with its concomitant assumptions about gender roles, power dynamics and relationship longevity), there has been a move towards a situation in which individuals are able to adopt a 'do-it-yourself biography'. This trajectory frees people from the expectations of traditional family life, and is closely associated with the process of individualisation wherein the individual rather than the family or the community becomes the primary focus of contemporary life. Do-it-yourself biographies have been given (albeit unintentional) support by welfare states by the provision of minimum incomes for households which do not correspond to those of the traditional family, thus making alternative lifestyles economically possible. At the same time, a radical separation of conception from heterosexual procreative sex has also become an option for heterosexuals and non-heterosexuals alike. Some commentators maintain that this has allowed new opportunities for personal autonomy and for choosing ways of being, thus transforming heterosexual life and making possible greater freedom in non-heterosexual life.

We believe this analysis has a great deal of validity. It certainly accords with the experiences of many of the non-heterosexuals who we interviewed. In the life stories recounted in this book, we have seen a vital emphasis on choice and creativity, and a firm belief that self-invention is a necessary part of non-heterosexual lives. But we have witnessed something else: a striving for autonomy in the context of mutuality, the attempt to shape individual freedom through a sense of belonging. Families of choice and the other life experiments we have analysed underline a point that often seems to be underplayed in Giddens' (1991, 1992) and Beck and Beck-Gernsheim's (1995) work – that is, the transformation of intimate life is about more than simply realising *individual* potentialities. Ultimately, it is about the possibilities for new forms of *relationships* that can transcend the rigidities and inequalities of traditional forms of life. In this context, it is surely significant that within the non-heterosexual world, alongside older claims for individual rights, we are seeing a new emphasis on relational rights, for the full recognition of same sex intimacies.

The possibilities for achieving such rights are greater than ever before, and at most levels of public life there is an increasing visibility of non-heterosexuals. One significant example is the fact that the British public seems unfazed at having openly lesbian and gay politicians, when as recently as a couple of decades ago overt homosexuality would have meant the end of a politician's career (see Rayside 1998). One British opinion poll has even suggested that 70 per cent of the population would accept a prime minister with a homosexual past, and 60 per cent would accept one who was currently homosexual (*Mail on Sunday*, 12 September 1999). Recently, there has been an explosion of non-heterosexual fictional and non-fictional literature, magazines and newspapers. Lesbian and gay characters have appeared in every major British television soap opera, as well as in other mainstream television programmes, and specialist programming, such as the drama *Queer as Folk*, has specifically targeted a non-heterosexual audience. Further, a political constituency of non-heterosexuals has begun to campaign for the recognition and legitimation of non-heterosexual lives in all spheres of society, and it is a constituency which both local and national politicians find increasingly necessary to woo.

These developments have resulted in an expanding range of what we call community knowledges about the possibilities and resources for non-heterosexual living (see Chapter 4). Though access to community knowledges may be limited by such factors as gender, geography, ethnicity, socio-economic resources and physical access issues, their existence has been responsible for the growing confidence of non-heterosexuals not only to live openly non-heterosexual lives, but to do so with a sense of pride rather than apology. It is therefore not surprising that the emerging generation of unapologetic non-heterosexuals often react with a sense of outrage at being denied the same protections and legitimation afforded to other groups in society, especially to those in traditional heterosexual intimate relationships. For many non-heterosexuals, the pace of change is too slow.

The pace of change is slowest in those parts of public policy that most clearly embody the heterosexual assumption: the nexus between marriage and entitlements in the welfare state, immigration rights, and the benefits and spousal rights attached to certain types of employment, insurance and leisure. Here a different sort of story remains dominant. A number of analyses have pointed out the extent to which the post-war welfare state was predicated upon traditional heterosexual family norms and relationships (e.g., Turner 1993). Similarly, in order to protect Britain from a supposed 'influx' of black people, immigration laws developed a concept of citizenship based on the biological and legal relationships of the traditional family. In both cases, the traditional family remained the key organising unit for social policy. In this scenario there are few opportunities for do-it-yourself biographies, and one result is that government policy frequently trails behind everyday practice. During the 1980s and early 1990s, as we saw in Chapter 1, various governmental efforts were made in Britain and the United States to halt the tide of sexual liberalisation – without notable success, it has to be said. Despite the existence from the late 1990s of a British Labour government committed to equality in a common age of consent for heterosexual and non-heterosexual alike, legislation became bogged down in parliamentary procedure and blocking tactics by a small group of moral conservatives (Waites 1999). Recent Labour government policy to do with the family skirts delicately around the question of non-traditional families, and affirms the importance of marriage in bringing up children (see Chapters 2 and 7). Other parts of the equality agenda have been signalled (for example, on adoption, gays in the military, and even some sort of acknowledgement of same sex partnerships), but they remain low on the government's list of priorities.

Most gains in the formal recognition of non-heterosexuals' intimate relationships – especially parenting relationships – are a result of individual or collective efforts to force the legal system to reflect more accurately contemporary demographics, for example in recognising the validity of (for the most part) lesbian parenting (Harne and Rights of Women 1997). Although other individual attempts to secure the same legal standing as heterosexual couples initially had mixed results, for instance in the areas of employment benefits and tenancy succession (see, for example, Northmore 1997, 1998), they eventually met with some success. However, this was largely due to legal challenges and the intervention of the European courts, rather than deliberate action by the British government (O'Hanlon 1999). Despite a new recognition of same sex relationships in immigration regulations, which allow the entry of lesbian or gay partners to the United Kingdom, there are stringent qualifying criteria to prove the authenticity of the relationship for both same sex relationships and unmarried heterosexual couples, in order to protect the 'special position of marriage' (Travis 1997: 7). Changes are occurring on the ground, but these are taking place in an inconsistent and often haphazard fashion, and they lack a consistent legal framework or philosophy, and unambiguous political support. The homosexual 'age of consent' was finally reduced to 16 (the same as the heterosexual age) on 30 November 2000, following the Labour government's use of the Parliament Act to bypass opposition in the House of Lords. By a nice historical touch, it was the exact centenary of the death of Oscar Wilde, the most famous 'martyr' of the homosexual struggle. A full official review of British sex offences promised more radical changes (Smith 2000), and a new Human Rights Act offered the hope of greater protection for private life and for the recognition of the validity of different family forms (Campbell 2000: 54–5). Alongside these promising signs, however, went a mobilisation of morally conservative forces threatening to block the repeal of Section 28 (for example, see Hogg 2000: 56; McSmith and Reeves 2000: 10). A broad liberalisation of attitudes has in turn stimulated a new articulation of strong 'traditional values' by a number of social forces, from conservative churches to opportunistic politicians seeking to shore up their political base. Thus, non-heterosexuals must necessarily continue to insist on their rights to be family and 'do' intimacy and commitment, while at the same time they are acutely aware of the risks.

The risks

A sense of risk is a characteristic feature of late modern societies (Beck 1992), as individuals are faced with a growing number of choices and the need to weigh a flood of possible options, threats and opportunities. This sense of risk is heightened for those whose lives remain on the margins. Even in more liberal times, it is difficult to escape the scars of discrimination, real or feared, and the risks that remain in many areas of life. Most non-heterosexuals have experienced either direct or indirect hostility or discrimination because of their sexuality. And the knowledge that it is a possibility can have a significant impact, as Alex explains:

> it does have quite an impact on my fear of people, or fear of being attacked (which is quite high) – just because I know it happens to a lot of people ... although it's never happened to me and there's no particular reason why I think it should. (M26)

Many non-heterosexuals feel their position in society is precarious. Jenny (F21), for example, says that 'a lot of us still live in fear of losing our jobs, fear of losing our children, people still get ... driven out of their homes'. These fears place very real limits on the freedoms of individuals to express their non-heterosexuality. Many non-heterosexuals we interviewed felt they could not hold hands with their partner in public, and others expressed fears of what might happen when they stepped outside their front door (see Donovan, Heaphy and Weeks 1999 for further analysis). Thus, the simple pleasures of everyday life are constrained by the knowledge of continuing stigma. This means that some individuals consider many of their decisions to be openly non-heterosexual in terms of risk calculations. They feel they must continually make an assessment of the amount of risk they will take to keep safe on the streets and in their homes; to keep their jobs, and to maintain relationships with families of origin or heterosexual friends. Martina explains:

> for me, it's like constantly assessing the risks really. You know, whether [they're the] sort of risks when you're walking down the street with your

girlfriend … risks about what you say to a colleague at work … about your sex – you know, not even about your sexuality – about who you live with even and about lifestyle and that. So I think … [why] I'm always assessing the risks is because I experience it as being quite a homophobic society really. And I do take risks, you know. It's not like I'm sort of gonna be closeted or anything, but it's about weighing it up really. (F26)

Living in fear of hostility and/or a continual state of anxiety about rejection is not helped by the fact that many non-heterosexuals feel they receive little legal protection. The negative reactions of other people are, it seems to some non-heterosexuals, given credence by this. Here, Malika discusses how she feels about living in a society she considers is heterosexist:

it forces me to hide parts of myself to various people at various times. And it effects me on a political level because there's no legislation, there's no social policy, there's no protection offered by society that validates who I am and who we are and that … allows us to be positive about who we are. (F03)

For the majority of people who live on the sexual margins of society, there are layers of their lives where they can feel safe to be themselves, and then there are layers where they feel that the risks attached to being found out as non-heterosexual are too great, and they must conceal their sexual lives. Due to the constant need to self-monitor in order not to be caught out, the effort of moving between these disparate layers can be exhausting. This contrast of feelings between the safe and dangerous parts of life can be experienced as permanently oppressive, as Annie very clearly articulates:

It's very oppressive to be inside and be totally yourself and feel very powerfully who you are and [then have to] step outside. And sometimes it's so extreme that it literally feels like a slap in the face, that you've got to suddenly change. Or, if we're going to a lot of lesbian events, it's like one world where you're safe and then you step out and suddenly you've got to be on your guard. … I find it really difficult. So it's like you've got one reality – your reality – and then there's the rest of the world. You're sort of moving between these two realities. There's the whole issue of safety and fear and it's very oppressive. (F41)

Annie's sense of the different realities forces her to enact a guarded performance, one which she feels is not the real her, but instead is that of a pretend heterosexual (see Butler 1990). This remains a very common personal reaction, involving a careful consideration of the circumstances and the probable responses of the heterosexual world. In the following quotation, Alex cites examples of situations in which he calculates that being openly gay could be either risky or risked:

I have ... quite a pronounced fear of being attacked both outside and in my own home. It would stop me wearing a T-shirt saying 'I'm queer' in the street. I wouldn't do it. Not because I'm in any way ashamed of being queer, but because it seems like a very obvious situation to put yourself in where you're going to be exposed to physical assault ... sat in a restaurant I will hold hands across the table because I think people are less likely to punch me in a restaurant. So it's about testing the limits of where you think something untoward is going to happen. (M26).

Here Alex makes it clear that, depending on the context of the situation, different behaviours can carry different levels of risk. Consequently, it is useful to think in terms of layers of 'being out' – layers which continually need to be negotiated and re-negotiated. If you are comfortably middle class, live in a cosmopolitan city and work in a liberal profession, then it is probably easier to be open about your life than if you are working class and live in a tight-knit community. Members of minority ethnic communities frequently have to balance loyalty to their communities of origin, which provide support against racism however 'traditional' their values, with attempts to explore their sexual desires and identities. In our interviews, several black non-heterosexuals pointed out that in some situations non-heterosexuals can choose to pass as heterosexual in a way that black people are unable to pass as white; and, as such, black non-heterosexuals often experience further dimensions of risk in terms of navigating everyday life.

Most non-heterosexuals have to choose how open they can be after consideration of the likely costs: they may be out only to themselves and a sexual partner; to some but not all of their family of origin; to some or all of their work colleagues (indeed, they may be out to an individual colleague but not out in their workplace); they may be out and involved in lesbian, gay and/or bisexual political, social or community activities, but not out to their parents, doctor or neighbours. The 'closet' that has trapped non-heterosexuals in a cycle of secrecy and self-hatred may be changing its meaning, but for many it is still necessary (cf. Seidman, Meeks and Traschen 1999; Bech 1999; Reynolds 1999). Regardless of which layer(s) of one's life one chooses to be out in, the decision is dependent on what the perceived consequences are for one's life and livelihood, and those of one's loved ones. The most difficult areas are those where society remains most anxious about non-heterosexual ways of life, where the boundaries are still most heavily policed. Parenting, as we have seen, remains on this disputed border (see Chapter 7). Perhaps because here the risks are highest.

Practices of freedom

However, while it would be easy to paint a picture of continuing victimisation and oppression of non-heterosexuals, this is not the main story that people tell. For at the same time as various practices of exclusion do undoubtedly continue to operate, we cannot fail to acknowledge the existence of ever-expanding spaces in society in which same sex intimacies are able to thrive. These have more to do with the informal revolution taking place in everyday life, as documented throughout this book, than with any formal changes in society. What we have called 'life experiments' amount to everyday 'practices of freedom', which are the real measure of the transformation of intimate life.

Practices of freedom are about the ethical choices available to people in the late modern world (see discussion in Weeks 1995: 50–8). Michel Foucault has argued that the contemporary challenge is not to seek a new morality, but to invent practices which reject models of domination and subordination, to resist the normalising pressures of modern life, and to allow the exploration of what he calls an 'aesthetics of existence': practices of life which allow the exploration of pleasure, friendship and autonomy. From this perspective, freedom is not a given or a goal but a continuous process, so that, in Foucault's words, 'the practices of freedom are what people try to make of themselves when they experience the existence of freedom in the history that has formed them' (quoted in Weeks 1995: 57).

Foucault (1979) maintains that the apparatus of sexuality lies at the heart of the workings of power in modernity, and the heterosexual assumption, based on a binarism of domination and submission, is central to this. Practices of freedom, in Foucault's usage, are oppositional to the binarism embedded in the heterosexual assumption because they both challenge taken-for-granted givens about traditional ways of life, and develop new ways of living emotional and intimate lives. It is clear from many of the non-heterosexual stories we have recounted in this book that many people believe they are actively engaged in practices of freedom, which potentially liberate them from this binarism and allow them to explore the possibilities of living in intimate relationships and families of choice that reach beyond the heterosexual assumption. These stories can be characterised as ones of *private* practices, through which meaning and *meaningfulness* is given to intimate life (Weeks 1995). What is significantly new, however, is the appearance of *public* stories that circulate these everyday experiences, and expand the community of meaning which receives and recirculates them.

We can identify three common public stories told by non-heterosexuals about practices of freedom: stories of coming out; stories of free spaces and informal separatism; and stories of direct challenges to the heterosexual assumption. They are not exclusive strategies – people might adopt different strategies in different situations, or they might develop a different strategy over time. The decision about which strategy to adopt is often dependent on a calculation of the risks involved.

The first story is the oldest in the post-1960s' repertoire: the practice of declaring one's homosexuality in order to affirm it – coming out (Weeks 1977). An openness about one's desires, identities and relationships means testing the power of the heterosexual assumption – the expectation in every aspect of life, whether in the community, at work, in places of worship or in leisure activities, that one is 'normal', that is heterosexual. Even in the most liberal and tolerant of societies, the fact that homosexual desires and identity are not transparent dictates that this assumption of 'normality' must be tested in order to freely express a sense of self. Sometimes the expectation of heterosexuality is not benign, and the pressure to be heterosexual can feel immense. The assumption of heterosexuality is so deeply embedded in the language of everyday life that even to disrupt the flow of conversation to correct people's assumptions about one's identity and most fundamental relationships can feel enormously exposing.

Confidence about coming out grows with friendships (see Chapter 3), the gaining of access to community knowledges (see Chapter 4), and in love relationships (see Chapter 5). Naturally, a sense of freedom to be open is dependent on one's socio-economic, gender or ethnic positioning. Consequently, some non-heterosexuals feel able to use their occupational power to challenge the heterosexual panorama. William is one such example:

> being an openly gay [health professional] is a role I have, and that's less to do with sex than very publicly being a rebel ... I think being a maverick suits me. So I'm very out. I mean, I'm out to everybody. The powers that be. I mean, I had occasion to address a meeting the other day and it was about HIV and trying to get the message across of why we had so many people with HIV on the books, [and] I put my 'queer as fuck' T-shirt on – under my jumper. And at the right moment, [I] took my jumper off to be under-stood. And this was a group of health care workers and GPs and other health professionals, so they got the message. (M03)

Being out can be transformative for the self, especially as it forces others to come to terms with misconceptions based on the heterosexual assumption. It also makes it possible for other individuals to come out, and for the creation of a culture of support. Here, Angela tells how she feels supported by the new atmosphere in her place of employment:

> I mean, I'm very out recently, so I don't think anybody dares do anything. I feel quite protected, really, because I'm out – because we have policies that protect us and harassment wouldn't be tolerated in the workplaces I've had in the past few years. (F28)

As argued in Chapter 1, coming out as lesbian or gay was perhaps *the* defining shift in homosexual consciousness in the 1970s, and has led to a greater climate of acceptance. But the case remains that in everyday life the heterosexual assumption has to be constantly tested, and constantly risked.

The second public practice of freedom we want to highlight is the creation of spaces in which to live, socialise and sometimes work, in an informal separatism from the heterosexual assumption (see Chapter 4). In such spaces, non-heterosexuals can be themselves, without having to explain who they are or wait anxiously for a misunderstanding about their lives. And in this way they can protect themselves from hostility or rejection. Peter is someone who has a strong sense of non-heterosexual space:

> I only socialise with lesbians and gay men, which I know is funny because I don't really think of myself as being separatist, but I don't actually have any straight friends if I think about it. I get on really well with the straight people I work with, but they're not friends. (M11)

The strong sense of identity and self-confidence that is provided by close non-heterosexual friends and sympathetic others means there is less of a need for approval from heterosexual society, and the restrictions imposed by the heterosexual assumption. A space for experimentation is created. Joan's story clearly illustrates this point. It is very important for Joan, who is bisexual, that her non-heterosexual family is seen as being different from a traditional one:

> I have less of a sense of family relating to me and my daughter, or me and my daughter and Giles [her daughter's father]. And I'm not quite sure what that's about. I think it's about me wanting to sort of get away from conventions – and wanting to kind of break new ground and enable a kind of greater number of possibilities to exist. Because, I think, you know, what is seen as acceptable is really quite narrow. And actually, the reality is that a lot of people are living quite different lives from the kind of accepted norm – but we're sort of not acknowledging that really, or valuing it. (F32)

Joan has chosen to share a house with a bisexual woman, and Joan's daughter spends half the week with her and the other half with her father, a bisexual man who shares his home with two bisexual friends. Their bisexual identities are integrally linked to the way in which they have organised their living arrangements and their friendship networks. Joan's political understanding of her identity results in her positively choosing the company of other bisexuals, with whom she can build a life, both for her and her wider family of choice.

The development of non-heterosexual social circles and friendship networks are not only instrumental in developing mutual support against the opprobrium of the heterosexual assumption, they are also celebrated and chosen over the company of heterosexuals. Jill, for example, talks about her recent experience of a package holiday:

> I came back thinking, 'I'm not going on another package holiday, I've done it'. I'm fed up with being with straights, you know, and listening to their inane conversation [laughs] and [I] feel that I don't have to be doing this any more. The world has got so big now and there's so much going for us in our own ways that we don't have to put up with this any longer. … No, I'm very intolerant of straights [laughs] these days. … and I actively search out lesbian and gay things. (F22)

This attitude of not 'putting up with this any more' can lead to direct challenges to particular manifestations of hostility or discrimination. Many nonheterosexuals tell of the anger they feel at being verbally abused on the street and how they fight back. Sue explains one strategy that she and her girlfriend Julie have used:

> I think the thing is that they think it's wounding to call you names and if you can turn that round and say … well, it's like with us the other night, we were walking down the street and a gang of little white boys were going, 'Dykes!' [and we said,] 'Thank you, thank you – you got it right, you didn't call us lesbians'. (F15)

Some non-heterosexuals get involved in more organised strategies for transformation that challenge the inequalities which exist for non-heterosexuals, and may provide opportunities for others to explore their sexual identity in safety. Friendships and a sense of common involvement, as Nardi (1999) argues, provide the spur to collective action. Many of the non-heterosexuals we interviewed are, or have been, involved in a range of community-based activities, from working on telephone help-lines or in lesbian and gay centres to campaigning on local or national issues. There are many who take an active part in lesbian, gay, bisexual and transgender Pride celebrations. More frequently, inappropriate behaviour, harassment and/or discrimination at work is being challenged, as are discriminatory welfare practices. Such strategies can reap rewards at the individual level. Miriam (F44), for example, was able to get her deceased partner's (Sacha) pension agency to recognise Miriam's son as well as Sacha's own son as equal dependants and therefore beneficiaries of Sacha's pension (see Chapter 7). Sam (M20) told us about encountering a sympathetic judge who recognised his parenting role and confirmed his right to access to his son. Jane (F16) won care and control of her two young children from their father, who had unsuccessfully tried to use the fact that she is a lesbian to argue for custody (see Chapter 7). And here, Thomas (M01) and James (M02) reveal their struggle with an insurance agency, leading to a significant victory as declared partners:

James: The lifestyles questionnaire. I mean, it was like a case of either you're not going to get this or it's going to be so bloody heavily loaded that it's going to be …

Thomas: … too expensive.

James: … not [a] financially viable proposition. So I thought, right I'm going to take this bloody insurance company head on. And I wrote them a two- or three-page letter detailing everything about my sexual past, everything about the work that I do – my knowledge of HIV and AIDS and my role in counselling. And I basically said, if they load my premium like I know they're going to – or force me to have an HIV test – then it will just show what a bunch of wankers they really are. And they responded well! They wrote back and they underwrote the premium without me having to do anything. … But I think it's about challenging, and there are some people that are not in a position to challenge.

Many non-heterosexuals take available legal steps to make visible and safeguard their intimate relationships. Some people make wills to try and secure their wishes in issues of guardianship or property inheritance, others draw up contracts with co-parents and donors, take out deeds of trust to protect housing, get powers of attorney, or become each other's next of kin. Many of these practices are contingent on personal resources, and on the self-confidence of the person to put his or her head above the parapet. But the fact that some non-heterosexuals do engage in any or all of these practices of freedom is indicative of the growing confidence in the legitimacy of non-heterosexuals' demands for the recognition and validation of their intimate lives. At the same time, local successes serve to underline the continuation of discriminatory practices and the need for wider social and legal changes to safeguard claims to relational rights. It is here that the debate about same sex marriage comes to the fore.

Assimilation or difference?

Throughout the stories of the search for recognition and validation for their intimate relationships, we see non-heterosexuals struggling with their desire to retain choice and creativity. In imagining what could be, most of the non-heterosexuals we interviewed use heterosexual marriage as the marker for comparison, and many find it wanting – despite the huge public salience of the issue (Sullivan 1997). Malika sums up this feeling when she says:

> Of course we want the same rights as heterosexuals – but I don't know if we do really. … We create our own lifestyles and … relationships that are different from heterosexual relationships. But I think in terms of … not just legislation, but in terms of civil rights and the right to participate in society … we should have those rights. But I don't think that we should be wanting to mimic everything … that heterosexual relationships have … it's about having choice[s] and to have those validated. (F03)

The debate within non-heterosexual communities focuses on a dilemma: is the general goal one of wanting to be included in a society still dominated by a strong heterosexual assumption; or is it to seek a recognition of different ways of life? This is often posed as a choice between assimilation and difference. However, the reality is more complex, as our earlier discussion of citizenship and transgression suggests (see Chapter 1; and also below). Despite the high profile of campaigns for the legal recognition of same sex partnerships, or indeed even marriage, there have been many dissenters within the lesbian, gay and bisexual communities about the movement for recognition of intimate relationships (e.g., Bersani 1995; see also Chapters 1 and 5, this volume). Many feminist and queer commentators are worried that, in seeking recognition, many non-heterosexuals have been assimilated into the dominant heterosexual culture, in other words that same sex families are beginning to 'look like' heterosexual ones (e.g., Bowen 1990; Saalfield 1993; Jackson 1995). Warner (1999), a major queer theorist, argues that the campaigns for gay marriage will inescapably lead to a new form of normalisation in which the queer challenge is vitiated.

This debate has been characterised as one between boundary-defenders, who argue for a social movement based on a collective identity, and boundary-strippers, who argue for the deconstruction of identity and binary categories, such as queer theorists and activists (Gamson 1994). Some of our interviewees showed affinity for the boundary-defenders in terms of arguing in favour of an equal rights approach to policy and legislative change; and the overwhelming majority supported the individual's right to choose to have access to legitimising institutions, such as marriage. However, most of the participants in our study, in response to questions about seeking validation for their lives and families of choice, displayed more in common with the boundary-strippers. Their concepts of family and relationships are characterised by the two themes of flexibility and choice. For example, many of the arguments against same sex marriage are based on our interviewees' own experiences of marriage and feminist-influenced understandings of marriage being a patriarchal institution, with rigid gendered expectations about power, and roles which they found undermining and/or restrictive. For instance, Angela comments on her marriage:

> I mean, I've been married for ten years and I'm actually not particularly in favour of heterosexual marriages in [their present] form … because it's all around property and ownership and roles, the roles that people play in it. (F28)

Most of our interviewees want equal rights but are not convinced that this should mean only being the 'same as', or having access to the same rights, as heterosexuals. As Will (M23) comments, the question is 'whether absolute equality … fits in with assimilation and whether a degree of invisibility comes with that'. This tension between wanting to be treated equally, yet not really desiring the heterosexual option of marriage, was a common theme we encountered. Angela, again, notes that,

> there are benefits to having certain status … I think we all have the right to them, whether they're good or bad. … I actually don't want to have to go through a marriage ceremony … so I'm a bit unclear about whether it's a good thing to have certain rights. … In principle, yes, we should all have the same [rights]. But then if we want something different, maybe everyone should have something different. (F28)

While most non-heterosexuals in this study think people should have the choice to get married, and a small minority would like to get married, there are also those who feel that, like marriage, formal recognition of cohabitation is inappropriate for same sex relationships. David (M12) feels that tailoring heterosexual laws and understandings towards gay relationships 'is bound to fail'. Many non-heterosexuals feel that their intimate relationships are – or have the potential to be – radically different from heterosexual relationships. And thus, marriage is perceived as a restrictive institution of the state, epitomising the worst aspects of heterosexuality with its prescribed gendered roles and unequal power balance. Warren (M34) says that 'marriage in heterosexual terms is such an oppressive institution, and I wouldn't like to see lesbians or gay men simply kind of reflecting that'.

In other words, there is a fear that conforming to traditional marriage-based models of family life means non-heterosexuals will sacrifice the creativity and egalitarianism which have characterised the development of their intimate lives. Pat, for example, believes that,

> we should all be treated equally in the eyes of the law. But … I believe now that we're not the same as straight people; that we do have differences, that we are diverse, and that we are creative and we take a lot more risks around lots of things. I believe we're almost like a tribe [laughs] – I think we create things in society and we help society move forward. (F36)

In considering partnership rights, several people make the point that cohabiting heterosexuals are often in the same position as same sex couples – that is, they are also excluded from rights and responsibilities which accrue to married couples. There is a general perception of an underlying hierarchy of value and status, along with social, legal and economic rights attached to couple relationships and family types, with marriage at the top (Van Every 1991/1992; Carabine 1996). A way to resolve the tension, some believe, is to separate marriage from legal rights and privileges, so that anyone can choose to take part in a public or private, religious or secular commitment or marriage ceremony, and to give all ceremonies equal validity. Many non-heterosexuals – especially women – have had experiences of living both inside and outside the traditional family, as many of them have been married or have lived in heterosexual relationships. This opportunity to compare lives that have had legitimation with those that have none make many wary of unquestioningly adopting the framework of traditional marriage. They warn that the perceived benefits of this type of legitimation is purchased at a price: it restricts people's opportunities to experiment with a diversity of living arrangements and family and caring practices. For most non-heterosexuals, the bottom line is that they want to open up opportunities, not restrict choices.

This can mean making the most of an existing situation. Living outside the heterosexual norms carries pains and risks, but for some it can also mean material advantages. As Andrew (M13) says, '[there are] benefits in not being recognised as well'. Several non-heterosexuals who receive, or have received, state benefits tell how – because their relationships are not recognised legally – they are assessed as single people, and therefore receive more money. If same sex couples were considered on a par with heterosexual couples, then one member of the couple would have to be assessed as the dependant of the other, and his/her benefit would then be dependent on the income of the partner. One example is Dee (F06), who is blind, and her partner Jane (F07). They are financially better off not being considered a valid couple:

Dee: Because I'm a lesbian, and because I'm blind, and because my relationship is not recognised as a valid relationship in the eyes of the DSS and the government, I can get away with having my own income. Now if we were a heterosexual couple and I was married, or if I wasn't married and had a male partner, then that would not apply.

Jayne: Because Dee still gets exactly the same amount of benefits as she would do … if I wasn't living here, basically.

Dee: So, you know, I really have mixed doubts when people sort of insist on having our relationships validated. I think, 'Oh, bloody hell – fuck off! No thanks!' [laughs]. I'm quite happy [with] the way things are. And why shouldn't I be financially independent?

While some are prepared, *faute de mieux*, to use the system, others not only look beyond traditional heterosexuality, but beyond the primacy of the couple in thinking about how non-heterosexual intimate relationships could be given legitimacy. In this case, the route to equal rights is to be found in taking away the privilege of the couple. As Melanie (F29) says, equal rights 'shouldn't be on a marriage model'. Charles (M25) feels it is 'bullshit' for gay couples to get married. 'I think it shows a distinct lack of imagination', he comments. Amy (F27) agrees: 'I think people shouldn't be given advantages for being couples, it just further boosts the institution of couples really – coupledom'. These advantages are articulated not only in financial terms, but also in terms of status and validation. Some non-heterosexuals are also concerned that these advantages should not fall automatically only to sexual partners, but that friends and other members of families of choice might equally be chosen or nominated to benefit from formal recognition. We interviewed several non-heterosexuals who considered the centrality of the couple relationship to be problematic, either because they value individual friendships very highly, or are celibate and thus wary of a model that reinforces the importance of a sexual relationship.

For many non-heterosexuals, one of the key assumptions of traditional heterosexuality has little meaning: monogamy. From this perspective, any legislative framework that privileges the couple necessarily negates the validity of non-monogamous relationships. Mollie (F30), a lesbian who has two partners, comments that, 'I imagine they wouldn't allow us to register as a multiple set-up'. For other non-heterosexuals who are involved in non-monogamous relationships, rights based on joint partnership are largely irrelevant in their own lives. As Joan (F32), a bisexual, says, 'my life is just a million miles away from that'. For these non-heterosexuals, and others like them, the challenge is to find formal practices of inclusion that allow for as much choice, flexibility and pluralism as possible in arrangements for intimate relationships.

A small number of non-heterosexuals in our sample, however, say they would marry if they were allowed. They feel that this would give their relationships the required recognition and validity which they seek. Jonah explains how hard it can be living in a relationship that is not given recognition and validity:

> it would be good for people and the quality of their relationships to know they had that kind of security with each other. I think it might make quite a difference to people, you know. Certainly there's an awful lot of insecurity rife in gay relationships 'cos nothing validates them except themselves. I mean, it's entirely up to yourself, constantly, and it must be a huge fucking burden and responsibility *always*, you know, that there's nothing ... there's no framework, [I mean] no foundation outside of yourself that validates you – you're constantly 24-hours a day involved in validating yourself, you know, and it's bloody hard work. (M41)

This sense of it being a constant struggle to live outside society's norm is the main factor behind calls for partnership rights and same sex marriage. It has led to a reorientation of the lesbian and gay political agenda. But among the participants in our research, at least, this remains a minority voice. Same sex marriage is understood by many to be largely irrelevant to their lives, since it is based on the heterosexual assumption. Others point out their unwillingness to be part of an institution that reinforces a hierarchy of relationships and to which are attached differential privileges, benefits, rights and responsibilities. Yet it is also widely recognised that being excluded from same sex marriage underlines how far non-heterosexuals are excluded from society. For Martina, as for many others, it is ultimately a question of equal citizenship:

> it's about being a citizen. It's about having full rights as a citizen really, and other citizens – every citizen has the right to certain things you know. It feels like, as lesbians, we haven't got the right to, you know, publicly declare or have a state sanction for a relationship. So it feels like it's almost depriving me of an aspect of my citizenship, really. (F26)

Martina's comments capture a key point in debates about legalised same sex partnerships and marriages. That is, regardless of the different attitudes people may have, it is important to engage with these debates because they touch on fundamental issues to do with social recognition and belonging. So long as concepts of citizenship, entitlements and responsibilities continue to be largely organised around marriage, family and the heterosexual assumption, non-heterosexuals will inevitably be marginalised in key aspects of their lives. The ideas of citizenship that are prevalent in the culture are crucial markers of inclusion and exclusion in society for non-heterosexuals.

Intimate citizenship

Earlier, we argued that the new sexual movements of the past generation, particularly feminism and the lesbian and gay movement, have had two characteristic elements: a moment of transgression, and a moment of citizenship (Weeks 1995). The moment of transgression is characterised by the constant invention and reinvention of new senses of the self, and new challenges to the inherited institutions and traditions that hitherto had excluded these new subjects. The aim, whether conscious or not, is to challenge the *status quo* and various forms of social exclusion by acts of public celebration of difference. The early lesbian and gay movement, like more recent queer politics, represents the moment of transgression. Yet contained within these movements is also a claim to inclusion, to the acceptance of diversity, and a recognition of and respect for alternative ways of being – a broadening of the definition of belonging. This is the moment of citizenship: the claim to equal protection of the law, to equal rights in employment, parenting, social status, access to welfare provision, and partnerships rights and same sex marriage (Donovan, Heaphy and Weeks 1999). Without the transgressive moment, the claims of the hitherto excluded would barely be noticed in the apparently rigid and complacent structures of old and deeply entrenched societies. Transgression is necessary in order to face traditional ways of life with their inadequacies, to expose their prejudices and fears. But without the claim to full citizenship, difference can never be fully validated (Weeks 1998).

Citizenship is about belonging, and the nexus of rights and responsibilities which entitle the individual to be included within the polity. Until recently, discussion of citizenship has tended to concentrate on three specific aspects: the civil or legal, the political, and the social (Marshall 1950). More recent critiques and developments of the idea of citizenship have demonstrated the gaps in the traditional definitions. They have done so by broadening the scope of the discussion (Turner 1993; Stevenson 1998); by uncovering the gendered nature of the concept (Walby 1994; Lister 1996, 1997; Feminist Review 1997); and laying bare its national and racialised dimensions (Anthias and Yuval-Davis 1992). It is now apparent that the citizenship discourse embraces a variety of interlocking strands which reveal the intricate interconnections of class, race, nationality gender – and sexuality (Weeks 1998).

The notion of sexual or 'intimate' citizenship (Plummer 1995) is an attempt to give meaning to the recognition of diversity and its implications for full recognition of individual needs and patterns of relationships. It is a useful metaphor for new claims of rights, and for rethinking the balance of entitlement, recognition, acceptance and responsibilities. Plummer argues that sexual or intimate citizenship is about:

> the *control (or not) over* one's body, feelings, relationships: *access (or not) to* representations, relationships, public spaces etc.; and *socially grounded choices (or not) about* identities, gender experiences.
>
> (Plummer 1995: 151. Emphasis in the original)

Superficially, at least, the idea of the sexual citizen seems to be a contradiction in terms. The sexual has traditionally been seen as a focus of our most intimate personal life, an arena of pleasure and pain, love and violence, power and resistance, separated away from the public gaze (Giddens 1992). Citizenship, on the other hand, is about involvement in a wider society (Marshall 1950). The citizen operates in the public sphere, carrying rights but also responsibilities to fellow citizens and to the community which defines citizenship. The sexual citizen, therefore, is a hybrid being, breaching the public–private divide which western culture has long held to be essential (Weeks 1998).

Yet this intermingling of the personal and public is precisely what makes the idea of intimate citizenship so important. Before the 1960s, no one would have publicly said, 'I am gay/lesbian', or 'sadomasochist', or 'transgendered', or 'queer', or anything remotely similar as a defining characteristic of personal and collective identity, and of social involvement and political commitment. Today, it is commonplace for those belonging to sexual minorities to define themselves both in terms of personal and collective identities by their sexual attributes, and to claim recognition, rights and respect as a consequence. The idea of sexual or intimate citizenship alerts us to new concerns, hitherto marginalised in public discourse: with the body, its possibilities, needs and pleasures; with sexualised identities; and with relational rights (Evans 1993; Waites 1996; Richardson 1998; Weeks 1998). It poses acutely the question of what we mean by 'sexual justice' (Kaplan 1997).

We have discussed elsewhere how public policy could more adequately reflect the plurality of living arrangements that exist in the contemporary world (Donovan, Heaphy and Weeks 1999). We argue that the social policies that currently underpin our active participation as citizens are based on a family model that is no longer necessarily appropriate, or indeed relevant for many people, whatever their sexuality. Many believe an approach to policy formation based on individualisation might be more appropriate (Waaldijk 1994). This would mean that any benefits an individual accrues are attributed to her-/himself as an independent person, and those benefits can then be distributed as she or he sees fit, regardless of the existence of blood relation- ships. As we have seen, most non-heterosexuals have important relationships in their lives for which they feel responsibility and commitment. A model based on individualisation does not mean licence to avoid responsibility and commitment, on the contrary it requires the reflexive working out of those chosen ties in everybody's 'do-it-yourself biography'. This model does not come without its own risks, and there may be valuable alternatives. The campaigns for same sex marriage offer the most obvious alternatives (Sullivan 1997; see also Chapter 5). The point is that, given the will, public policy can be creatively rethought to match the needs of diverse ways of life.

However, policy changes are not necessarily the only or immediate route for broadening concepts of citizenship for non-heterosexuals. The advances of the last thirty years have been achieved largely in the absence of any specific legislative or policy changes in favour of non-heterosexual lives. Indeed, often it was retrograde legislation, like Section 28, that mobilised and politicised non-heterosexual communities across Britain to become actively and visibly engaged in debates about what constitutes family (Weeks 1991). Living against the odds, moving inwards from the margins, opens up new possibilities for alternative ways of life. In this scenario, citizenship is not so much something that is claimed or given, but a process that is lived *as if* there were full equality. The creation of grass-roots realities, and the circulation of stories about them to audiences ready to hear them, is reshaping the meaning of what it is to be a full citizen. Political and legal changes, however painfully slow they might often appear, will surely follow.

We have sought to show in this book how, despite the limitations and restrictions that continue to exist, we are living in a period where there are ever-widening possibilities for non-heterosexuals to live openly in their chosen relationships. These expanding spaces and possibilities, we have argued, have enabled many non-heterosexuals to engage in practices of freedom which are oppositional to the heterosexual assumption. In coming out, developing and thriving in informal separatism, and directly taking on and challenging the heterosexual assumption, many non-heterosexuals create the opportunities through which the traditional ways of doing family and intimacy are turned on their heads.

We have explored the way in which many non-heterosexuals are experimenting with ways of living that challenge all the assumptions of traditional heterosexual family life. Friendships – including those with ex-lovers – are being celebrated, and held in an esteem comparable with that of kin in traditional families. For many who do not necessarily believe in the romantic story of monogamy, it is friendships that form the bedrock of their intimate lives. The centrality of the couple is being questioned, for fear of colluding with a hierarchy of values attached to different ways of living, with the couple at the top reaping privileges, benefits and status as well as formalised responsibilities at the expense of others. Notions of home and community have the potential to embrace a plurality of ways of sharing households, and deciding where those households should be, as well as often transcending bricks and mortar and geographical location. Many non-heterosexuals engage in relationships based on trying to achieve an egalitarian ideal, where power inequalities, though often expected, are not necessarily accepted without discussion and compensatory behaviours. Gender expectations are being questioned and explored, so that divisions of emotional and household labour in relationships are the subject of negotiation, flexibility and mutuality. Commitments and responsibilities are positively embraced as expressions of binding involvements with members of families of choice. There is a widespread understanding that relationships cannot be assumed, but must be worked at and negotiated, allowing for changes and the movement in and out of families of choice. The possibilities for parenting, motherhood and fatherhood, are being innovatively explored, to the extent that parenting practices do not necessarily depend on biological relationships, and gendered notions of mothering and fathering are held up for scrutiny. There is a widespread belief in the need to protect and nurture difference, diversity and the choices offered by pluralist ways of living and the sharing and creating of community knowledges. Practices of freedom are being explored through everyday experiments.

By engaging in practices of freedom, the non-heterosexuals whose lives and personal narratives we have explored not only challenge the givens of the heterosexual assumption but also invent new ways of living that can influence the available possibilities for thinking and doing citizenship. Citizenship thus becomes more than just a legal, policy or academic concept, it is also a practice. By reflexively living as non-heterosexuals and engaging in these practices of freedom, non-heterosexuals are continually experimenting with what citizenship could be and might mean in their everyday lives.

In so doing they are proclaiming the authenticity of their chosen ways of being. Inauthenticity, philosophers have argued, signals a passivity before life, waiting for a fate that will overwhelm us (Weeks 1995: 67). Authenticity, on the other hand, signifies a willingness to take hold of the present possibilities and to anticipate the future bravely and positively, as something that we have the ability to make. The unexplored life may be something not worth living. But the life that is created reflexively, with full awareness of the opportunities and risks, can become a meaningful life. In the meaningful life, Agnes Heller (1984: 268) has suggested, 'the role of conscious conduct of life is constantly expanding, leading the individual on in confrontation with new challenges, in perpetual re-creation of life and personality'. In this book, we have explored the structure and meanings of non-heterosexual lives in their diversity. Through this, we hope we have shown how people who still live their lives at odds with the dominant, if faltering, norms are able to live meaningful lives, connected lives, through their chosen families and other life experiments. That is the ultimate significance of same sex intimacies.

Appendix 1

Researching *Same Sex Intimacies*

This book is based on the findings of a research project, 'Families of Choice: The Structure and Meanings of Non-heterosexual Relationships', which was carried out in 1995 and 1996. It was funded by the British Economic and Social Research Council (ESRC; reference L315253030) as part of its 'Population and Household Change' programme (see McRae 1999). In studying emerging narratives of non-heterosexual relationships, the aim was to provide empirical insights into the changing nature of forms of domestic organisation, the shifting meanings of identity and belonging, and the developing culture of non-heterosexual ways of life. Because there has been very little systematic empirical research on these themes in Britain (see Weeks, Donovan and Heaphy 1996), we had no existing baseline from which to work. Therefore, it was necessary to generate the data which would allow us to analyse what we believe are dramatic changes in non-heterosexual ways of life. In this appendix, we outline the approach that we took to the study. A more detailed discussion of our methodological approach can be found in Heaphy, Donovan and Weeks (1998).

Researching non-heterosexuals

The main body of the research was based on qualitative interviews with 96 individuals, divided equally between men and women. Of this number, 32 were interviewed as 'couple' units (13 same sex couples; 2 household units; 1 parenting unit). In addition, we conducted four group interviews (a lesbian and gay youth group; a group of parents of lesbian and gay men; and two groups of women in communal living situations). A qualitative approach was adopted for various reasons.

Quantitative studies based on surveys are notoriously difficult in relation to homosexuality, not least because of the problems of establishing a sampling frame for a 'hidden' population, and defining what is meant by a homosexual lifestyle (Plummer 1981; Weston 1991; see also Davies *et al.* 1993: 66–71; Dunne 1997). Also, work on the nature of non-heterosexual identities that has been carried out over the past twenty years (e.g., Plummer 1981, 1992; Porter and Weeks 1990; Weeks 1991, 1995) has demonstrated the shifting and problematic nature of such identities (as indeed all identities), and the central importance given to self-definition. As researchers, we felt it was crucial to acknowledge that if identities, and the patterns of relationships which are built around them and sustain them, are 'contingent', 'emergent' and 'processual' (Giddens 1991, 1992; Weeks 1995), then reflexive research techniques which can begin to uncover that complexity were needed. Therefore, we rationalised that a questionnaire survey, even of a self-defining sample, would fail to reveal the complexity of meanings around identity and relationships. A methodology based on semi-structured interviews, on the other hand, could provide a way of exploring shifting nuances of identity by providing brief life-histories of the subjects, and allow for the development of narratives of 'intimate' and 'family' life (see also Dunne 1997).

The geographical scope of the research was mainland Britain. The national nature of the research had important implications for recruiting research participants. Parallel research on lesbian and gay relationships (e.g., McWhirter and Mattison 1984; Weston 1991) has tended to have a limited geographical focus (on particular urban areas), and has recruited through 'snowballing' or by accessing friendship networks in an effort to include a diversity of experience (see Weston 1991). Like Weston (1991), we aimed to avoid the race, class and organisational bias that has characterised other studies on non-heterosexualities (Weston 1991). While we employed some 'snowballing', to enable us to get in touch with 'hard to reach' non-heterosexuals, our recruiting strategies were primarily based on advertising in the local and national lesbian, gay and bisexual press, in conjunction with the contacting of over 150 local information, support and social groups. By using a mix of recruitment methods, it was hoped at least to touch a diversity of experience in terms of different social and cultural positioning *and* geographical location (though we recognised that the concentration of non-heterosexuals in urban areas, and particularly in London, should be reflected in our sample – see Chapter 4).

In practice this entailed contacting groups of lesbians, gay men, bisexuals and other non-heterosexuals that were organised around 'race' and ethnicity, disability, religious belief, recreational interests, and so on. We found the *Pink Directory* (Cassell 1994) to be a particularly useful resource in identifying groups and organisations to contact. We wrote to the groups, providing information about the study and enclosing leaflets with a tear-off return slip for those interested in taking part. In our communications with information centres and organisations, we requested that they assist us by displaying the leaflets in a public place. We also placed a notice in *The Pink Paper*, a free national newspaper for lesbians and gay men.

From the outset we anticipated difficulties in recruiting certain populations, and compensated for this by sending leaflets to almost all of the groups for black and disabled individuals listed in the *Pink Directory*. In an endeavour to contact rural non-heterosexuals, we contacted local activity groups (e.g., walking groups) in areas where there were few other non-heterosexual organisations. Due to the (relatively) limited formal organising outside of England (as listed in the *Pink Directory*), we contacted most of the relevant addresses listed under 'Wales' and 'Scotland'. We also specifically targeted almost all the organisations listed for older individuals, including a range of religiously and politically affiliated groups, and placed particular focus on parenting groups.

These strategies were relatively successful, and by the end of the project we had received responses from over 150 individuals who wished to participate in the research. Practically all the community publications we approached responded to our requests for assistance by publishing a notice about the research. We also learned that in some cases one or two individuals from particular local organisations had taken it upon themselves to inform others of the project. A youth group worker had also asked his group if they would like to be interviewed, and a group of parents of lesbians and gay men invited us to interview them.

In selecting participants to interview, and to offset the type of 'bias' problems identified by Weston, we adopted theoretic sampling (Weston 1991; Holland *et al.* 1994). That is, from the wealth of possible participants, we deliberately based our selection in terms of various social and cultural positionings. This was not in an attempt to claim 'representativeness' as such, but to include identities considered important by respondents themselves.

Interviewing and recruiting were not distinct stages. Throughout the research we continued to snowball for 'hard to reach' non-heterosexuals (particularly with regard to age, ethnicity and disability). Towards the end of the research we also made a concerted effort to increase the number of older respondents and black respondents. In order to do so, we occasionally employed our own networks to make contact with potential interviewees, and posted further notices in particular interest newsletters (for example, a newsletter circulated by a Quaker group). We also made a particular effort to interview people who lived in specific areas (who may or may not have been aware that others in the area were being interviewed) to capture a sense of the operations of geographically based communities.

Our recruitment strategy, and particularly the issue of theoretic sampling, raises the question of 'who' is included in the research. In terms of the sexual, class and ethnic identities of our interviewees, self-identification was the key to our sampling approach. In the profiles outlined in Appendix 2, we have used the respondents' own understanding of their sexuality, ethnicity and class (and have assigned nationality based on the birthplace of the participant). While many of our interviewees framed their accounts in terms of lesbian and gay life, the research concern with 'non-heterosexuals' was adopted in an attempt to acknowledge the existence of a diversity of subordinate sexual identities (see also Dunne 1997). While all the male interviewees described themselves as gay in one sense or another (sometimes in conjunction with 'queer'), the majority of women defined themselves as lesbian, 6 described themselves as bisexual, 2 as queer, and 1 declined to define herself in terms of sexual identity.

While 48 of the research participants identified clearly as middle class, there were 4 who identified more vaguely as middle class. Twenty-five identified firmly as working class, while 10 identified in more complex terms as working class. The remainder presented accounts of their class identities that were too complex to reduce to either/or classifications, or did not identify with any social class at all. As many of the profiles in Appendix 2 indicate, self-identifying in terms of class was often described as 'difficult', 'a struggle' or 'impossible'. The class categories should, therefore, be understood as an (inadequate) reduction of often detailed and complex discussion. This is also the case with ethnicity, where such terms as 'white/Celtic' and 'bi-racial' were used by research participants to conjure up a sense of 'who they are'.

While the profiles in Appendix 2 underplay the complexity of these identity categories (but see Heaphy, Donovan and Weeks 1998), they are provided to assist the reader in 'placing' the narrators to some extent. Self-definition is not unproblematic, but it can demonstrate the complexity of identities *and* the problems of sampling that attempts to rely on neat categories and definitions. In the end, we believe that allowing respondents the time to develop complex accounts of their class, ethnic, and sexual identities provided us with information which is highly relevant to 'realities' of sexuality, identity and relationships in today's world.

The interview

The interview 'schedule' was compiled following the writing of an in-depth review of the relevant literature (Weeks, Donovan and Heaphy 1996). As indicated above, we used a semi-structured style for the interviews. The most appropriate strategy for exploring the issue seemed to be to adopt a flexible and reflexive approach, which would enable the unfolding of interviewees' viewpoints and narratives of experiences (Plummer 1983; Anderson and Jack 1991). The focus was on an approach that would allow us to engage with participants in a 'conversational' style. In essence, interviewing entailed developing a 'checklist' of areas and topics that we wished to address in the interview. While these were not necessarily covered in any particular order, at the beginning of the interview we tended to focus on general issues relating to the individual's biography. The remainder of the interview was then organised around particular themes: personal life and identity; friendships; household; partners; children; caring; HIV and AIDS; legalities, partnerships and marriage; families; trust and obligations; intimacy; love; sex and sexuality; stigma; general.

A pilot study of ten interviews was undertaken, and the checklist/schedule was revised in light of this. At the pilot stage, we realised that the interviews could entail between three to seven hours of conversation, depending on the degree to which participants engaged with the questions. This raised serious issues in terms of revising the time allocated for transcription and the quantity of data that would have to be managed and analysed. Other issues that were presented at the pilot stage were related to the appropriate unit of study (the couple, individual or group narrative) and the nature of the narratives that the interview was attempting to access. While the research design for the study initially proposed that the most significant unit would be the same sex couple, and 63 of the 96 subjects interviewed were members of couple-type relationships, the pilot research suggested two important issues to be taken into account, one methodological, the other substantive.

In terms of the methodological question, the problem arose whether couples should be interviewed together or separately. The question as to whether the research was studying collective or individual stories became a key issue (cf. Duncombe and Marsden 1996). As we were concerned with the reflexive nature of stories of the intimate, including individual and collective stories, a dual strategy was adopted: some couples were interviewed as couples, others were interviewed as individual members of couples. While this was partly a matter of what couple members wanted, or were able within time constraints to offer, it was also a strategy employed to enable an exploration of differences in response (see Heaphy, Donovan and Weeks 1998 for a more detailed discussion).

In the analysis we have approached both couple and individual accounts as examples of emerging narratives of relating (see below). The adoption of a dual strategy offered considerable comparative possibilities, and the significant degree to which couple and individual narratives are consistent in their descriptions of the operation of same sex relationships (in terms of negotiation, the egalitarian ideal, and so on) is noteworthy. But the strategy also provided the opportunity to access narratives that were unlikely to be provided in couple interviews (for example, where individuals were withholding opinions or information about their activities from partners). Furthermore, this approach offered the opportunity to witness the active construction of the narrative of relating from two different perspectives – as a task for the individual and for the couple (see Heaphy, Donovan and Weeks 1998 on the role of the interviewer in this construction).

This in turn raises the substantive issue. It became apparent during the course of the research that while couple formation and membership were intensely important to many of our interviewees, this did not exhaust the range of relationships that were identified as important. To concentrate either on the individual story of the couple, or the couple narrative, was to risk losing the sense that relationships emerge as part of collective stories: of friendship circles, social networks and sexual communities. Hence, it proved necessary and productive for the research to interview people who were not in couple relationships at the time of interview. While 63 research participants identified as members of couples, 6 were members of multiple relationships, and the remainder were single. All had stories of same sex relationships to tell, even if these were not centred on (current) coupledom. Including this diversity of accounts enabled the research to consider a number of experiments in living that challenge the primacy of the couple as assumed in much of the literature on same sex relationships (see Weeks, Donovan and Heaphy 1996). It further allowed us to go beyond the widely employed definitions of 'lesbian and gay families' that refer exclusively, or primarily, to extended networks which contain same sex couples at the core (McWhirter and Mattison 1984; Cruikshank 1992).

The 'doing' of interviews began when potential participants contacted us (as individuals or couples) by mail or phone. At this stage we provided information about the nature of the research, and informed the contact about issues of confidentiality and time. We also asked if he or she wanted to be interviewed alone or with a partner/friend, and for permission to record the interview. We then enquired as to whether they were still interested in taking part in the research. If they did want to continue, we asked for basic personal details (age, ethnicity, location, relationship status, and so on). In the majority of cases we contacted the participant at a later date to check that he or she was still willing to participate, and to arrange a time and location (usually the participant's home, but in a few cases a university interview room).

The interview proper began by explaining the purpose and background of the research. Participants were again assured of confidentiality (within the research team and transcribers), and reminded of the time the interview might take. The subjects were assured that they could stop the interview whenever they wished, and they did not have to talk about particular issues which might be raised if they did not want to do so. They were then reminded that the interview would be recorded and transcribed. When it was agreed that the participant wished to go ahead, he or she was asked which research name they would like to use. Many suggested the use of their own names. We initially accepted this, but following further consideration of the issue of confidentiality, and arguments against the use of actual names, the research team decided that pseudonyms should be allocated to *all* participants (cf. Holland *et al.* 1994). On some occasions participants would (unexpectedly) ask if a friend or family member could sit in or take part in (some or all of) the interview. Our approach was to allow the interviewee to decide who could take part.

The length of interview conversations (sometimes over seven hours) occasionally meant that the interview took place over two meetings. We had initially developed the interview schedule with the problem of 'getting interviewees to talk' in mind. However, in practice we discovered that most of the individuals were very willing, and eager, to tell their stories (see also Dunne 1997: 31). This is likely to have been influenced, in part, by the fact that we had disclosed our own non-heterosexual identities to respondents. The existence of perceived commonalties between respondents and researchers can have a significant role to play in determining the extent to which trust develops within the interview (Oakley 1981; Finch 1984; Dunne 1997). This in turn influences the kind of narratives that are provided. We were, however, aware of the danger in overemphasising these commonalties. While respondents and researchers may share identities in terms of gender and sexuality, other differences, such as those relating to class, nationality and ethnicity can be at play in the research situation (Edwards 1993; Song and Parker 1995). There may also be other reasons for participants' enthusiastic telling of their stories. As we have discussed elsewhere in this book, the willingness to talk to researchers can be indicative of the increasing confidence that non-heterosexuals have in their ways of living, and the desire to have these validated (see Heaphy, Donovan and Weeks 1998 for a discussion of the implications for validity).

While the core of the research is made up of the narratives gathered through these interviews, informal interviews with other individuals and groups concerned with non-heterosexual relational issues were also undertaken. In Britain, we had various meetings with representatives of campaigning, policy and political groups (for example, Stonewall, and Rights of Women). Study trips to the Netherlands, Denmark and North America offered the opportunity to meet with a broad range of researchers, community activists and those involved in policy formation relevant to same sex relationships. Together these provided us with the opportunity to familiarise ourselves with developments both inside and outside of Britain, and provided part of the backdrop against which we have theorised and analysed the more personal narratives of non-heterosexuals.

Analysis and validity

Throughout the research, we found ourselves 'constantly' analysing in many respects (cf. Coffey and Atkinson 1996). But in terms of the formal aspects of analysis, a primary challenge was to manage the very large data set. Interviews were transcribed in full where possible, and *The Ethnograph V4* (Qualis Research Associates) software package was used to store and manage the coded data (cf. Coffey and Atkinson 1996). The approach to analysis was one that was based on themed readings of the participants' narratives (cf. Mason 1996). Initially, we produced general analyses for the funding body and for initial overview papers (see Weeks, Donovan and Heaphy 1996; Weeks, Donovan and Heaphy 1999; Weeks, Heaphy and Donovan 1999a and b). We also produced more issue-focused analyses (for example, on families of choice and AIDS, non-heterosexual parenting, the policy implications of families of choice, and so on).

A discussion of methodology would not be complete without some reference to the issue of validity. As discussed in Chapter 1 and elsewhere in this book, the concepts of 'stories' and 'narratives' have been of crucial importance to the research. Throughout we have highlighted the value of seeing these as part of emerging narratives of the intimate that have a key role to play in the organisation of everyday life. We have been influenced in this by Plummer's (1995) work, and by his defence of the validity of analysing narratives less for their 'truth' telling or 'aesthetic' qualities than for what can be said at a particular time. This involves taking narratives seriously in their own right, not as historical truth (though historical truths do become apparent through them), but as narrative truth. This is what Plummer (1995) calls the 'pragmatic connection', by which stories can now be examined for the roles they play in lives, in contexts, in social order. Hence, the concern is with the role a certain kind of story plays in the life of a person or society (Plummer 1995: 172). It is precisely this pragmatic connection – between the relational stories and the lived lives of non-heterosexuals – that was the foundation for our research (and this book).

Appendix 2

Biographies of interviewees

We interviewed 48 women and 48 men for this research. The participants were drawn from a variety of backgrounds. In the following, we provide brief biographical notes on each of the 96 people. They are listed in order of interview: first the female interviewees (coded F), and then the male interviewees (coded M). The numerical order is the basis for the references to the interview (F01, M01, etc.). We also indicate whether the participants were interviewed individually, or as part of couple interviews.

The women

F01 Juliet is a 39-year-old white lesbian. She is English, working class, and works in the voluntary sector. She is single and lives by herself in a city in the north of England. The most important people in her life are her lesbian friends. (Individual interview)

F02 Rachel is a 32-year-old black, middle-class, Jewish lesbian. She is English and lives alone in a city in the north of England. She has been in a relationship with Malika (see F03) for three years. She is employed in the voluntary sector. The most important people in Rachel's life are her partner, her friends, a child of an ex-lover, and her mother. (Individual interview)

F03 Malika is a 28-year-old black, Asian lesbian. She is English, middle class and lives alone in a city in the north of England. She has been in a relationship with Rachel (see F02) for three years. She is employed in the voluntary sector. The most important people in her life are her partner and friends. (Individual interview)

F04 Sam is a 31-year-old white lesbian. She is English, working class and lives in a city in the south of England with her partner Jackie (see F05). She has been in her current relationship for almost three years, and for most of this time has lived with her partner and her partner's child. Sam works in nursery education. The most important people in her life are her partner and her daughter, and her brother. (Couple interview with F05)

F05 Jackie is 42 and prefers not to identify in terms of sexuality. She is English, white working class and lives with her partner, Sam (see F04), and her daughter in a city in the south of England. She works in primary education. The most important people in her life are her partner, her daughter, her mother, and a male heterosexual friend. (Couple interview with F04)

F06 Dee is a 41-year-old white, disabled lesbian. She is working class, English and lives with her partner, Jayne (see F07), in a village in the north of England. She has a daughter from a previous marriage and two granddaughters. She is currently living on disability living allowance. The most important people in her life are her partner, her daughter, her two grandchildren and a small group of lesbian friends. (Couple interview with F07)

F07 Jayne is a 31-year-old white lesbian. She is English and middle class. She lives with her partner, Dee (see F06), in a village in the north of England. She has lived with Dee for four and half years. Jayne works in the voluntary sector. The most important people in her life are her partner, a group of lesbian friends, her partner's two grandchildren, her mother and an aunt. (Couple interview with F06)

F08 Jody is a 25-year-old white lesbian. She is English, middle class and lives with her partner of nearly eighteen months, Michelle (see F09), in the south-east of England. Jody has recently started paid full-time work with a voluntary project and is also a part-time student. (Couple interview with F09)

F09 Michelle is a 25-year-old white lesbian. She is English and middle class. She lives with her partner, Jody (see F08), in a small village in the south-east of England. Michelle is a part-time student and lives on income support. (Couple interview with F08)

F10 Caroline is a 32-year-old white lesbian. She is Welsh and middle class. She lives in a town on the south coast of England with her partner Pam (see F11). Caroline works full-time in the care profession. The most important people in her life are her partner, her family, her partner's son and family, and close friends. (Couple interview with F11)

F11 Pam is a 43-year-old white lesbian. She is working class and English. She lives with her partner Caroline (see F10). She has an adult son from a previous marriage and a grandchild. She is a full-time student in a vocational course. The most important people in her life are her partner, her son and his family. (Couple interview with F10)

F12 Pippa is a 33-year-old white lesbian. She is English, middle class and was born in the north of England. She lives with her partner in a town on the south coast of England. She is currently completing a course in an ancillary health care profession. The most important people in her life are her partner and her family of origin. (Individual interview)

F13 Coral is a 26-year-old white lesbian. She is Australian, but has lived in Britain for five years. She does not identify in terms of class. She lives alone in a city in the south of England, and works part-time for the local authority. She is single and has recently come out of an 'abusive' relationship. The most important people in her life are three friends. (Individual interview)

F14 Julie is 34, white and identifies as queer. She is English, middle class and works for the civil service. She has been in a relationship with Sue (see F15) for over two years and lives with her in a city in the south-east of England. She was adopted when she was 4 years old. The most important people in her life are Sue and a group of queer friends. (Couple interview with F15)

F15 Sue is 28, white and identifies as queer. She is English, and although she finds the concept of social class confusing, would identify as middle class. She is in a relationship with Julie (see F14), and they live together in a city in the south-east of England. Sue works as an administrator. The most important people in her life are Julie, her sister (who is lesbian), her family of origin, and a group of queer friends. (Couple interview with F14)

F16 Jane is a 31-year-old white lesbian. She is English, working class and disabled. She lives in a town on the south coast of England with her partner of almost one year and her two children from a previous marriage. She has recently been made redundant from her job as an HIV/AIDS trainer. The most important people in Jane's life are her partner and her children. (Individual interview)

F17 Catherine is 27, white and bisexual. She is English, middle class and works as a civil servant. She lives in a city in the south of England with her male partner. She is also in a relationship with a bisexual woman. The most important people in her life are her two sexual partners, her father, and a group of friends (two of whom she has occasional sex with). (Individual interview)

F18 Jo is a 40-year-old white lesbian. She is English and middle class. She lives with her partner and her children in a city in the south-east of England. She is employed in higher education. The most important people in her life include her partner and her children. (Individual interview)

F18 Alex is a 24-year-old white lesbian. She is English, and sees herself as somewhere between working class and middle class. Alex is single and shares a house in a city in the Midlands with Janet (see F19) and a heterosexual woman. She currently works part-time for a local authority. The most important person in her life is her sister. (Interviewed with F19)

F19 Janet is a 27-year-old white lesbian. She is English, middle class and is currently employed in office work. She is single and shares a house with Alex (see F18) in a city in the Midlands. The most important person in her life is her mother. (Interviewed with F18)

F21 Jenny is a 45-year-old white lesbian. She is middle class and has American nationality. She lives in a city in the Midlands with her partner and one of her adopted daughters. She and her partner have six children between them, and live between two homes. Jenny is currently caring for her children, and is engaged in part-time university studies. The most important people in her life are her partner, her children, her partner's children, and a small group of friends. (Individual interview)

F22 Jill is a 46-year-old white lesbian. She is English, middle class and an education professional. She has lived with her partner (of eleven years) for ten years in a town in the south-east of England. The most important people in her life are her partner, her family of origin, and a group of friends. (Individual interview)

F23 Sarah is 31, white and bisexual. She is disabled, English, middle class and Christian. She is in two relationships: one with a heterosexual man, the other with a lesbian. Sarah has just finished a degree in social work, and is about to move to begin a job in social work. The most important people in her life are God, her two partners and her twin sister. (Individual interview)

F24 Karen is a 25-year-old white lesbian. She grew up in South Africa and has lived in Britain for three years. She lives in a town in the south-east of England where she is completing her part-time studies and working part-time. She has been in a relationship for sixteen months, but does not live with her partner. The most important people in her life are various members of her extended family of origin and a friend. (Individual interview)

F25 Katrina is a 29-year-old white lesbian. She identifies as Irish Catholic born and brought up in England, and working class. She lives with her partner of three years, Martina (see F26), in the north-west of England. Katrina works in the voluntary sector. The most important people in her life are her partner, her brother and sister, and two friends. (Individual interview)

F26 Martina is a 35-year-old white lesbian. She is English, middle class and lives in a city in the north-west of England. She lives with her partner Katrina (see F25). Martina is employed as an education professional. The most important people in her life are her partner, her mother, her two sisters, and two friends. (Individual interview)

F27 Amy is a 31-year-old white lesbian. She is English, middle class and lives in a city in the north-west of England. She is in a relationship with Angela (see F28), and currently lodges with another lesbian. She is employed as an information officer in the public sector. The most important people in her life are her partner, a group of friends, and the child of an ex-lover. (Individual interview)

F28 Angela is a 41-year-old white lesbian. She is disabled, English and working class. She lives alone in a city in the north-west of England and is in a relationship with Amy (see F27). She has two adult children and one granddaughter. She is employed as a youth worker. The most important people in her life are her partner, her children and granddaughter, and a group of friends. (Individual interview)

F29 Melanie is a 52-year-old white lesbian. She is English, middle class and employed full-time in research. She has four children and one grandson. She is involved in sexual relationships with two lesbians (one is Mollie, see F30) and lives alone in a city in the south-west of England. The most important people in her life are her two partners and an ex-lover. (Individual interview)

F30 Mollie is a 51-year-old white lesbian. She is English, working class and disabled. She lives alone in a flat that she rents from Melanie (see F29), who is one of her sexual partners. She is currently unemployed. She has two daughters (one is a lesbian) and two grandchildren. The most important people in her life are her lesbian daughter and her two sexual partners. (Individual interview)

F31 Ruby is a 35-year-old white bisexual. She is English and identifies as working class. Ruby is intimately involved with three men. She lives with her son in a city in the Midlands, and works in nursery education. The most important people in her life are her son, a group of friends, and a friend's child. (Individual interview)

F32 Joan is 30, white and bisexual. Born in England, she grew up in South Africa and now lives in a city in the Midlands. She is middle class and has a daughter from a bisexual relationship that has recently split up. She lodges with a bisexual woman and works part-time in nursery education. The most important people in her life are her daughter, and five adults – three of whom are occasional lovers (one woman and two men). (Individual interview)

F33 Marilyn is a 45-year-old white lesbian. She is English, middle class and works as an administrator. She lives with her partner and three of their four children in a town in the south-east of England. The most important people in her life are her partner and their four children, and her family of origin. (Individual interview)

F34 Niamh is a 42-year-old white lesbian. She is Irish and middle class. She lives alone in a city in the south-east of England, and has recently begun a sexual relationship. Niamh is employed as a therapist. The most important people in her life are her best friend (an ex-lover), her lover, certain members of her family of origin, a work colleague, and a group of friends. (Individual interview)

F35 Sue is a 32-year-old white lesbian. She is Scottish, and lives in a city in Scotland where she shares a flat with a heterosexual woman. She has recently begun a relationship. She works part-time as a development worker for a voluntary organisation. (Individual interview)

F36 Pat is a 34-year-old white lesbian (though she prefers to use the terms 'dyke' or 'gay'). She is Scottish, Jewish and middle class. She lives with her partner and baby boy (who is co-parented with two gay male friends) in a town on the west coast of Scotland. Pat is a full-time mother. The most important people in her life are her partner and son. (Individual interview)

F37 Naseem is a 33-year-old black, Asian lesbian. She grew up in Pakistan and moved to Britain in the mid-1970s. She works in the voluntary sector. She lives with her husband and daughter in a city in the north-east of England. She is not in a relationship with a woman. The most important people in her life are her daughter, her parents, and her 'made family' – Rachel and Malika (see F02 and F03). (Individual interview)

F38 Josephine is a 38-year-old white lesbian. She is Irish and middle class. She lives with her partner, Jess (see F39), in a city in the south-east of England. She is employed full-time as a trainer in social care. The most important people in her life are her partner, her brother and sisters, and her partner's parents (her own parents are dead). (Couple interview with F39)

F39 Jess is a 32-year-old lesbian. She is English, Jewish and middle class. She lives with her partner, Josephine (see F38), in a city in the south-east of England, and works as a counsellor/trainer. The most important people in her life are her partner, her parents, a group of close friends, her partner's nieces, nephews and older sister. (Couple interview with F38)

F40 Annie is 38, white and identifies as a dyke. She is English and describes herself as 'educated working class'. She lives with her daughter and her partner of four years, Frankie (see F41), in a city in the south-east of England. Annie is currently unemployed but is doing a sign language interpreter's course. The most important people in her life are her partner, her daughter, and a small group of single parents. (Couple interview with F41)

F41 Frankie is 32, black and identifies as a dyke. She is English and 'struggling' class. She has lived with her partner, Annie (see F40), in a city in the south-east of England for three years. Frankie works part-time as a graphic designer. The most important people in her life are Annie and their daughter. (Couple interview with F40)

F42 Diane is 28, white and gay. She is working class, English and lives with her partner of two years in south Wales. They each have two children and co-parent all four. Diane is a full-time student and currently works in manual labour. The most important people in her life are her partner, their four children, and her mother. (Individual interview)

F43 Mo is a 22-year-old white lesbian. She is English, middle class and lives in a town in the Midlands with her partner. Mo is currently completing a full-time Masters degree. The most important people in her life are her partner, two close friends, her mother, and her grandmother. (Individual interview)

F44 Miriam is a 42-year-old white lesbian. She is English, Jewish and middle class. She lives with her two children in a city in the south-east of England. Miriam's partner, Sacha, is dead and Miriam is now the guardian of Sacha's son. She works as a counsellor/trainer. The most important people in her life are her children, her family, and a small group of friends. (Individual interview)

F45 Ebony is a 34-year-old black dyke ('technically a bisexual lesbian'). Born in England, she is African-Caribbean/British/American, and does not identify in terms of class. Ebony lives in a city in the south-east of England and co-parents her son with her ex-partner, Toni (see F46), and the child's father. She works part-time as a counsellor/development worker. The most important people in her life are Toni, her son, her partner, her close friends, and members of her family of origin. (Interviewed with F46)

F46 Toni is a 32-year-old white/Celtic dyke. She is Irish, working class and grew up in the city in the south-east of England where she currently lives. She co-parents with her ex-partner Ebony (see F45). Toni has recently completed a degree and is currently unemployed. The most important people in her life are Ebony, her son, her brother and her parents. (Interviewed with F45)

F47 Lilly is 67, white and gay. She is English and reluctantly identifies as middle class. Her partner (of thirty-nine years) died seven years ago. Lilly is now retired and lives alone. The most important people in her life are four close friends who live in another city. (Individual interview)

F48 Virginia is a 62-year-old white homosexual/lesbian. She is English and upper-middle class. She lives with her partner of thirty-four years, a heterosexual woman. She is retired from paid employment (past positions included research and teaching). The most important people in her life are her partner, her partner's children and grandchildren, her sister and brother, and close friends. (Individual interview)

The men

M01 Thomas is 29, white and gay. He is Irish and identifies as working class. He lives with his partner of seven years, James (see M02), in a city in the north-west of England. He currently works for James' company. The most important people in his life are his partner, certain members of his family of origin, and close friends. (Couple interview with M02)

M02 James is a 31-year-old white gay man. He is English and sees himself as middle class in terms of his profession, but not in terms of his 'philosophy and approach'. He grew up in London and now lives with his partner, Thomas (see M01), in a city in the north-west of England. He is currently running his own consultancy company. The most important people in his life are his partner, his family of origin, and close friends. (Couple interview with M01)

M03 William, a white gay man of 40, is English and lives in a city in the north-west of England. He is a medical professional and identifies as middle class. He has been in a relationship with his 'spouse', Luke (see M04), for five years. The most important people in his life are his partner, his mother, and close friends. (Individual interview)

M04 Luke is a 30-year-old white gay man who lives with his 'spouse' William (see M03) in a city in the north-west of England. Scottish and from a working-class background (but now unsure of his class), he is a health professional. The most important people in Luke's life are his partner, his parents, his sister, and certain friends. (Individual interview)

M05 Simon is a 32-year-old white gay man who has recently moved to London, where he lives alone. He is English and working class (but is sometimes uncertain about his class status). He is currently unsure of his relationship status – though 'officially' single, he is still very involved with his ex-partner of nine years. He identifies his (ex-)'boyfriend' and friends as the most important people in his life. (Individual interview)

M06 Rob is a 30-year-old white gay man. He is English and identifies as middle class. He has been in a relationship with Scott (see M07) for seven years, and lives with him in a small village in the Midlands. He is currently a mature student. He identifies his partner, his family of origin, and his friends as the most important people in his life. (Couple interview with M07)

M07 Scott is a 31-year-old white gay man. He is English and identifies as working class. He lives with his partner, Rob (see M06), with whom he has been in a relationship for seven years. He identifies his partner, his family of origin, and his friends as the most important people in his life. (Couple interview with M06)

M08 Colin is a 24-year-old white gay man. He is English. Although unsure of his class identity, he would opt for middle class. He is single and lives with Ed (see M09) who is one of his closest friends. He is currently unemployed. He has a biological son, but has no contact with him. The most important people in his life are his father, his father's partner, Ed (M09), and particular friends. (Interviewed with M09)

M09 Ed is 29, white and gay. He is English and working class. He is currently single and lives with his friend Colin (see M08) in a city in the east of England.

He is employed in manual labour. The most important people in his life are his friends. (Interviewed with M08.)

M10 Matt is 22, white and a 'straight identified' gay man. He is English, 'part Italian' and middle class. A full-time student in higher education, he lives in a shared house during term time, and the rest of the time with his mother in a city in the Midlands. He is single. The most important people in his life are his mother and three friends. (Individual interview)

M11 Peter is a 32-year-old white gay man who lives in a city in the north-east of England. He is English, middle class and works in public relations. He has been in a relationship with David (see M12) for one year. He lives with a lesbian friend in a house which he owns. The most important people in Peter's life are his partner and friends. (Individual interview)

M12 David is a 24-year-old gay man who lives in the north-east of England. He is white, English and working class. He is currently unemployed. His relationship with Peter (see M11) is his first major relationship. He identifies the most important people in his life as his partner and his parents – even if he is 'moving away' from the latter. (Individual interview)

M13 Andrew is a 28-year-old white gay man, who lives in the north-east of England with his partner of seven years, Tom (see M15 below). He is English and works in social services. He comes from a working-class family, but does not identify in terms of class. The most important people in his life are his partner and friends. (Individual interview)

M14 Craig is a 56-year-old gay man who lives with his female partner of twenty years and his three teenage children. He is white, British, working class and lives in the north-east of England. He is a religious minister. His partner and children are the most important people in his life. (Individual interview)

M15 Tom is a 39-year-old gay man who lives with his partner of seven years, Andrew (see M13), in the north-east of England. He is English and middle class. He works in the voluntary sector. The most important people in his life are himself, Andrew and some close friends. (Individual interview)

M16 John is a 37-year-old gay man. He identifies as 'bi-racial' and lives alone in the area where he grew up, a city in the south-east of England. He is currently semi-employed and strongly identifies as working class. John is single. The most important people in his life are his parents, sister, niece, nephew, godchildren, and particular friends. (Individual interview)

M17 Greg is a 38-year-old white gay/queer man. He is English, middle class and lives in a large town in the south-east of England. He lives with his partner of three years, Mark (see M18). He co-parents his biological daughter with her lesbian parents and Mark. He is currently unemployed. The most important people in his life are his daughter, Mark, and key friendships. (Couple interview with M18)

M18 Mark is a 22-year-old white gay/queer man. He is English and is unsure about his class identity/positioning. He is employed as a care worker. He lives with his partner, Greg (see M17), and Greg's biological daughter, Becky. The most important people in his life include Greg, Becky, and his mother. (Couple interview with M17)

M19 Darryl is 44, white and gay. He is English, and has lived in a town in the Midlands for ten years with his partner of twelve years, Sam (see M20), his informal 'foster' son and his boyfriend. He is middle class and part-time self-employed. He also has another 'foster' son who now lives in another city. The most important people in his life are his partner, his 'stepsons', his partner's son, and friends. (Couple interview with M20)

M20 Sam, a white gay man of 42, is English. He lives with his partner Darryl (see M19), his foster son and his boyfriend. He is employed part-time in the law. He is an 'official' (i.e., he is named on the birth certificate), but not biological, parent with a lesbian. The most important people in his life are his partner, his two stepsons and his son. (Couple interview with M19)

M21 Paul is a 36-year-old black gay man. He is English, and has lived in a city in the south-east of England for the past fourteen years. He is from a working-class background, but considers class to be a complex and vague issue. He is an artist and lives alone. He has been in his present relationship for three months. The most important people in Paul's life are his family of origin, special close friends, and his new boyfriend 'in a particular way'. (Individual interview)

M22 Ronnie is a 73-year-old white gay man. He is English and has lived in London most of his life. He is middle class. His long-term partner died recently, and he has employed a live-in care worker. The most important person in his life was his partner. (Individual interview)

M23 Will, a 29-year-old white gay man, is English. He lives in the city where he was born, in the south-west of England. He is presently unemployed, but is preparing to start work as a mature student. He 'struggles' with the idea of class, but when pushed, he would identify as working class. He has been in a relationship for three years, and has lived with his partner for two years. The most important people in Will's life are his partner, two lesbian friends, a gay friend, and his brother and sister. (Individual interview)

M24 Kevin, a 52-year-old white gay man, is English and lives in a small town in the south of England. He has been in his current relationship for twenty-two years, and has lived with his partner in their jointly owned home for most of this time. He is employed in the health/caring profession. The most important person in his life is his partner. (Individual interview)

M25 Charles, a 30-year-old white gay/queer man, was born in Britain, but grew up in Africa. He now lives in London in a house that is rented with friends. He is from an upper-middle-class background, and studies and works part-time. He has a small income from inherited money. Charles has been in a relationship with his partner (who lives in another country) for three years. The most important people in his life are his partner and various friends. (Individual interview)

M26 Alex is a 29-year-old white gay man. He is English and has lived in a city in the south-east of England for seven years. He has lived with his partner, Warren (see M34), for one year (in Warren's house). He is from a mixed class background, and identifies as middle class, but is 'informed by working-class values'. He works in the area of gay community services. (Individual interview)

M27 Phillip is a 45-year-old white gay man. He is English and lives alone in a city in the south-east of England. He has been in a relationship for three years with a black man who is fourteen years his younger. He works in the community sector. He is from a working-class background, but now considers himself to be middle class due to his income and interests. The most important people in his life include his partner and his partner's nephew, whom he helps care for. (Individual interview)

M28 Matthew is 41, white and married. He has recently begun to identify as gay. He is English and middle class. Matthew works in education and lives in a Midlands city with his wife and their two children. In terms of who is important in his life, he feels that he is 'in transition'. (Individual interview)

M29 Richard is a 36-year-old white gay man. He grew up in Wales and now lives in a city in the south-east of England. He describes his background as 'bourgeois middle class'. Richard has been in a relationship for seven years. He and his partner live apart but plan to live together within the next year. The most important people in his life include his partner, his sister, a straight friend, and gay friends. (Individual interview)

M30 Roy is a 57-year-old white American gay man who lives in a Midlands city. He lives with his ex-wife (whom he has known for over twenty years), her male partner, her male partner's mother, and some of his four children. He does not identify in terms of class. The most important people in his life are a friend, his sons (one of whom is adopted), his foster daughter, his wife and her mother, and other friends. (Individual interview)

M31 Liam, a 29-year-old white gay man from Northern Ireland, lives in a city in Scotland. He lives alone, though his boyfriend of eight months, Alain (see M32), is staying with him temporarily. He works in the voluntary sector. He is from a working-class background, but 'can't escape' the fact that he is now middle class. The most important people in his life are his boyfriend, his best friend and other friends, 'with family in the background'. (Couple interview with M32)

M32 Alain is a 27-year-old white gay man. He is French, but has lived in Scotland for the past five years. He is living temporarily with his boyfriend Liam (see M31) while he finds a place of his own. He works in the catering industry. He does not identify in terms of class. The most important people in his life are his boyfriend and his best friend. (Couple interview with M31)

M33 Anthony is a 33-year-old white gay man who lives in a city in the north-east of England. He is English, identifies as working class and works in the community sector. He has recently finished a four-year relationship, and is currently having a 'very casual' sexual relationship with someone. The most important people in his life are his parents, his 17-month-old child, the child's lesbian parents, and his closest friends. (Individual interview)

M34 Warren is a 28-year-old white gay man. He lives in the south-east of England, is English and identifies as middle class. Warren works in publishing and owns a house, which he shares with his partner of two years, Alex (see M26).

The most important people in his life include his partner and a few friends. (Individual interview)

M35 Bernard is a 36-year-old white gay man who divides his life between two cities, one in the south-east of England, and one in the Midlands. He is British, middle class and works in transport. He is single and has recently finished a two-year relationship. He lives alone at the weekends and with friends midweek. The most important people in his life are his sister and brother, two gay friends, his mother, and a female heterosexual friend. (Individual interview)

M36 Frank is a 47-year-old gay man who lives with his partner of eighteen years in a city in the south-east of England. He is originally from North America, and does not identify in terms of class. Frank has been unemployed for ten months. The most important people in his life are his partner, his brother and sister, and very close friends. (Individual interview)

M37 Sean is a 42-year-old white Scottish gay man who lives in a city in the south-east of England. Though 'technically' he lives alone, he spends the majority of his time at the home of his partner, Arthur (see M38). He is from a lower middle-class background, and works in the public service industry. He has been in a relationship for over ten years. The most important people in his life are his partner, his family of origin, and friends. (Couple interview with M38)

M38 Arthur is a 64-year-old black gay man. He identifies as Caribbean/British, and has lived in a city in the south-east of England for thirty-four years. He is working class and works in a manual trade. He has been in a relationship with Sean (see M37) for over ten years. He has four biological children, and is also a grandparent and a soon to be great-grandparent. (Couple interview with M37)

M39 Alan is a 44-year-old white gay man. He is English and lives in a city in Wales. He identifies as middle class and works in education. He lives alone, but often has his biological sons to stay. He has been married and has regular contact with his ex-wife. He is currently single. The most important people in his life include his children and friends. (Individual interview)

M40 John Peter is a 47-year-old white gay/homosexual man. He lives in the same Welsh town where he was born. He is single and lives alone. He does not work and comes from a lower middle-class background. The most important people in his life are, first, his friends, and then his parents. (Individual interview)

M41 Jonah is a 30-year-old white gay/queer man. He is Irish, and though his 'roots' are working class, he does not identify in terms of class. An artist, and currently unemployed, he shares his flat with a friend. He is single. The most important people in his life are a network of long-term friends who live nearby. (Individual interview)

M42 Aubrey is a 72-year-old white gay man. He is American and does not identify in terms of class. He used to work in education, but is now retired. He is single and lives with a gay male care worker. He is presently involved in a casual sexual relationship. The most important people in his life are his care worker and a friend who is also a neighbour. (Individual interview)

M43 Bob is a 61-year-old white gay man. He is English and working class. He does not work due to illness. He lives in warden-assisted housing near a city in the south-east of England. He is single. The most important people in his life are a male friend, and some heterosexual couple friends. (Individual interview)

M44 Dan is a 71-year-old white gay man. He is English and middle class. He is retired from work in local government, and lives in a city in the south-east of England with his partner of ten years. He is the biological parent of two sons from a heterosexual marriage. The most important people in his life are his partner and friends. (Individual interview)

M45 Jonathan is a 57-year-old white gay/homosexual man. He is Scottish, working class and lives in a city in the south-east of England. He works in the retail industry. He is single and lives alone. (Individual interview)

M46 Tony, who is 60, was brought up working class, but is now middle class 'through and through'. He is retired from paid employment. He is English and lives alone in a city in the south-east of England. He is single, but has two biological sons from a previous heterosexual marriage. (Individual interview)

M47 Harry is a 32-year-old white gay man who lives in a city in the north of England. He is English and middle class, and works in a caring profession. He lives with his partner of eight years, George (see M48). The most important people in his life are his partner, his brother, and some close friends. (Individual interview)

M48 George is a 36-year-old Chinese-British gay man. He works in education and lives in a city in the north of England with his partner of eight years, Harry (see M47). He is middle class in terms of his profession and lifestyle. The most important people in his life are his partner and very close friends. (Individual interview)

Bibliography

Adam, B. D. (1992) 'Sex and Caring among Men', in Plummer, K. (ed.) *Modern Homosexualities: Fragments of Lesbian and Gay Experience*, London: Routledge.

—— (1994) *The Rise of a Gay and Lesbian Movement*, New York: Twayne Publishers.

Ali, T. (1996) *We Are Family: Testimonies of Lesbian and Gay Parents*, London and New York: Cassell.

Alibhai-Brown, Y. (1999) 'The importance of family dining', *Independent* (Thursday review), 2 September: 4.

Allan, G. (1989) *Friendship: Developing a Sociological Perspective*, Boulder, CO: Westview.

—— (1996) *Kinship and Friendship in Modern Britain*, Oxford: Oxford University Press.

Altman, D. (1971/1993) *Homosexual Oppression and Liberation*, New York: New York University Press.

—— (1979) *Coming Out in the Seventies*, Sydney and Eugene, OR: Wild and Woolley.

—— (1982) *The Homosexualization of America, the Americanization of the Homosexual*, New York: St Martin's Press.

Anderson, K. and Jack. D. (1991) 'Learning to Listen: Interview Techniques and Analyses', in Gluck, S. B. and Patai, D. (eds) *Women's Words: The Feminist Practice of Oral History*, London: Routledge.

Anthias, F. and Yuval-Davis, N. (1992) *Racialized Boundaries: Race, Nation, Gender, Colour and Class, and the Anti-racist Struggle*, London: Routledge.

Arnup, K. (1995) *Lesbian Parenting. Living with Pride and Prejudice*, Charlottetown, P.E.I., Canada: Gynergy.

Aylewell (1998) *Pink Parenting*, Timewatch series, BBC Television.

Barrett, M. and McIntosh, M. (1982) *The Anti-Social Family*, London: Verso.

Barrington, J. (ed.) (1991) *An Intimate Wilderness: Lesbian Writers on Sexuality*, Portland, OR: The Eighth Mountain Press.

Bauman, Z. (1993) *Postmodern Ethics*, Oxford: Blackwell.

Bech, H. (1992) 'Report from a Rotten State: "Marriage" and "Homosexuality" in "Denmark" ', in Plummer, K. (ed.) *Modern Homosexualities: Fragments of Lesbian and Gay Experience*, London and New York: Routledge.

—— (1997) *When Men Meet: Homosexuality and Modernity*, Cambridge: Polity Press.

—— (1999) 'After the Closet', *Sexualities* 2 (3): 343–5.

Beck, U. (1992) *Risk Society: Towards a Modern Modernity*, London: Sage.

—— (2000) 'Zombie Categories', in Rutherford, J. (ed.) *The Art of Life*, London: Lawrence and Wishart.

—— and Beck-Gernsheim, E. (1995) *The Normal Chaos of Love*, Cambridge: Polity Press.

Beck-Gernsheim, E. (1998) 'On the Way to a Post-familial Family: From a Community of Need to Elective Affinities', *Theory, Culture and Society* 15 (3–4): 53–70.

Bell, A. P. and Weinberg, M. S. (1978) *Homosexualities: A Study of Diversity among Men and Women*, London: Mitchell Beazley.

Bell, H. (1991) 'Insignificant Others: Lesbian and Gay Geographies', *Area* 23: 323–9.

Benjamin, O. and Sullivan, O. (1996) 'The Importance of Difference: Conceptualising Increased Flexibility in Gender Relations at Home', *Sociological Review* 44 (2): 225–51.

Benkov, L. (1994) *Reinventing the Family: The Emerging Story of Lesbian and Gay Parents*, New York: Crown.

Berger, R. M. (1990) 'Men Together: Understanding the Gay Male Couple', *Journal of Homosexuality* 19 (3): 31–49.

Bersani, L. (1995) *Homos*, Cambridge, MA, and London: Harvard University Press.

Bev Jo (1996) 'Lesbian Friendships Create Lesbian Community', in Weinstock, J. S. and Rothblum, E. D. (eds) (1996) *Lesbian Friendships: For Ourselves and Others*, New York and London: New York University Press.

Bhatt, C. (1997) *Liberation and Purity: Race, New Religious Movements and the Ethics of Postmodernity*, London: UCL Press.

Bigner, J. and Bozett. F. W. (1989) 'Parenting by Gay Fathers', *Marriage and Family Relations* 14 (3/4): 155–76.

—— and Jacobson, R. B. (1989) 'Parenting Behaviour of Homosexual and Heterosexual Fathers', *Journal of Homosexuality* 18 (12): 173–86.

Binnie, J. (1995) 'Trading Places: Consumption, Sexuality and the Production of Queer Space', in Bell, D. and Valentine, G. (eds) *Mapping Desire*, London: Routledge.

Blasius, M. (1994) *Gay and Lesbian Politics: Sexuality and the Emergence of a New Ethic*, Philadelphia, PA: Temple University Press.

Blumstein P. and Schwartz, P. (1983) *American Couples*, New York: William Morrow.

Boswell, J. (1994) *Same Sex Unions in Pre-modern Europe*, New York: Villard Books.

Bourdieu, P. (1977) *Outline of a Theory of Practice*, Cambridge: Cambridge University Press.

Bowen, A. (1990) *Children in Our Lives: Another View of Lesbians Choosing Children*, Brookline, MA: Profile Productions.

Bozett, F. W. (1980) 'Gay Fathers: How and Why They Disclose their Homosexuality to their Children', *Family Relations: Journal of Applied Family and Child Studies* 29: 173–9.

—— (1981a) 'Gay Fathers: Identity Conflict Resolution through Integrative Sanctioning', *Alternative Lifestyles* 4: 90–107.

—— (1981b) 'Gay Fathers: Evolution of the Gay-Father Identity', *American Journal of Orthopsychiatry* 51: 522–59.

—— (ed.) (1987) *Gay and Lesbian Parents*, New York: Praeger.

Bray, A. (1982) *Homosexuality in Renaissance England*, London: Gay Men's Press.

—— (1990) 'Homosexuality and the Signs of Male Friendship in Elizabethan England', *History Workshop Journal* 29: 1–19.

—— (1997) 'Report Back: Partnership Blessings in Church History – Past and Present', *History Workshop Journal* 43: 283–4.

Brewer, J. D. (1994) 'The Ethnographic Critique of Ethnography: Sectarianism in the RUC', *Sociology* 28 (1): 231–44.

Bristow, J. and Wilson, A. R. (eds) (1993) *Activating Theory: Lesbian, Gay and Bisexual Politics*, London: Lawrence and Wishart.

Bronski, M. (1988) 'Death and the Erotic Imagination', in Preston, J. (ed.) *Personal Dispatches: Writers Confront AIDS*, New York: St Martin's Press.

Buntzly, G. (1993) 'Gay Fathers in Straight Marriages', *Journal of Homosexuality* 24 (1/2): 193–203.

Burrell, I. (1999) 'Gay man wins landmark decision on housing rights', *Independent*, 29 October: 1.

Butler, J. (1990) *Gender Trouble: Feminism and the Subversion of Identity*, London: Routledge.

Califia, P. (1988) *Sapphistry: The Book of Lesbian Sexuality*, Tallahassee, FL: Naiad.

Callen, M. (ed) (1988) *Surviving and Thriving with AIDS: Collected Wisdom*, volume 2, New York: People with AIDS Coalition.

Campbell, R. (2000) 'No kidding', *Gay Times*, 263 (August): 54–5.

Cant, B. (ed.) (1997) *Invented Identities? Lesbians and Gays Talk about Migration*, London: Cassell.

Carabine, J. (1996) 'Heterosexuality and Social Policy', in Richardson, D. (ed.) *Theorising Heterosexuality*, Buckingham: Open University Press.

Carpenter, E. (1902) *Iolaus: An Anthology of Friendship*, London: Swan Sonnenschein.

Carrington, C. (1999) *No Place Like Home: Relationships and Family Life among Lesbians and Gay Men*, Chicago, IL and London: University of Chicago Press.

Cartledge, S. and Ryan, J. (eds) (1983) *Sex and Love: New Thoughts on Old Contradictions*, London: Women's Press.

Cassell (1994) *The Pink Directory*, London: Cassell.

Castells, M. (1983) *The City and the Grassroots: A Cross Cultural Theory of Urban Social Movements*, Berkeley, Consortium Agreement, and London: University of California Press/Edward Arnold.

—— (1993) *The City and the Grassroots*, Berkeley, CA: University of California Press.

—— (1996) *The Information Age: Economy, Society and Culture. Volume I: The Rise of Network Society*, Oxford: Blackwell.

—— (1997) *The Information Age: Economy, Society and Culture. Volume II: The Power of Identity*, Oxford: Blackwell.

—— (1998) *The Information Age: Economy, Society and Culture. Volume III: End of Millennium*, Oxford: Blackwell.

Chauncey, G. (1994) *Gay New York: Gender, Urban Culture, and the Making of the Gay Male World, 1890–1940*, New York: Basic.

Clausen, J. (1987) 'To Live outside the Law You Must Be Honest: A Flommy Looks at Parenting', in Pollack, S. and Vaughn, J. (eds) *Politics of the Heart: An Anthology of Lesbian Parenting*, Ithaca, NY: Firebrand Books.

Clunis, D. M. and Green, G. D. (1993) *Lesbian Couples: Creating Healthy Relationships for the '90s*, Seattle, WA: Seal Press.

Coffey, A. and Atkinson, P. (1996) *Making Sense of Qualitative Data*, London: Sage.

Colwin, M. and Hawksley, J. (1991) *Section 28: A Practical Guide to the Law and its Implications*, London: National Council for Civil Liberties.

Connell, R. W. (1987) *Gender and Power*, Cambridge: Polity Press.

—— (1995) *Masculinities*, Cambridge: Polity Press.

Cooper, D. and Herman, D. (1995) 'Getting "the Family Right": Legislating Heterosexuality in Britain, 1986–91', in Herman, D. and Stychin, C. (eds) *Legal Inversions: Lesbians, Gay Men and Politics of Law*, Philadelphia, PA: Temple University.

Coward, R. (1989) *The Whole Truth: The Myth of Alternative Health*, London: Faber and Faber.

Coyle, A. (1991) *The Construction of Gay Identity*, unpublished PhD thesis, University of Surrey.

Cramer, D. W. and Roach, A. J. (1988) 'Coming Out to Mom and Dad: A Story of Gay Males and their Relationships with Parents', *Journal of Homosexuality* 15 (3/4): 79–92.

Cruikshank, M. (1992) *The Lesbian and Gay Liberation Movement*, New York: Routledge.

Dalley, G. (1988) *Ideologies of Caring: Rethinking Community and Collectivism*, London: Macmillan.

Davies, P. (1992) 'The Role of Disclosure in Coming Out among Gay Men', in Plummer, K. (ed.) *Modern Homosexualities: Fragments of Lesbian and Gay Experience*, London: Routledge.

Davies, P. M., Hickson, F. C., Weatherburn, P. and Hunt, A. J. (1993) *Sex, Gay Men and AIDS*, London: Falmer.

Davis, E. and Phillips, M. (1999) 'Debate: Gay Marriage', *Prospect* April: 16–20.

D'Emilio, J. (1983) *Sexual Politics, Sexual Communities: The Making of a Homosexual Minority in the United States, 1940–1970*, Chicago, IL and London: University of Chicago Press.

Dench, G. (1996) *The Place of Men in Changing Family Attitudes*, London: Institute of Community Studies.

Dennis, N. and Erdos, G. (1993) *Families without Fatherhood*, London: Institute for Economic Affairs Health and Welfare Unit.

Deverell, K. and Prout, A. (1995) 'Sexuality, Identity and Community – Reflections on the MESMAC Project', in Aggleton, P., Davies, P. and Hart, G. (eds) *AIDS: Safety, Sexuality and Risk*, London: Taylor & Francis.

Donoghue, E. (1993) *Passions between Women: British Lesbian Culture 1668–1801*, London: Scarlett Press.

Donovan, C. (1992) *Keeping It in the Family: Doctors' Decision-making about Access to Donor Insemination*, unpublished PhD thesis, University of Edinburgh.

—— (1997) 'UK', in Griffin, K. and Mulholland, L. (eds) *Lesbian Motherhood in Europe*, London: Cassell.

—— (2000) 'Who Needs a Father? Negotiating Biological Fatherhood in British Lesbian Families Using Self-insemination', *Sexualities* 3 (2): 149–64.

——, Heaphy, B and Weeks, J. (1999) 'Citizenship and Same Sex Relationships', *Journal of Social Policy* 28 (4), 689–709.

Dowsett, G. W. (1996) *Practising Desire: Homosexual Sex in the Era of AIDS*, Stanford, CA: Stanford University Press.

Driggs, J. H. and Finn, S. E. (1991) *Intimacy Between Men: How to Find and Keep Gay Love Relationships*, London: Plume.

Drucker, J. (1998) *Families of Value: Gay and Lesbian Parents and their Children Speak Out*, New York: Insight Books/Plenum Press.

Duncombe, J. and Marsden, D. (1993) 'Love and Intimacy: The Gender Division of Emotion and Emotion Work', *Sociology* 27 (2): 221–41.

—— (1996) 'Can We Research the Private Sphere? Methodological and Ethical Problems in the Study of the Role of Intimate Emotion in Personal Relationships', in Morris, L. and Lyons, S. (eds) *Gender Relations in Public and Private: Research Perspectives*, London: Macmillan.

Dunne, G. A. (1997) *Lesbian Lifestyles: Women's Work and the Politics of Sexuality*, London: Macmillan.

—— (1998) 'Opting into Motherhood: Blurring the Boundaries and Redefining the Meaning of Parenthood', *Gender Institute Discussion Paper*, series no. 6 (December), London School of Economics.

—— (1999) 'A Passion for "Sameness"?: Sexuality and Gender Accountability', in Silva, E. B. and Smart, C. (eds) *The New Family?*, London: Sage.

—— (2000) 'The Different Dimensions of Gay Fatherhood: Exploding the Myths'. Online. Available: http:www.lse.ac.ukdeptsGENDERgaydads.htm

Dworkin, A. (1987) *Intercourse*, London: Arrow Books.

The Economist (2000) 'Gay weddings for Germany', 29 July: 45.

Edwards, R. (1993) 'An Education in Interviewing: Placing the Researcher and the Research', in Renzetti, C. M. and Lee, R. M. (eds) *Researching Sensitive Topics*, London: Sage.

Eisenstadt, K. and Gatter, P. (1999) 'Coming Together: Social Networks of Gay Men and HIV Prevention', in Aggleton, P., Hart, G. and Davies, P. (eds) *Families and Communities Responding to AIDS*, London: UCL Press.

Epstein, S. (1990) 'Gay Politics, Ethnic Identity: The Limits of Social Constructionism', in Stein, E. (ed.) *Forms of Desire: Sexual Orientation and the Social Constructionist Controversy*, New York and London: Garland Publishing.

Eskridge, Jr., W. N. (1997) 'Beyond Lesbian and Gay "Families We Choose" ', in Estlund, D. M. and Nussbaum, M. C. (eds) *Sex, Preference, and Family: Essays on Law and Nature*, New York and Oxford: Oxford University Press.

Estlund, D. M. and Nussbaum, M. C. (eds) (1997) *Sex, Preference, and Family: Essays on Law and Nature*, New York and Oxford: Oxford University Press.

Etzioni, A. (1995) *The Spirit of Community: Rights, Responsibilities and the Communitarian Agenda*, London: Fontana Press.

Evans, D. (1993) *Sexual Citizenship: The Material Construction of Sexualities*, London: Routledge.

Faderman, L. (1981) *Surpassing the Love of Men*, London: Junction Books.

Falk, P. J. (1989) 'Lesbian Mothers: Psychosocial Assumptions in Family Law', *American Psychologist* 44 (6): 941–7.

Farquhar, C. (2000) ' "Lesbian" in a Post-lesbian World? Policing Identity, Sex and Image', *Sexualities* 3 (2): 219–36.

Feminist Review (1997) 'Citizenship: Pushing the Boundaries', *Feminist Review* 57 (Autumn).

Finch, J. (1984) 'It's Great to Have Someone to Talk to', in Bell, C. and Roberts, H. (eds) *Social Research: Politics, Problems, Practice*, London: Routledge and Kegan Paul.

—— (1989) *Family Obligation and Social Change*, London: Polity Press.

—— and Groves, D. (1983) *A Labour of Love: Women, Work and Caring*, London: Routledge and Kegan Paul.

—— and Mason, J. (1993) *Negotiating Family Responsibilities*, London: Routledge.

Foucault, M. (1979) *The History of Sexuality. Volume 1: An Introduction*, Harmondsworth: Penguin.

French, M. (1992) 'Loves, Sexualities, and Marriages: Strategies and Adjustments', in Plummer, K. (ed.) *Modern Homosexualities: Fragments of Lesbian and Gay Experience*, London: Routledge.

Frye, M. (1991) 'Lesbian "Sex" ', in Barrington, J. (ed.) *An Intimate Wilderness: Lesbian Writers on Sexuality*, Portland, OR: The Eighth Mountain Press.

Fukuyama, F. (1995) *Trust: The Social Virtues and the Creation of Prosperity*, London: Hamish Hamilton.

Gagnon, J. and Simon, W. (1974) *Sexual Conduct: The Social Sources of Human Sexuality*, London: Hutchinson.

Gamson, J. (1994) 'Must Identity Movements Self-destruct? A Queer Dilemma', *Social Problems* 42 (3): 390–407.

Garber, M. (1995) *Vice Versa: Bisexuality and the Eroticism of Everyday Life*, London: Hamish Hamilton.

Gatter, P. (1999) *Identity and Sexuality: AIDS in Britain in the 1990s*, London: Cassell.

George, S. (1993) *Women and Bisexuality*, London: Scarlet Press.

Gibbs, E. D. (1988) 'Psychosocial Development of Children Raised by Lesbian Mothers: A Review of Research', *Women and Therapy* 8: 65–8.

Giddens, A. (1991) *Modernity and Self-identity*, Cambridge: Polity Press.

—— (1992) *The Transformation of Intimacy: Sexuality, Love and Eroticism in Modern Societies*, Cambridge: Polity Press.

—— (1994) *Beyond Left and Right: The Future of Radical Politics*, Cambridge: Polity Press.

Gilligan, C. (1982) *In a Different Voice: Psychological Theory and Women's Development*, Cambridge, MA, and London: Harvard University Press.

Gorna, R. (1996) *Vamps, Virgins and Victims: How Women Can Fight AIDS*, London: Cassell.

Goss, R. E. (1997) 'Queering Procreative Privilege: Coming Out as Families', in Goss, R. E. and Strongheart, A. S. (eds) *Our Families, Our Values: Snapshots of Queer Kinship*, Binghampton, NJ: The Harrington Park Press.

—— and Strongheart, A. S. (eds) (1997) *Our Families, Our Values: Snapshots of Queer Kinship*, Binghampton, NJ: The Harrington Park Press.

Graham, H. (1991) 'The Concept of Caring in Feminist Research: The Case of Domestic Service', *Sociology* 25 (1): 61–78.

Griffin, K. and Mulholland, L. (eds) (1997) *Lesbian Motherhood in Europe*, London: Cassell.

Grundy, E. and Glaser, K. (1997) 'Intergenerational Relationships and Household Change', *Research Results*, no. 5 (ESRC Population and Household Change Research Programme), Swindon: ESRC.

Haggerty, G. E. (1999) *Men in Love: Masculinity and Sexuality in the Eighteenth Century*, New York: Columbia University Press.

Hall Carpenter Archives (1989a) *Inventing Ourselves: Lesbian Life Stories*, London: Routledge.

—— (1989b) *Walking After Midnight: Gay Men's Life Stories*, London: Routledge.

Hall, R. and Ogden, P. E. (1997) 'One Person Households in England and Wales and France', *Research Results*, no. 7 (ESRC Population and Household Change Research Programme), Swindon: ESRC.

Hall, R., Ogden, P. E. and Hill, C. (1999) 'Living Alone: Evidence from England, Wales and France for the Past Two Decades', in McRae, S. (ed.) *Changing Britain: Families and Households in the 1990s*, Oxford: Oxford University Press.

Halperin, D. M. (1995) *Saint Foucault: Towards a Gay Hagiography*, New York: Oxford University Press.

Hamer, E. (1996) *Britannia's Glory: A History of Twentieth-Century Lesbians*, London: Cassell.

Hammersley, M. and Atkinson, P. (1983) *Ethnography: Principles in Practice*, London: Routledge.

Hanscombe, G. and Forster, J. (1982) *Rocking the Cradle: Lesbian Mothers. A Challenge in Family Living*, London: Sheba Feminist Publishers.

Harne, L. and Rights of Women (1997) *Valued Families: The Lesbian Mothers' Legal Handbook*, London: Women's Press.

Harris, M. D. and Turner, P. H. (1986) 'Gay and Lesbian Parents', *Journal of Homosexuality* 12 (2): 101–13.

Harry, J. (1984) *Gay Couples*, New York: Praeger.

—— and DeVall, W. B. (1978) *The Social Organisation of Gay Males*, New York: Praeger.

Healey, E. (1996) *Lesbian Sex Wars*, London: Virago Press.

Heaphy, B. (1999) *Reinventing the Self: Identity, Agency and AIDS*, unpublished PhD thesis, University of the West of England, Bristol.

—— (2000) 'Living with Death', in Rutherford, J. (ed.) *The Art of Life*, London: Lawrence and Wishart.

—— (2001) 'The (Im)Possibilities of Living with AIDS: Incorporating Death into Everyday Life', in Cunningham Burley, S. (ed.) *Exploring the Body*, London: Macmillan.

——, Donovan, C. and Weeks. J. (1998) ' "That's Like My Life": Researching Stories of Non-heterosexual Relationships', *Sexualities* 1 (4): 453–70.

—— (1999) 'Sex, Money and the Kitchen Sink: Power in Same Sex Couple Relationships', in Seymour, J. and Bagguley, P. (eds) *Relating Intimacies: Power and Resistance*, London: Macmillan.

——, Weeks, J. and Donovan, C. (1999) 'Narratives of Love, Care and Commitment: AIDS/HIV and Non-heterosexual Family Formations', in Aggleton, P., Hart, G. and Davies, P. (eds) *Families and Communities Responding to AIDS*, London: UCL Press.

Heller, A. (1984) *Everyday Life*, London: Routledge and Kegan Paul.

Hemmings, C. (1999) 'Locating Bisexual Identities: Discourses of Bisexuality and Contemporary Feminist Theory', in Storr, M. (ed.) *Bisexuality: A Critical Reader*, New York and London: Routledge.

Henriksson, B. (1995) *Risk Factor Love: Homosexuality, Sexual Interaction and HIV Prevention*, unpublished PhD thesis, Goteborg University, Department of Social Work, Sweden.

Herdt, G. (ed.) (1992) *Gay Culture in America: Essays from the Field*, Boston, MA: Beacon Press.

Herman, D. (1997) *The Anti-gay Agenda: Orthodox Vision and the Christian Right*, Chicago, IL and London: University of Chicago Press.

—— and Strychin, C. (eds) (1995) *Legal Inversion: Lesbians, Gay Men, and the Politics of Law*, Philadelphia, PA: Temple University Press.

Hexter, R. (1997) 'Same Sex Unions in Pre-modern Europe: A Response', in Sullivan, A. (ed.) *Same Sex Marriage: Pro and Con – a Reader*, New York: Vintage Books.

Hicks, S. and McDermott, J. (1998) *Lesbian and Gay Fostering and Adopting. Extraordinary yet Ordinary*, London: Jessica Kingsley Publishers.

Hidalgo, H. and Christensen, E. H. (1976/1977) 'The Puerto Rican Lesbian and the Puerto Rican Community', *Journal of Homosexuality* 2 (20): 19–22.

Higgs, D. (ed.) (1999) *Queer Sites: Gay Urban Histories since 1600*, London and New York: Routledge.

Hochschild, A. (1983) *The Managed Heart: The Commercialization of Human Feeling*, Berkeley: University of California Press.

—— (1989) *The Second Shift*, New York: Avon.

Hocquenghem, G. (1978) *Homosexual Desire*, London: Allison and Busby.

Hogg, M. (2000) 'Half the battle', *Gay Times*, 263 (August): 56.

Holland, J., Ramazanoglu, C., Scott, S., Sharpe, S. and Thomson, R. (1994) 'Methodological Issues in Researching Young People's Sexuality', in Boulton, M. (ed.) *Challenge and Innovation: Methodological Advances in Social Research on AIDS/HIV*, London: Taylor & Francis.

——, Ramazanoglu, C., Sharpe, S. and Thomson, R. (1998) *The Male in the Head: Young People, Heterosexuality and Power*, London: Tufnell Press.

International Lesbian and Gay Association (ILGA) (1999a) World Legal Survey. Online. Available: www.ilga.org Information legal_survey europedenmark.htm

—— (1999b) World Legal Survey. Online. Available: www.ilga.org Information legal_survey europefrance. htm

Jackson, S. (1995) 'Gender and Heterosexuality: A Materialist Feminist Analysis', in Maynard, M. and Purvis, J. (eds) *(Hetero)sexual Politics*, London: Taylor & Francis.

—— (1996) 'Heterosexuality as a Problem for Feminist Theory', in Adkins, L. and Merchant, V. (eds) *Sexualizing the Social: Power and the Organization of Sexuality*, London: Macmillan.

Jamieson, L. (1998) *Intimacy: Personal Relationships in Modern Society*, Cambridge: Polity Press.

—— (1999) 'Intimacy Transformed: A Critical Look at the "Pure Relationship" ', *Sociology* 33 (3): 477–94.

Jeffreys, S. (1985) *The Spinster and her Enemies: Feminism and Sexuality, 1880–1930*, London: Pandora.

—— (1990) *Anti-climax: A Feminist Perspective on the Sexual Revolution*, London: Women's Press.

Johnson, S. E. (1990) *Staying Power: Long-term Lesbian Couples*, Tallahassee, FA: Naiad Press.

Johnston, L. and Valentine, G. (1995) 'Wherever I Lay my Girlfriend, That's my Home: The Performance and Surveillance of Lesbian Identities in Domestic Environments', in Bell, D. and Valentine, G. (eds) *Mapping Desire*, London: Routledge.

Kaplan, M. B. (1997) *Sexual Justice: Democratic Citizenship and the Politics of Desire*, New York and London: Routledge.

Katz, J. N. (1995) *The Invention of Heterosexuality*, New York: Dutton.

Kehoe, M. (1988) 'Lesbians over 60 Speak for Themselves', *Journal of Homosexuality* 16 (3/4): 1–111.

Kelly, L. (1988) *Surviving Sexual Violence*, Cambridge: Polity Press.

Keogh, P., Holland, P. and Weatherburn, P. (1998) *The Boys in the Backroom: Anonymous Sex among Gay and Bisexual Men*, London: Sigma Research.

King, E. (1993) *Safety in Numbers*, London: Cassell.

Kiss and Tell: Blackbridge, P., Jones, L. and Stewart, S. (1994) *Her Tongue on my Theory, Images, Essays and Fantasies*, Vancouver: Press Gang Publishers.

Kitzinger, C. (1996) 'Towards a Politics of Lesbian Friendship', in Weinstock, J. S and Rothblum, E. D. (eds) *Lesbian Friendships: For Ourselves and Others*, New York and London: New York University Press.

Knopp, L. (1995) 'Sexuality and Urban Space: A Framework for Analysis', in Bell, D. and Valentine, G. (eds) *Mapping Desire*, London: Routledge.

Kramer, J. L. (1995) 'Bachelor Farmers and Spinsters: Gay and Lesbian Identities and Communities in Rural North Dakota', in Bell, D. and Valentine, G. (eds) *Mapping Desire*, London: Routledge.

Kurdek, L. and Schmitt, J. D. (1987) 'Perceived Emotional Support from Families and Friends in Members of Homosexual, Married and Heterosexual Cohabiting Couples', *Journal of Homosexuality* 14 (3/4): 57–68.

Laner, M. R. (1977) 'Permanent Partner Priorities: Gay and Straight', *Journal of Homosexuality* 3 (1): 21–40.

Lash, S. (1994) 'Reflexivity and its Doubles: Structure, Aesthetics, Community', in Beck, U., Giddens, A. and Lash, S. *Reflexive Modernization*, Cambridge: Polity Press.

Levine, M. (1979) 'Gay Ghetto', in Levine, M. (ed.) *Gay Men: The Sociology of Male Homosexuality*, New York: Harper and Row.

—— (1991) 'AIDS and Changing Concepts of Family', in Nelkin, D., Willis, D. P. and Parris, S. V. (eds) *A Disease of Society: Cultural and Institutional Responses to AIDS*, New York: Cambridge University Press.

Lewin, E. (1984) 'Lesbianism and Motherhood: Implications for Child Custody', in Dary, T. and Potter, S. (eds) *Women-Identified-Women*, Palo Alto, CA: Mayfield Publishing Co.

—— (1993) *Lesbian Mothers: Accounts of Gender in American Culture*, Ithaca, NY and London: Cornell University Press.

—— (1998) *Recognizing Ourselves: Ceremonies of Lesbian and Gay Commitment*, New York: Columbia University Press.

Lewis, J. (2001) *The End of a Marriage? Individualism versus Commitment*, Cheltenham, Glos. and Northampton, MA: Edward Elgar.

Liddington, J. (1993) 'Anne Lister of Shibden Hall, Halifax (1791–1840): Her Diaries and the Historians', *History Workshop Journal* 35 (Spring): 45–77.

—— (1999) *Female Fortune: Land, Gender and Authority. The Anne Lister Diaries 1833–36,* London: Rivers Oram Press.

Lister, R. (1996) 'Citizenship Engendered', in Taylor, D. (ed.) *Critical Social Policy: A Reader,* London: Sage.

—— (1997) *Citizenship: Feminist Perspectives,* Basingstoke and London: Macmillan.

London Gay Liberation Front (1971) *Manifesto,* London: Gay Liberation Front.

Lorde, A. (1987) Man Child: A Black Lesbian-Feminist Response', in Pollack, S. and Vaughn, V. (eds) *Politics of the Heart: A Lesbian Parenting Anthology,* Ithaca, NY: Firebrand Books.

Loulan, J. (1987) *Lesbian Passion: Loving Ourselves and Each Other,* San Francisco, CA: Spinsters Ink/Aunt Lute.

McGee, C. (2000) *Childhood Experience of Domestic Violence,* London: Jessica Kingsley.

McGlone, F., Park, A. and Roberts, C. (1999) 'Kinship and Friendships: Attitudes in Britain', in McRae, S. (ed.) *Changing Britain,* Oxford: Oxford University Press.

McSmith, A. and Reeves, R. (2000) 'Gay law row that ignited Middle England', *Observer,* 30 January: 10–11.

McRea, S. (ed.) (1999) *Changing Britain: Families and Households in the 1990s,* Oxford: Oxford University Press.

McWhirter, D. and Mattison, A. M. (1984) *The Male Couple: How Relationships Develop,* New Jersey: Prentice Hall.

Mansfield, P. and Collard, J. (1988) *The Beginning of the Rest of your Life: A Portrait of Newly Wed Marriage,* London: Macmillan.

Marcus, E. (1992) *The Male Couples' Guide: Finding a Man, Making a Home, Building a Life,* New York: Harper Perennial.

Marshall, A. (1995) *Together Forever? The Gay Guide to Good Relationships,* London: Pan Books.

Marshall, T. H. (1950) *Citizenship and Social Class,* Cambridge: Cambridge University Press.

Martel, F. (2000) *The Pink and the Black: Homosexuals in France since 1968,* Stanford, CA: Stanford University Press.

Martin, A. (1993) *The Guide to Lesbian and Gay Parenting,* London: Pandora.

Martinac, P. (1998) *The Lesbian and Gay Book of Love and Marriage,* New York: Broadway Books.

Mason, J. (1996a) *Qualitative Researching,* London: Sage.

—— (1996b) 'Gender, Care and Sensibility in Family and Kin Relationships', in Holland, J. and Adkins, L. (eds) *Sex, Sensibility and the Gendered Body,* London: Macmillan.

Mellor, P. A. and Shilling, C. (1993) 'Modernity, Self-identity and the Sequestration of Death', *Sociology* 27 (3): 411–31.

Melucci, A. (1996) *The Playing Self: Person and Meaning in the Planetary Society,* Cambridge: Cambridge University Press.

Mendola, M. (1980) *The Mendola Report: A New Look at Gay Couples in America,* New York: Crown Publishers.

Miller, B. (1978) 'Adult Sexual Resocialization: Adjustments toward a Stigmatized Identity', *Alternative Lifestyle* 1: 207–34.

—— (1979) 'Gay Fathers and their Children', *The Family Coordinator* 28: 544–52.

—— (1986) 'Identity Resocialization in Moral Careers of Gay Husbands and Fathers', in Davies, A. (ed.) *Papers in Honour of Gordon Hirabayashi,* Edmondton: University of Alberta Press.

Ministerial Group on the Family (1998) *Supporting Families: A Consultation Document*, London: HMSO.

Mirza, H. S. (1997) *Black British Feminism: A Reader*, London and New York: Routledge.

Morgan, D. H. J. (1985) *The Family, Politics and Social Theory*, London: Routledge and Kegan Paul.

—— (1996) *Family Connections*, Cambridge: Polity Press.

—— (1999) 'Risk and Family Practices: Accounting for Change and Fluidity in Family Life', in Silva, E. B. and Smart, C. (eds) *The New Family?*, London: Sage.

Morgan, P. (1995) *Farewell to the Family? Public Policy and Family Breakdown in Britain and the USA*, London: The Institute of Economic Affairs Health and Welfare Unit.

Mort, F. (1987) *Dangerous Sexualities*, London: Routledge and Kegan Paul.

Mulgan, G. (1997) *Connexity: How to Live in a Connected World*, London: Chatto and Windus.

Muller, A. (1987) *Parents Matter: Parents' Relationships with Lesbian Daughters and Gay Sons*, Tallahassee, FA: Naiad Press.

Muncie, J., Wetherell, M., Dallos, R. and Cochrane, A. (1995) *Understanding the Family*, London: Sage.

Nardi, P. (1992a) 'That's What Friends Are For: Friends as Family in the Lesbian and Gay Community', in Plummer, K. (ed.) *Modern Homosexualities. Fragments of Lesbian and Gay Experience*, London: Routlege.

—— (1992b) 'Sex, Friendship and Gender Roles among Gay Men', in Nardi, P. (ed.) *Men's Friendship*, London: Sage.

—— (ed.) (1992c) *Research on Men and Masculinities*, London: Sage.

—— (1999) *Gay Men's Friendships: Invincible Communities*, Chicago, IL: Chicago University Press.

National Lesbian and Gay Survey (1992) *What a Lesbian Looks Like. Writings by Lesbians on their Lives and Lifestyles*, London: Routledge.

—— (1993) *Proust, Cole Porter, Michelangelo, Marc Almond and Me*, London: Routledge.

Nestle, J. (1987) *A Restricted Country: Essays and Short Stories*, London: Sheba.

Northmore, D. (1997) 'Cherie Blair slams British government's poor record on gay equality', in *The Pink Paper* 489 (11 July): 1–2.

—— (1998) ' "Legislation not litigation" goes the post-Grant rights battlecry', *The Pink Paper* 521 (27 February): 9.

Nussbaum, M. C. (1997) 'Preference and Family: Commentary on Parts III and IV', in Estlund, D. M. and Nussbaum, M. C. (eds) *Sex, Preference, and Family*, New York and Oxford: Oxford University Press.

Oakley, A. (1981) 'Interviewing Women: A Contradiction in Terms', in Roberts, H. (ed.) *Doing Feminist Research*, London: Routledge and Kegan Paul.

Oerton, S. (1997) ' "Queer Housewives?": Some Problems in Theorising the Division of Labour in Lesbian and Gay Households', *Women's Studies International Forum* 20 (3): 421–30.

O'Hanlon, K. (1999) 'Homosexual couple can be members of a family', *Independent* (Tuesday review), 2 November: 7.

Pahl, R. (2000) *On Friendship*, Cambridge: Polity Press.

—— and Spencer, L. (1997) 'The Politics of Friendship', *Renewal* 5 (34): 100–7.

Parker, P. (1989) *Ackerley: A Life of J. R. Ackerley*, London: Constable.

Patterson, C. J. (1992) 'Children of Lesbian and Gay Parents', *Child Development* 63: 1025–42.

Peplau, L. A. (1981) 'What Homosexuals Want in Relationships', *Psychology Today* (March): 28–38.

—— (1982) 'Research on Homosexuality: An Overview', *Journal of Homosexuality* 8 (2): 3–8.

——, Venigas, R. C. and Miller Campbell, S. (1996) 'Gay and Lesbian Relationships', in Savin-Williams, R. C. and Cohen, K. M. (eds) *The Lives of Lesbians, Gays, and Bisexuals*, New York: Harcourt Brace College.

Phillips, M. (1998) 'The truth that dare not speak its name', *Observer*, 27 February: 25.

—— (1999) *The Sex-change Society: Feminised Britain and Neutered Male*, London: The Social Market Foundation.

Phillipson, C., Bernard, M., Phillips, J. and Ogg, J. (1998) 'The Family and Community Life of Older People: Social Networks and Social Support in Three Urban Areas', *Research Results*, no. 9 (ESRC Population and Households Change Research Programme), Swindon: ESRC.

—— (1999) 'Older People in Three Urban Areas: Household Composition, Kinship and Social Networks', in McRae, S. (ed.) *Changing Britain*, Oxford: Oxford University Press.

Pies, C. (1988) *Considering Parenthood*, San Francisco, CA: Spinsters/Aunt Lute.

Plummer, K. (1978) 'Men in Love: Observations on Male Homosexual Couples', in Corbin, M. (ed.) *The Couple*, Harmondsworth: Penguin.

—— (ed.) (1981) *The Making of the Modern Homosexual*, London: Hutchinson.

—— (1983) *Documents of Life: An Introduction to the Problem and Literature of a Humanistic Method*, London: Allen and Unwin.

—— (ed.) (1992) *Modern Homosexualities: Fragments of Lesbian and Gay Experience*, London and New York: Routledge.

—— (1995) *Telling Sexual Stories: Power, Change and Social Worlds*, London: Routledge.

Polikoff, N. D. (1987) 'Lesbian Mothers, Lesbian Families: Legal Obstacles, Legal Challenges', in Pollack, S. and Vaughn, V. (eds) *Politics of the Heart*, Ithaca, NY: Firebrand Books.

Pollack, S. (1987) 'Lesbian Mothers: A Lesbian Feminist Perspective on Research', in Pollack, S. and Vaughn, V. (eds) *Politics of the Heart*, Ithaca, NY: Firebrand Books.

—— and Vaughn, V. (eds) (1987) *Politics of the Heart. A Lesbian Parenting Anthology*. Ithaca, NY: Firebrand Books.

Porter, K. and Weeks, J. (1990) *Between the Acts*, London: Routledge (see also Weeks and Porter, 1998).

Prieur, A. (1990) 'Gay Men: Reasons for Continued Practice of Unsafe Sex', *AIDS Education and Prevention* 2 (2): 110–17.

Qualis Research Associates (1995) *The Ethnograph V4: A User's Guide*, Amherst, MA: Qualis Research Associates.

Radford, J. (1991) 'Immaculate Conceptions', *Trouble and Strife* 21 (Summer): 8–12.

Raphael, S. and Robinson, M. (1984) 'The Older Lesbian: Love Relationships and Friendship Patterns', in Darty, T. and Potter, S. (eds) *Women Identified Women*, Palo Alto, CA: Mayfield Publishing Co.

Rapp, R. (1982) 'Towards a Nuclear Freeze? The Gender Politics of Euro-American Kinship Analysis', in Collier, J. F. and Yanagisako, S. (eds) *Gender and Kinship. Essays toward a Unified Analysis*, New York: Stanford University Press.

Raymond, J. (1986) *A Passion for Friends: Towards a Philosophy of Female Affection*, Boston, MA: Beacon Press.

Rayside, D. (1998) *On the Fringe: Gays and Lesbians in the Political Process*, Ithaca, NY and London: Cornell University Press.

Rednour, S. (1995) *Virgin Territory*, New York: Richard Kassel.

Reynolds, M. (1999) 'Fury over gay couple who are having surrogate twins', *Evening Standard*, 1 September: 9.

Reynolds, R. (1999) 'Postmodernizing the Closet', *Sexualities* 2 (3): 346–50.

Rich, A. (1983) 'On Compulsory Heterosexuality and Lesbian Existence', in Snitow, A., Stansell, C. and Thompson, S. (eds) (1983) *Desire: The Politics of Sexuality*, London: Virago Press.

Richardson, D. (1992) 'Constructing Lesbian Sexualities', in Plummer, K. (ed.) *Modern Homosexualities: Fragments of Lesbian and Gay Experience*, London: Routledge.

—— (ed.) (1996) *Theorising Heterosexuality*, Buckingham: Open University Press.

—— (1998) 'Sexuality and Citizenship', *Sociology* 32 (1): 83–100.

Rights of Women Lesbian Custody Group (1986) *Lesbian Mothers' Legal Handbook*, London: Women's Press.

Roberts, C. and McGlone, F. (1997) 'Kinship Networks and Friendship: Attitudes and Behaviour in Britain, 1986–1995', *Research Results*, no. 3 (ESRC Population and Household Change Research Programme), Swindon: ESRC.

Roberts, Y. (2000) 'A nation ill at ease with itself', *Independent on Sunday*, 30 January: 18.

Rofes, E. (1997) 'Dancing Bears, Performing Husbands, and the Tyranny of the Family', in Goss, R. E. and Strongheart, A. S. (eds) *Our Families, Our Values*, Binghampton, NJ: The Harrington Park Press.

Romans, P. (1992) 'Daring to Pretend: Motherhood and Lesbians' in Plummer, K. (ed.) *Modern Homosexualities*, London and New York: Routledge.

Rothblum, E. D. and Brehony, K. A. (1993) *Boston Marriages: Romantic But Asexual Relationships among Contemporary Lesbians*, Amherst: University of Massachusetts Press.

Rubin, G. (1984) 'Thinking Sex: Notes for a Radical Theory of the Politics of Sexuality', in Vance, C. (ed.) *Pleasure and Danger: Exploring Female Sexuality*, London and Boston, MA: Routledge and Kegan Paul.

Rubin, L. (1985) *Just Friends. The Role of Friendship in Our Lives*, New York: Harper and Row.

Saalfield, C. (1993) 'Lesbian Marriage ... (K)not', in Stein, A. (ed.) *Sisters, Sexperts, Queers: Beyond the Lesbian Nation*, London and New York: Penguin Books.

Saffron, L. (1994) *Challenging Conceptions. Planning a Family by Self-insemination*, London: Cassell.

—— (1996) *'What About the Children?': Sons and Daughters of Lesbian and Gay Parents Talk about their Lives*, London: Cassell.

Schulenberg, J. (1985) *Gay Parenting*, New York: Doubleday.

Schuyf, J. (1992) 'The Company of Friends and Lovers: Lesbian Communities in the Netherlands', in Plummer, K. (ed.) *Modern Homosexualities*, London and New York: Routledge.

Scott, J. (1999) 'Family Change: Revolution or Backlash?', in McRae, S. (ed.) *Changing Britain*, Oxford, Oxford University Press.

Sebag-Montefiore, S. (1997) 'Pregnant with implications', *Sunday Times*, 1 June: 7.

Sedgwick, E. K. (1985) *Between Men: English Literature and Male Homosocial Desire*, New York: Columbia University Press.

—— (1990) *Epistemology of the Closet*, Berkeley and Los Angeles: University of California Press.

Seidman, S. (1997) *Difference Troubles: Queering Social Theory and Sexual Politics*, Cambridge: Cambridge University Press.

——, Meeks, C. and Traschen, F. (1999) 'Beyond the Closet? The Changing Social Meaning of Homosexuality in the United States', *Sexualities* 2 (1): 9–34.

Selbourne, D. (1994) *The Principle of Duty: An Essay on the Foundations of the Civic Order*, London: Sinclair-Stevenson.

Seymour, J. and Bagguley, P. (eds) (1999) *Relating Intimacies: Power and Resistance*, London: Macmillan.

Shakespeare, T. (1996) *The Sexual Politics of Disability. Untold Desires*, London: Cassell.

Sherman, S. (1992) *Lesbian and Gay Marriage: Private Commitments, Public Ceremonies*, Philadelphia, PA: Temple University Press.

Shilling, C. (1993) *The Body and Social Theory*, London: Sage.

Silva, E. B. and Smart, C. (eds) (1999a) *The New Family?*, London: Sage.

—— (1999b) 'The "New" Practices and Politics of Family Life', in Silva, E. B. and Smart, C. (eds) *The New Family?*, London: Sage.

Silverstein, C. (1981) *Man to Man: Gay Couples in America*, New York: Morrow.

Sinfield, A. (1999) *Gay and After*, London: Serpent's Tail.

Smart, C. (1999) 'The "New" Parenthood: Fathers and Mothers after Divorce', in Silva, E. B. and Smart, C. (eds) *The New Family?*, London: Sage.

Smith, D. (2000) 'The law is an arse', *Gay Times*, 263 (August): 23–5.

Smith-Rosenberg, C. (1985) 'The Female World of Love and Ritual', in *Disorderly Conduct: Visions of Gender in Victorian America*, New York and Oxford: Oxford University Press.

Smyth, C. (1992) *Lesbians Talk Queer Notions*, London: Scarlet Press.

Snitow, A., Stansell, C. and Thompson, S. (eds) (1983) *Desire: The Politics of Sexuality*, London: Virago Press.

Song, M. and Parker, D. (1995) 'Commonality, Difference and the Dynamics of Disclosure in In-depth Interviewing', *Sociology* 29 (2): 241–56.

Stacey, J. (1996) *In the Name of the Family: Rethinking Family Values in the Postmodern Age*, Boston, MA: Beacon Press.

Stack, C. (1974) *Allow Kin*, New York: Harper and Row

Stanley, J. L. (1996) 'The Lesbian's Experience of Friendship', in Weinstock, J. S. and Rothblum, E. D. (eds) *Lesbian Friendships*, New York and London: New York University Press.

Stein, A. (1993) 'The Year of the Lustful Lesbian', in Stein, A. (ed.) *Sisters, Sexperts, Queers*, London: Penguin Books.

Stevenson, N. (ed.) (1998) *Cultural Citizenship*, London: Sage.

Stonewall (1997) *Equality 2000*, London: Stonewall.

Storr, M. (ed.) (1999) *Bisexuality: A Critical Reader*, New York and London: Routledge.

Strasser, M. (1997) *Legally Wed: Same Sex Marriage and the Constitution*, Ithaca, NY: Cornell University Press.

Straus, M. A. and Gelles R. J. (1990) *Physical Violence in American Families*, London: Transaction.

Straus, M. A., Gelles, R. J. and Steinmetz, S. (1981) *Behind Closed Doors: Violence in the American Family*, New York: Anchor.

Stuart, E. (1995) *Just Good Friends: Towards a Lesbian and Gay Theology of Relationships*, London: Mowbray.

—— (1997) 'Just a Perfect Blendship: Friendship and Sexuality', in Goss, R. E. and Strongheart, A. S. (eds) *Our Families, Our Values*, Binghampton, NJ: The Harrington Park Press.

Sullivan, A. (1995) *Virtually Normal: An Argument About Homosexuality*, London: Picador.

—— (ed.) (1997) *Same Sex Marriage: Pro and Con – a Reader*, New York: Vintage Books.

—— (1998) *Love Undetectable: Reflections on Friendship, Sex and Survival*, London: Chatto and Windus.

Tanner, D. M. (1978) *The Lesbian Couple*, Lexington, MA: Lexington Books.

Tasker, F. L. and Golombok, S. (1991) 'Children Raised by Lesbian Mothers. The Empirical Evidence', *Family Law* (May): 184–7.

—— (1995) 'Adults Raised as Children in Lesbian Families' *American Journal of Orthopsychiatry* 65 (2): 203–15.

—— (1997) *Growing up in a Lesbian Family. Effects on Child Development*, New York: Guilford Press.

Taylor, J. and Chandler, T. (1995) *Lesbians Talk: Violent Relationships*, London: Scarlet Press.

Thynne, L. (1996) *Child of Mine*, Channel 4 television production.

Travis, A. (1997) 'Gays win right to bring foreign partners to Britain', *Guardian*, 11 October: 7.

Troiden, R. R. (1993) 'The Formation of Homosexual Identities', in Garnets, L. D. and Kimmel, D. C. (eds) *Psychological Perspectives on Lesbian and Gay Male Experiences*, New York: Columbia University Press.

Trumbach, R. (1998) *Sex and the Gender Revolution. Volume 1: Heterosexuality and the Third Gender in Enlightenment London*, Chicago, IL and London: Chicago University Press.

—— (1999) 'London', in Higgs, D. (ed.) *Queer Sites: Gay Urban Histories since 1600*, New York and London: Routledge.

Turner, B. (ed.) (1993) *Citizenship and Social Theory*, London: Sage.

Uhrig, L. J. (1984) *The Two of Us: Affirming, Celebrating and Symbolizing Lesbian and Gay Relationships*, Boston, MA: Alyson Publications.

Van Every, J. (1991/1992) 'Who is "the Family"? The Assumptions of British Social Policy', *Critical Social Policy* 11 (3): 62–75.

—— (1995) *Heterosexual Women Changing the Family: Refusing to be a Wife*, London: Taylor & Francis.

Velu, C. (1999) 'Faut-il "pactiser" avec l'universalisme? A short history of the PACS', *Modern and Contemporary France* 7 (4): 429–42.

Verere, V. A. (1982) 'The Role of Friendship in the Development and Maintenance of Lesbian Love Relationships', *Journal of Homosexuality* 8 (2): 51–65.

Vicinus, M. (1985) *Independent Women: Work and Community for Single Women, 1850–1920*, London: Virago.

—— (1996) ' "They wonder to which sex I belong": The Historical Roots of the Modern Lesbian Identity', in Vicinus, M. (ed.) *Lesbian Subjects: A Feminist Review Reader*, Bloomington: Indiana University Press.

Vida, G. (ed.) (1996) *The New Right to Love: A Lesbian Resource Book*, New York: Touchstone.

Waaldijk, K. (1994) 'Homosexuality, European Community Issue', in Zijlstra, G., Odijk M. and Ketelaar, G. (eds) *Family? Partners? Individuals?*, Amsterdam: RoseLinks.

Waites, M. (1996) 'Lesbian and Gay Theory, Sexuality and Citizenship: Review Article' *Contemporary Politics* 2 (3): 139–49.

—— (1999) *The Age of Consent, Homosexuality and Citizenship in the United Kingdom (1885–1999)*, unpublished PhD thesis, South Bank University, London.

Wakeling, L. and Bradstock, M. (1995) *Beyond Blood: Writings on the Lesbian and Gay Family*, Leichhardt, NSW: Blackwattle Press.

Walby, S. (1994) 'Is Citizenship Gendered?' *Sociology* 28 (2): 379–95.

Wan, M. (1995) *Building Social Capital: Self-help in the 21st Century Welfare State*, London: IPPR.

Warner, M. (ed.) (1993) *Fear of a Queer Planet: Queer Politics and Social Theory*, Minneapolis and London: University of Minnesota Press.

—— (1999) 'Normal and Normaller: Beyond Gay Marriage', *GLQ* 5 (2): 119–71.

Watney, S. (1994) *Practices of Freedom: Selected Writings on HIV/AIDS*, London: Rivers Oram Press.

Weeks, J. (1977/1990) *Coming Out: Homosexual Politics in Britain from the Nineteenth Century to the Present*, London: Quartet.

—— (1985) *Sexuality and its Discontents: Myths, Meanings and Modern Sexualities*, London: Routledge and Kegan Paul.

—— (1989) *Sex, Politics and Society: The Regulation of Sexuality since 1800*, Harlow: Longman.

—— (1991) *Against Nature: Essays on History, Sexuality and Identity*, London: Rivers Oram Press.

—— (1993) 'AIDS and the Regulation of Sexuality', in Berridge, V. and Strong, P. (eds) *AIDS and Contemporary History*, Cambridge: Cambridge University Press.

—— (1995) *Invented Moralities: Sexual Values in an Age of Uncertainty*, Cambridge: Polity Press.

—— (1996) 'The Idea of a Sexual Community', *Soundings* 2: 71–83.

—— (1998) 'The Sexual Citizen', *Theory, Culture and Society* 15 (3–4): 35–52.

—— (1999) 'Supporting Families', *The Political Quarterly* 70 (2): 225–30.

—— (2000) *Making Sexual History*, Cambridge: Polity Press.

——, Donovan, C. and Heaphy B. (1996) *Families of Choice: Patterns of Non-heterosexual Relationships – a Literature Review*, Social Science Research Papers, School of Education and Social Science, South Bank University, London.

—— (1999) 'Everyday Experiments: Narratives of Non-heterosexual Relationships', in Silva, E. and Smart, C. (eds) *The 'New' Family?*, London: Sage.

Weeks, J., Heaphy, B. and Donovan C. (1999a) 'Families of Choice: Autonomy and Mutuality in Non-heterosexual Relationships', in McRae, S. (ed.) *Changing Britain*, Oxford: Oxford University Press.

—— (1999b) 'Partnership Rites: Commitment and Ritual in Non-heterosexual Relationships', in Seymour, J. and Bagguley, P. (eds) *Relating Intimacies*, London: Macmillan.

Weeks, J. and Porter, K. (1998) *Between the Acts: Lives of Homosexual Men 1885–1967*, London: Rivers Oram Press.

Weinstock, J. S. and Rothblum, E. D. (eds) (1996) *Lesbian Friendships: For Ourselves and Others*, New York and London: New York University Press.

Wellings, K., Field, J., Johnson, A.M. and Wadsworth, J. (1994) *Sexual Behaviour in Britain: The National Survey of Sexual Attitudes and Lifestyles*, London: Penguin.

Weston, K. (1991) *Families We Choose: Lesbians, Gays, Kinship*, New York: Columbia University Press.

—— (1993) 'Parenting in the Age of AIDS', in Stein, A. (ed.) *Sisters, Sexperts, Queers*, London: Penguin Books.

—— (1995) 'Get Thee to a Big City: Sexual Imaginary and the Great Gay Migration' *GLQ* 2: 253–77.

Whitbread, H. (ed.) (1988) *'I Know my Own Heart': The Diaries of Anne Lister, 1791–1840*, London: Virago.

—— (ed.) (1992) *'No Priest But Love': The Journals of Anne Lister, 1824–1826*, Otley: Smith Settle.

Whitworth, D. (2000) 'Homosexual marriages approved by Vermont', *The Times*, 17 March: 21.

Wilson, E. (1983) 'I'll Climb the Stairway to Heaven: Lesbianism in the Seventies', in Cartledge, S. and Ryan, J. (eds) *Sex and Love*, London: Women's Press.

—— (1998) 'Bohemian Love', *Theory, Culture and Society* 15 (3;4): 111–27.

Wilton, T. (1996) *Finger-Licking Good*, London: Cassell.

Wolf, D. (1984) 'Lesbian Childbirth and Women-controlled Conception', in Darty, T. and Potter, S. (eds) *Women-Identified-Women*, Palo Alto, CA, Consortium Agreement.: Mayfield Publishing Co.

Yip, A. T. (1997) *Gay Male Christian Couples: Life Stories*, Westport, CT: Praeger.

Zinn, M. B. and Eitzen, D. (1987) *Diversity in American Families*, New York: Harper and Row.

Index

abuse 78, 118–19
Adam, B. D. 14, 74, 83, 101
adoption 158–9, 167
adult life narratives 79–80
aesthetic theory, narratives 26
aesthetics of existence 187
age: friendship 68, 102; housing 102–3; lesbians 103; power relations 117; sexuality 140
age of consent 183
AIDS: care ethic 101–2; casual sex 142–3; community 74–5, 88, 90; ethics 101–2, 153–4, 156; gay men 153–4; insurance 190–1; kinship 17–18; lesbians 153–4; responsibility 74–5; Weeks 18, 90, 101, 153–4
Ali, T. 12, 160
Alibhai-Brown, Y. 77
alienation 91
Allan, G. 51, 56, 62
Altman, D. 5, 14, 15, 52, 65
anal sex 145–6, 155–6
Anglicans 92
Anthias, F. 196
anti-pornography movement 147
authenticity 39, 199
autonomy 22–3, 39

Barrett, Michele 15
Barrington, J. 147
Bauman, Z. 126
Bech, H. 25, 82, 83, 84, 85, 137, 158, 186
Beck, U.: do-it-yourself biography 181; family 43, 108, 167–8; individualisation 19, 107, 108, 113, 182; love 124; modernity 181; risk society 184
Beck-Gernsheim, E.: community of need 23; do-it-yourself biography 44, 181;

family 43, 71, 108, 167–8; individualisation 19, 107, 108, 182; love 124
bed death, lesbians 139–40
Bell, A. P. 106
Bell, H. 93
Benjamin, O. 99, 114, 115
Benkov, L. 59, 159, 163, 164, 166
Berger, R. M. 95, 96
Bersani, L. 16, 192
Bigner, J. 178
Binnie, J. 84
biography: do-it-yourself 44, 181, 197; interviewees 207–18; non-heterosexuals 6
bisexuality 194–5; friendship 64–5, 66; in history 13, 14; homosexuality 66–7, 68; identity 61, 135, 189; visibility 45, 141, 147; women 139
Blasius, M.: AIDS 90; community 86, 88; discrimination 41, 42; equality 149; friendship 58, 63, 71, 76; gender/sex 146; heterosexuality 80–1; identity 137; living practices 89; non-heterosexuals' ethos 46, 58, 63, 71; relationships 111
Blumstein, P. 100, 107, 108, 110, 120, 138–9, 150
body: intimacy 119–20; pleasure 133; sexuality 134–5
Boswell, J. 13, 51, 55
Bourdieu, Pierre 79
Bowen, A. 159, 192
Bozett, F. W. 48, 137, 138, 159, 160, 162, 164, 178
Bradstock, M. 9
Bray, A. 13, 43, 55
Brehony, K. A. 54
Brewer, J. D. 27

Smith, D. 184
Smith-Rosenberg, C. 13, 53, 54
Smyth, C. 146, 147
Snitow, A. 147
social capital 76, 90, 117–18
social class: parenthood 170; risk 186;
   sexual relations 56
social constructs 43–4, 161
social policy 197
socialisation 80, 83–4
sodomy 55, 145
Spencer, L. 4, 21, 52
sperm donation, gay men 166, 169, 175
Stacey, J. 11, 17, 21, 28
Stack, C. 49
Stanley, J. L. 57, 58, 87
Stansell, C. 147
state benefits 193–4
state/marriage 182–3
Stead, W. T. 56
Stein, A. 139, 147
Steinmetz, S. 78
stereotypes: gay men 104–5, 141, 142–3;
   gender 138
Stevenson, N. 196
Stonewall 3
Stonewall Parenting Group 165
Strasser, M. 2
Straus, M. A. 78
Straw, Jack 40–1
Strongheart, A. S. 92
Stuart, E. 53, 57, 70, 92
Sullivan, A.: commitment 109; friendship
   51, 64, 74; *Love Undetectable* 60; same
   sex marriage 2, 4, 17, 22, 127, 191,
   197
Sullivan, O. 99, 114, 115
support 60–1
surrogate parenthood 1, 166

Tanner, D. M. 65, 95, 106, 110, 130
Tasker, F. L. 158, 164, 174, 176, 178,
   179
Taylor, J. 118
tenancy rights 128, 183
Thompson, S. 147
tolerance 41–2, 178–9, 181, 182
transgression 14–15
Traschen, F. 186
Travis, A. 183
Troiden, R. R. 136, 137
Trumbach, R. 14, 55, 57

trust: commitment 107, 122, 123–4, 152;
   families of choice 38–9; gay men 155–6;
   lesbians 32–3
Turner, B. 182–3, 196
Turner, P. H. 160, 178

Uhrig, L. J. 104, 129, 131
unemployment 116–17
US: Defense of Marriage Act 4, 40;
   families of choice 5, 21; lesbian mothers
   159; lesbianism 147; love 70–1;
   partnership rights 127; same sex
   relationships 106; San Francisco life 83

Valentine, G. 78, 79, 93
values: community 75; family 40; home 79
Van Every, J. 99, 110, 115, 193
vanilla sex 147
Vaughn, V. 159, 166
Velu, C. 2, 40
Venigas, R. C. 99, 100, 111, 114, 117, 120,
   149
Verere, V. A. 56
Vicinus, M. 43, 54, 56
Vida, G. 104
violence 118
visibility: bisexuality 45, 141, 147;
   lesbianism 147, 159; marginalised
   people 6, 162; non-heterosexuals 81, 86,
   147, 159, 182; queer identity 141
visitation rights 164
Voeller, Bruce 79, 93

Waaldijk, K. 96, 197
Waites, M. 183, 197
Wakeling, L. 9
Walby, S. 196
Wan, M. 90, 117
Warner, M. 14, 41, 192
Watney, S. 18, 156
Weatherburn, P. 6, 143
Weeks, J.: AIDS 18, 90, 101, 153–4;
   authenticity 199; citizenship 196, 197;
   city life 84; coming out 187–8;
   commitment 107; community 86–90,
   91, 93; couples 95; equality 99; 'Families
   of Choice: The Structure and Meanings
   of Non-heterosexual Relationships'
   200–6; family 4, 5, 22, 198; freedom
   187; friendship 74; heterosexual
   assumption 81; homosexuality 55;
   hostility 184–5; identity 43, 44–5, 51,